SIGNS OF PERFORMANCE

Signs of Performance is a lucid and accessible introduction to the study of theatre as a signifying practice, focusing upon a range of key practitioners and movements of the twentieth century from Stanislavski to postmodernism. Colin Counsell addresses live theatre as 'readable', tracing a path from specific ideas and techniques through to the performance signs they produce, in order to examine the ways in which theatrical practices inscribe meaning upon the bodies, space and objects of the stage.

Eschewing traditional, abstract semiotic formulas, Counsell draws upon the work of a variety of theorists – from Saussure and Raymond Williams to Lyotard, Lacan and Patrice Pavis – to address theatre's unique signifying regime, its 'liveness' and the role of the audience. Theatre, Counsell argues, is inextricable from its historical, cultural and discursive contexts.

This straightforward, clear introduction assumes no previous knowledge of the subject or of the theories. It is the ideal starting point for undergraduate students embarking on the study of theatre semiotics.

Colin Counsell is Lecturer in English Literature and Theatre Studies at the University of North London. He has worked in the theatre both as a performer and as a director.

SIGNS OF PERFORMANCE

An Introduction to Twentieth-Century Theatre

Colin Counsell

Routledge
Taylor & Francis Group

LONDON AND NEW YORK

First published 1996
by Routledge
11 New Fetter Lane, London EC4P 4EE

Simultaneously published in the USA and Canada
by Routledge
29 West 35th Street, New York, NY 10001

Reprinted 2001, 2003, 2004

Routledge is an imprint of the Taylor & Francis Group

© 1996 Colin Counsell

Typeset in Palatino by Florencetype Ltd,
Stoodleigh, Devon
Printed and bound in Great Britain by
TJ International Ltd, Padstow, Cornwall

British Library Cataloguing in Publication Data
A catalogue record for this book is available from the British Library

Library of Congress Cataloguing in Publication Data
A catalogue record for this book has been requested

ISBN 0–415–10642–7 (hbk)
ISBN 0–415–10643–5 (pbk)

CONTENTS

ACKNOWLEDGEMENTS

For permission to quote from copyright material the author would like to thank the following: John Calder Press for extracts from 'Proust' and Three Dialogues (with Georges Duthuit) by Samuel Beckett and Georges Duthuit (1965); Methuen, London, for extracts from Stanislavski: An Introduction by Jean Benedetti (1982), from The Shifting Point (1987) by Peter Brook, from The Director and the Stage by Edward Braun (1979), from The Semiotics of Theatre and Drama (1980) by Keir Elam, and from The Conference of the Birds (1989) by John Heilpern; Farrar, Straus and Giroux Inc. for extracts from Brecht on Theatre by Bertolt Brecht, edited and translated by John Willett (1964); HarperCollins for the extract from The Empty Space (1972) and The Shifting Point (1987) by Peter Brook, and from An Actor Prepares by Constantin Stanislavski (1936), translated by Elizabeth Hapgood Reynolds; Paul Cohen for extracts from 'Peter Brook and the "Two Worlds" of Theatre' (1991); Macmillan for the extract from Cities on a Hill by Frances Fitzgerald (Pan, 1987); W. W. Norton and Co. and Foster Hirsch for extracts from his book A Method to their Madness (copyright 1984); MIT Press for the extract from Jindrich Honzl's essay 'Dynamics of the Sign in the Theatre' in Semiotics of Art (1984), edited by L. Matejka and I. R. Titunik; Routledge for the extract from Avant Garde Theatre by Christopher Innes (1993), and Experimental Theatre: From Stanislavski to Peter Brook (1989) by James Roose-Evans; Weidenfeld and Nicolson and the University of Chicago Press for the extract from The Savage Mind by Claude Lévi-Strauss (1966 edition); Manchester University Press for the extract from The Postmodern Condition by Jean-François Lyotard (1984); Performing Arts Journal Publications for the extract from Languages of the Stage by Patrice Pavis (1982);

ACKNOWLEDGEMENTS

Blackwell Publishers for the extract from *Literature, Politics and Culture in Post War Britain* by Alan Sinfield (1989); A. C. H. Smith for the extract from his book *Orghast at Persepolis* (1972); the estate of Constantin Stanislavski, The Bodley Head and Theater Arts Books for extracts from *Building a Character*, translated by Elizabeth Hapgood Reynolds (1950 edition); Bloomsbury Publishing for *A Dream of Passion* by Lee Strasberg (1988); Johns Hopkins University Press for extracts from *Shakespeare and the Popular Tradition* by Robert Weimann, translated by Robert Schwartz (1978).

Every effort has been made to trace all the copyright holders, but if any have been inadvertently overlooked the publishers will be pleased to make the necessary changes at the first opportunity.

Finally, the author would like to extend his heartfelt thanks to Talia Rodgers for her continued support over a long trek; to David Jarrett for being a mate; to Alan Sinfield for always seeming to know what I was talking about, no matter which hobby-horse I was riding that day; most of all, to Peri Stanley for her limitless patience and unfailing critical perceptions.

INTRODUCTION

The purpose of this book is twofold, both to examine the theatre of the West in the twentieth century, and to bring to bear upon it the analytical perspectives that have been developed in recent years and which are now central to work in other disciplines.

The notion of 'the West' is, of course, to some degree an artificial one. No insurmountable material barriers separate Europe and North America from the rest of the world, the divisions are political and ideological. This is particularly so in the theatre, since so many seminal theatrical producers have drawn upon the traditions of the Developing World, particularly Asia. But when a Brook or an Artaud borrows from other cultures, the borrowings are always redefined; they are placed alongside indigenous artefacts, used in new ways, and viewed by western audiences from a western cultural perspective. Meaning, whether in the theatre or elsewhere, is always culturally specific. This book will focus upon western theatre because to do otherwise, to operate under the assumption that 'Theatre' is an activity pursued and understood in the same way by all, is both to misconstrue the processes of meaning and to overlook the distinctness of cultures, our own and others'.

'Twentieth-century theatre' is a vast area and no single text can hope to cover the variety of theatrical practices implied. The practitioners addressed are merely a selection, and an orthodox one, being composed largely of canonical figures who might be expected to feature at some point on most courses of theatre study. Each is influential and stands within a broader tendency, so that many of our observations will apply not only to them but also to practitioners who follow similar paths. Equally, each creates a radically different form of theatre. The book seeks not

1

to be exhaustive, then, but to provide some representative signposts on a wide and diverse terrain.

Being comprised of the better known and more influential figures, the group inevitably features many Dead White Bourgeois Males, since such have historically dominated culture. The purpose of this book, however, is to offer an alternative to the orthodox view of these cultural producers. To counter such an orthodoxy there are broadly two strategies available. The first is to unearth and draw into the centre of enquiry practitioners who have been marginalised, ultimately redrafting the boundaries of the canon to include those who offer different perspectives, or who originate outside of traditional cultural elites. This option has been pursued most successfully by feminist critics, who have done much to reintroduce women until recently written out of theatre history. The second strategy is to view the existing canon critically; that is, to analyse what practitioners have achieved as opposed to what they claim to have achieved, and to view their works and opinions less as the fruits of individual creative genius than as cultural objects, artefacts which inevitably partake of and reproduce the ideas circulating in the societies from which they originate. It is this second course that will be followed here. Of necessity this means concentrating on Dead White Bourgeois Males: to counter an orthodoxy, it is necessary to address it.

This project is not without its difficulties. Theatre is a performing art, a *live* art, and its liveness poses two obstacles to study. First, it leaves us with no recallable text, no convenient and definitive reproduction we can take away and examine at leisure. As an alternative to analysing actual productions, then, we shall examine the theatrical models which inform them. Theatre is a cultural space, and the existing blueprints for theatrical production that circulate within it provide the ideas and parameters within which practitioners knowingly or unknowingly think and work.

But theatre's liveness also impacts upon the way audiences interpret the event, and this is the second obstacle. It is simple to reproduce the conditions in which films, paintings or novels are 'read' since they are very similar for the analyst and the everyday viewer. As a performing art, however, theatre involves the simultaneous presence of both spectator and performer. We must therefore develop a theoretical perspective able to account for the liveness of theatrical performance.

THE THEATRICAL SPACE

How can we describe theatre as an artform, what are its characteristic components? Perhaps the first thing we expect of it is a plot or, more accurately, a *narrative*, a series of events and actions which succeed each other according to a causal or developmental logic. In contrast to, say, film this narrative will be enacted live, by performers who occupy the same physical time/space as the audience. Each performer will use their everyday expressive resources – voice, gesture, movement and so on – to construct a fictional participant in the narrative, a character, which will function as the notional author of the actor's words and actions. Visual and spatial arts – painting, architecture, clothes design – will be employed in sets, props and costume not solely to complement narrative and character but also to establish a fictional time and space conceptually removed from the real site of performance, a hypothetical other-place in which the action will be deemed to have occurred. The whole performance will take place in an agreed venue for representation, in which the spaces and functions of spectators and actors are strictly separated.

This list might accord with most people's conception of theatre. Yet during the course of the twentieth century, with its wealth of formal experiment in all the arts, the indispensability of each of these components has been challenged. It is debatable whether even the first and most conventional of Samuel Beckett's plays, *Waiting for Godot*, has a narrative in the accepted sense, whereas some of his later, more experimental pieces lack plot and development entirely. Beckett's works are built of a predetermined sequence of events and actions, of course, but this cannot be said of Improvisational Theatre. The obvious riposte is that Improvisational Theatre is not real theatre, but it is precisely the parameters of 'real theatre' that are at issue.

In many of Beckett's plays the actor's communicative resources are markedly curtailed. *Happy Days* restricts movement by burying its central character, Winnie, in the earth, while *That Time* limits the expressivity of the voice by having its character's words recorded on tape. In *Not I* all that is visible of the central protagonist is a mouth; not only are the performer's expressive powers minimised, but 'character' itself is called into question. Indeed, the twentieth century has seen our customary notions of character challenged in a variety of ways. French theatrical visionary Antonin Artaud rejected psychological identity as a basis for character, populating his stage with figures who were fusions of primeval drives. Julian Beck and Judith Malina's Living Theatre developed towards a form of 'ritual' performance in which the actors themselves were the dramatic protagonists.

Theatre has been performed in bare spaces and with minimal props since Aeschylus, and directors such as Ingmar Bergman have made this practice commonplace on the modern stage. It is questionable whether picket lines and market places, both familiar theatre spaces, constitute 'agreed venues for representation', but even if they do we must still account for the Underground Theatre. There the audience meets the actors at a pre-arranged place and time, and accompanies them as they travel the London subway system and perform eccentric actions. The show itself consists of those actions and the reactions of unsuspecting commuters. The commuters are not aware that it is theatre and as a consequence the necessity for both an *agreed* venue and a hypothetical other-place disappears into a maze of qualifications.

The very separation of audience's and performers' spaces was questioned by experiments with so-called 'Environmental Theatre' in the United States. By staging action in the audience's space, and moving among spectators to get from one site to the next, the Performance Group under director Richard Schechner violated traditional spatial boundaries. Of course, it could be argued that the Performance Group's actors carried the borders of their special space around with them, by virtue of the fact that they were to be 'read' in a different way from members of the audience. Thus with the very distinction between actor and spectator a *perceptual* division of space was effected. However, the later work of Polish director Jerzy Grotowski problematised even this. In his 'paratheatre', participants collaborated to create the event, each effectively acting both as onlooker and actor, and so rejecting the distinction entirely.

It might appear that one distinctive characteristic of theatre, the physical presence of its actors, remains inviolable, but this is not so. Once again Beckett acts as a kind of one-man assault against theatrical norms. The curtain rises on his play *Breath* to reveal a stage filled only with 'miscellaneous rubbish', and the action consists of a light rising and falling, coordinated with the taped sound of breathing and of a child's birth cry. There is no story, set, hypothetical other-place, character, nor even a live performer. It is therefore perplexing that there are still clear grounds for viewing the piece as theatre.

How is it that, while a play such as *Breath* lacks so many of the features we deem characteristic of theatre, we still view it *as* theatre? The answer is that the event presents us with indications, signs, that it is to be addressed as such. If *Breath* were to be staged on a roadside, and without any further explanation, we would have difficulty knowing how to view it. But performed in a recognised theatrical venue, the circumstances themselves (the stage, curtains and so on, the arrangement of playing and viewing spaces, our foreknowledge of the building's purpose) would signal the identity appropriate to the piece. Indeed, the process of identification, of granting the event a given status, usually begins much earlier. We are likely to have read reviews, seen publicity material or at least have heard of Samuel Beckett before buying our ticket. If we inadvertently come upon a performance in a park or on a picket line, a host of other familiar indicators – the arrangement of actors/spectators, the way performers move and speak, the audience's passivity and so on – would tell us what species of event it was, and consequently how to view it.

Therefore theatre cannot adequately be defined with a checklist of its component parts. In 'recognising' theatre we perform what is essentially an *interpretative* act. We read its elements as 'signs', taking them to first signify the event's general cultural identity. The category 'theatre', then, depends on notions which we as spectators bring to the event, cultural 'frames' that tell us how it is to be addressed. All cultural artefacts are framed in this way. Be it a painting, dance, table or teapot, our recognition of the object/event brings with it socially derived expectations of how it should be read, what kinds of significance we should seek in it and how we should seek them. It is precisely because culture makes such frames available that theatre, like all categories of this kind, proves so malleable, for, once the correct identity, the correct categorisation, has been established, the production itself can interrogate it. This is how *Breath* challenges the category of theatre; it signals its theatrical status and so evokes expectations, only to disrupt them with its notable absence of narrative, performers and so on, subverting our customary conception of theatre *per se*.

The audience's interpretative role, however, goes beyond recognising theatre as a category. The audience is also active in manufacturing the meanings a theatrical event offers, for this too requires the spectator to use their cultural experience. In order to understand how theatre works, the meanings it constructs and the means by which it does so, we must now examine it and the audience's place within culture.

CULTURE AND DISCOURSE

We have described the spectator as a cultural interpreter. In our use of the term, 'culture' refers not solely to 'artistic' objects but also to the entire range of artefacts and activities that characterise a given society. This includes not only poetry and ballet, but also belief systems, language, the design of clothes and cars and consumer products, codes of behaviour and so on. The key characteristic of such products, the quality which makes them cultural, is that they all encode meaning. Cultural objects are readable.

That is not to say we perform a conscious act of interpretation each time we encounter a cultural product. Rather, 'reading' culture is part of the everyday process by which we operate in society. Because so much of that process is automatic, our activities can seem merely 'functional', but they in fact entail scrutinising the human world for meaning and producing meanings for others to read. This is the case with, for example, behavioural codes, those ways of acting that society deems appropriate to given situations. When in the presence of a social superior, say, a whole range of behavioural prescriptions come into play regarding proximity, gesture, posture, tone of voice, mode of eye contact and so on. These are not 'rules' that must be followed but *signs* to be 'written' and 'read', actions with conventionally agreed significance which are legible to both user and reader. Our social superior will use a different but corresponding set of signs, the two comprising a sign system, and with such systems we signify to each other, communicate our acceptance or refusal of given social positions.

Reading theatre involves a comparable process. Theatre proffers meaning not solely in its overt utterances – the character's words and actions, the 'author's message' – but also in the very form in which those utterances are conveyed, and we take meaning from that form without necessarily acknowledging that we are performing an act of interpretation. Our reading, however, is never entirely free. The example of behavioural codes also makes evident the fact that such 'messages' are not personal to either their author or their reader. They are cultural, re-articulating meanings drawn from the social pool. Just as those codes express existing social relationships, and so offer meanings which parallel those of other cultural objects and activities, so theatre customarily deals in concepts that already hold cultural currency.

The critical term we may use to describe this encoding of social meaning – *discourse* – is usually employed in reference to language alone. When we speak of 'a discourse' we mean both a type of language and a practice of language. It is a *type* of language because it deals with a recognised subject area and, more importantly, because its reservoir of words and concepts already incorporates a view of that subject, of what it is, how it can be spoken of and thought about. Discourse does not describe the world but manufactures it, encodes a view of reality in the very concepts out of which it is made. Moreover, different discourses encode different views; the discourse of microphysics tells us that a chair is made up of atoms, whereas the discourse of common sense allows us to think of it only as solid.

However, discourse is also a *practice* of language because such acts of conceptualisation are never abstract. Discourse is an activity, a process of *making* meaning, and it does so using not ethereal 'ideas' but concrete words, material components of language articulated by real social individuals. These linguistic acts take place in equally material and specific social and historical circumstances. They occur, that is, within given cultural *spaces* – an office, a university physics department, a theatre – sites wherein distinct species of social relationship already operate. Produced and articulated in those real socio-historical situations, discourse is inevitably moulded by, and expressive of, the political relations that feature in them.

Thus it is in discourse that *ideology*, the systems of ideas by which elite social groups maintain their positions of power, is inscribed. We often conceive of ideology as composed of ideas consciously held, and this is to some degree true. But it also consists of ideas adopted unconsciously, ways of understanding our world which may seem entirely 'natural', simply 'common-sense', but which in fact determine *what* we see and *how* we see it. Discourses do not reflect reality, they create it, each encoding a model of the real in the very terms of which it is composed. By controlling the mental tools with which human beings make sense of the world – by controlling their subjectivity – one effectively controls their ability to act upon the world. Discourse is thereby the medium in which ideology operates, and the means by which individuals in society, *social subjects*, are constructed.

We can best explain this process of construction by referring to the popular usage of the term *subject*. We commonly employ the word in two ways. In grammar the subject of a sentence is the active agent of events; with 'the boy jumps over the wall' it is the boy who does the jumping. In the second sense, the subject as topic – as in 'the subject of discussion' – it is the passive repository of intelligence brought from elsewhere. The critical use of 'subject' combines both these senses. The human subject is simultaneously the pad and the pen of discourse, the passive recipient of the concepts contained in it and their active reproducer in his/her actions and utterances.

Discourse, then, is not *imposed* upon the individual. Each of us requires a set of concepts to make-sense of the world, concepts which are shared and so permit communication. But when discourses are ideological – when they serve the interests of a ruling elite – their very concepts perform a political function, shaping our thoughts and behaviour, the way we view and act upon the world. The French theorist Louis Althusser termed this process 'interpellation' (for an excellent exposition of this issue, see Belsey 1980: 56–63). To employ a discourse – write or read, speak or understand it – the individual must adopt a predetermined position, as it is only from the vantage point of this 'subject position' that the discourse is usable and intelligible. However, in adopting that position, in assuming the guise of the discourse's 'I', the individual takes on the perspective and identity prepared for him or her. For Althusser, subjectivity is built of a matrix of these positions. The individual in society is 'hailed' by a variety of discourses so that one's identity consists of overlapping placements in language/ways of viewing the world. In providing the mental apparatus with which people function socially, discourse becomes not just a way of speaking/writing, but a way of thinking of and experiencing reality, and of conceiving of one's own place within it.

This does not mean that there is only one way of viewing the world. Societies are inherently pluralistic. Each is composed of a variety of social groups, distinguished on lines of class, ethnicity, gender and sexual preference at the very least. Nor is any one group defined by a single set of ideas and beliefs. As Raymond Williams has noted, societies are characterised by at least three ideological systems: the current ruling elites produce the *dominant ideology*, those coming to power adhere to the *emergent*, while the *residual* is held to by those whose formerly dominant position has waned (see Williams 1977). When we multiply these by the various peripheral and alternative world views that proliferate in modern cultures, it becomes apparent that there is no 'discourse', only discourse*s*, and that society incorporates a multiplicity of conflicting ways to make sense of the world. Culture provides a public platform for different social groups and the discourses they champion, and so is the arena in which the political, *ideological* struggle between these takes place.

Discourse proper, then, is a concrete thing, existing as written and spoken language. This makes it a useful concept for the analysis of theatre because on the stage discourses and ideologies are further physicalised. They become aesthetics: styles and genres, techniques and practices, designs for sets, costumes and the hypothetical 'individuals' that are the characters. All these constitute ways of representing the world, and so, like discourse proper, offer positions from which reality is construed. We now need to examine how it is that theatre becomes the bearer of such constructions.

PARITY AND DISPARITY

Theatre, then, encodes meaning not merely in its overt utterances, its content, but also in its form. To understand how theatrical form is able to bear discourse, we require a way of explaining how the objects of the stage signify, function as *signs*. We therefore need a theory of signs, a semiotics.

The theory most often used in the study of theatre is a simplified version of the semiotics of American philosopher Charles S. Peirce (1839–1914). Peirce distinguishes three kinds of sign: the *Icon*, where the sign resembles the referent, as the actor resembles a person or a stage table resembles the real thing; the

Index, with a causal or contiguous relationship to the referent, as smoke indicates a fire, a soldier's marching stride infers his profession or a knock signifies someone on the other side of the door; the *Symbol*, where the meaning is purely conventional and relies on the agreement of all parties involved, so that when an actor speaks the word *pig* we all understand that the sound refers to a particular four-legged animal despite its lacking any inherent quality of pig-ness (see Elam 1980: 21–7).

This simplified version of Peirce's theory (Peirce's complete semiotics is considerably more complex) is useful in naming the kinds of sign we find in the theatre, but it suffers limitations. In particular, it implicitly considers signs in isolation, focusing on the relationship between the single image and its sole referent. On the stage, however, signs are usually presented *en masse*, and it is *en masse* that we interpret them.

It is for this reason that semiotic paradigms of this kind cannot deal adequately with theatrical form, for *form* consists of different kinds of sign operating in combination, systematically. In the simplified Peircean view the sign stands-in-for an object in the real world, so that the relationship between sign and referent, the stage and reality, is one of simple parity; the stage reproduces the individual objects of the world and the meanings already attached to them. But while a marching stride does in some sense stand-in-for a soldier, realistic, surrealistic and expressionistic versions of that stride offer the audience different views of the soldier, construe him in different ways. It does not merely stand-in-for the world but also constructs it.

An alternative semiotic is offered by the work of the French theatre semiotician Patrice Pavis. In his essay 'The Discourse of (the) Mime' (Pavis 1982) Pavis argues that the mime artist's first and most important task is to establish a code or 'key' by which the mime in its entirety may be understood. A pig, for example, cannot be evoked with a single pose or gesture, only when a consistent sequence of such 'attitude-images' cohere into a regime of movement. The first few gestures must therefore map out that movement, the pig's 'gestural universe', signalling to spectators the logic by which all gestures must be read and so enabling them to weave the sequence of signs together in their interpretation. Mime does not work by 'imitation', Pavis argues, but 'musically'; the signs do not relate solely to the referent, do not stand-in-for a pig, but relate to one another to form a

10

systematic 'language', and it is this integrated whole that evokes the pig.

At the same time there is another effect, for it is this very systematicity which indicates that the mime artist's movements are to be read in a way different from ordinary behaviour. The artist's physical presence onstage, in the same space/time as the audience, brings the world of everyday movements into the spectator's interpretative frame. But when the elements of the mime hang together a 'gap' opens up between that ordinary gestural universe and the gestures of the mime. The very consistency of the gestures signals that they are to be interpreted symbolically, not representative of the mime artist but of something else. When the artist is recognised to be doing something other than simply 'behaving', his or her movements are addressed as signs. This gap is maintained throughout the performance, creating a 'dialogue' between the mime world and the world of everyday movement, with the audience constantly making the comparison and noting the difference.

The performance therefore produces two simultaneous and symbiotic effects. By relating to each other systematically, the pig-like movements signal their difference from ordinary human gesture, while it is this very gap which prompts the spectator to weave them into a symbolic, readable whole. Perhaps the key word of the essay is *coherence*, for in Pavis's use its two senses come together; it is in *cohering*, binding together to form a language, that the mime's individual gestures and movements become intelligible, become *coherent*. The relationship between sign and referent, gesture and pig, is not one of parity, it is one of dis-parity, for the signs must signal their difference from the world of ordinary behaviour in order to cohere together and say something *about* the world.

In emphasising the systematic way in which signs function, Pavis employs not the semiotic model of Peirce but that of Ferdinand de Saussure (1857–1913), the Swiss theorist whose work provided the basis for structuralism (Saussure 1974). For Saussure, the sign is composed of two parts, a material *signifier* (a spoken or written word, or an image) and a *signified* (a concept). There is no essential relationship between signifier and signified, no similarity or contiguity, only a culturally agreed link. But in culture they are joined inextricably like the two sides of a sheet of paper, so that the signifier immediately invokes the

11

idea associated with it. The sign, then, does not neutrally mirror reality but offers a conception of reality, for the concrete word/image always carries a socially agreed meaning.

For Saussure, however, signs can only operate as part of a system, for it is from the system as a whole that their meanings derive. Signs function like the colours in a spectrum of light. At one point the waveband of light we call 'orange' ends and at another the waveband 'green' begins, and since there is an area between these, we can confer upon it a name, a signifier, 'yellow'. Yellow does not exist as an objective entity, it is merely a name we give to an area the other signs have conceptually demarcated, so that the process entails both dividing the world into knowable units and granting those units meaning. Similarly each sign in a system ultimately relies on all other signs, both for the segment of reality it represents and for the concept attached to it. As a consequence the sign never functions in isolation, for it keys into, and brings with it, a whole systematic view of reality.

This for Saussure is the way in which human consciousness conceptualises the world. We do not passively perceive reality, we *make*-sense of it using sign systems, and those systems determine the kinds of sense we can make. The sign system operates like a grid held before the eyes; the world is divided up, quantified, into units with meanings attached, and each unit depends for its significance on its relationship with all the others. Thus the world enters the subject's consciousness only in a culturally shaped and mediated form. While the simplified Peircean theory implicitly viewed signification as the communication of *existing* meaning, Saussure views it as the *construction* of meaning.

This view underlies Pavis's analysis of mime, and we can use it to explain signification in theatre *per se*. Theatre, like mime, does not use atomised signs but signs which function together systematically. This systematicity places them in a relationship of *disparity* with the world of ordinary voice, movement, gesture and so on, signals to the audience that they are to be read to elicit symbolic meaning. They 'cohere', forming an integrated whole which is readable.

The principle of disparity explains how live actors on a physically present stage are able to bear meaning; it does not help us to decipher the particular discourses inscribed there, nor explain how they are read. As we saw, culture is composed not of a sign system but of a plurality of conflicting sign systems, a diversity of discursive positions from which the world may be construed. To understand how a particular discourse is inscribed in theatre and, more importantly, how it is interpreted, we need to position the 'coherent' theatrical production in culture's discursive arena.

THE LAW OF THE TEXT

We do not, of course, view theatrical events in the same way as events that take place in, say, the street. In the theatre the audience customarily assumes that everything on the stage is a meaningful sign. This assumption of meaning is to some degree self-realising. The spectator searches for significance in everything presented and so tends to 'find' it, with the result that even accidental occurrences – a stage thrown into darkness when a fuse blows, an actor dropping a cup – are usually viewed as purposeful parts of the production until proven otherwise. The audience simply weaves such wayward 'signs' back into the fabric of the piece by interpreting them as if they had been created intentionally.

In addition to regarding all signs as meaningful, then, the audience also assumes they are intentional. The stage is viewed as an *interlocutor*, a partner in the exchange of meaning. The spectator therefore addresses the theatrical event not as a disparate collection of words, actions and images with a multitude of authors (playwright, director, actors and so on) but as a semic unity; that is, it is assumed to express one organised meaning and so is viewed as a single *theatrical text*. This is so even in performances which deliberately court schism and fragmentation, for the resulting contradictions and discords are themselves relationships, offering ways of weaving disparate elements together within a single meaning.

How then does the audience read the specific meanings inscribed into the theatrical text? Viewed objectively, the stage presents its audience with a multitude of signs. Each sign has a number of possible meanings available to it, for, as we have seen, societies are inherently pluralistic, composed of a variety of discourses, ideologies, sign systems and so on, each of which is potentially able to construe the signifier in a different way. There will therefore be great potential for contradictory interpretations for any element of a theatrical event.

13

But the audience addresses the stage as the site of one unified meaning, and there is less potential for diverse interpretations of an entire theatrical text than for any particular part of it. This is due to the sheer scale of the act of sense-making that is required. The decoding of a whole text will require that each of its elements be interpreted according to a single logic. Some shared and consistent potential for meaning must be found for all the parts, a semic 'lowest common denominator' to unify them. We can term this the *Law of the Text*. The Law of the Text is simultaneously the area of potential meaning shared by all or most of the event's elements, and the logic which governs their interpretation. It is this which gives theatre proper its Pavisian coherence, for, being the logic for the interpretation of signs *en masse*, it unifies them *in* that interpretation.

The logic of the Law of the Text, however, is not personal to either author or audience. It is culturally derived, drawn once again from the pool of existing social meanings. This quality, which enables the theatrical text to mobilise extant social meanings, is termed *intertextuality*. In its narrowest sense, intertextuality refers to one text's explicit quotation or inference of another. Thus John Fowles made intertextual reference to the conventions of the Victorian novel in his modern novel *The French Lieutenant's Woman*, and Lawrence Kasdan called upon a whole tradition of *noir* thrillers, especially *Double Indemnity*, in his film *Body Heat*. But the principle of intertextuality has a much broader application. When reading any cultural text – a play, painting or advertising poster – we do not spontaneously create a means of interpreting it but employ the instruments our culture makes available. We call on our experience of other texts; not simply other plays, paintings and posters, but discourses and sign systems, iconographies and ideologies, using their logics to weave the work's parts into a single, coherent whole.

Thus it is not that texts perfectly communicate a theatrical practitioner's intentions. Rather, audiences and 'authors' – directors, actors and designers as well as playwrights – have access to shared discourses, and so can employ shared codes/logics in both 'writing' and reading; or if they do not, we can expect the audience's interpretation to differ markedly from the authors'. The meaning, then, is generated in the meeting of the theatrical text and the 'text' of the audience's culturally derived subjectivity. Just as the subject is 'hailed' by discourse proper, provided with a position from which that form of language is readable/ writable, so a particular form of theatre, with its characteristic repertoire of images and devices, prompts the spectators to draw upon his/her experience of other texts to find the discourse(s) with which it can be read. This does not mean that every member of an audience will respond to a play in precisely the same way. The Law of the Text defines the terms and parameters of our interpretative activities – not the specific meaning derived but the *kinds* of meaning. In watching a piece of realism on the stage, for example, we may respond to the characters in a variety of ways, viewing each as good or bad or any of a thousand shades between. But if we are experienced with realism and competent in its reading, we will view them as 'fully rounded individuals', for that is one of realism's precepts, one of the assumptions of its Law of the Text. Even in a pluralistic society, where individual signs may be interpreted in very different ways, individuals across the range of social groups possess competency in many of the same cultural forms – are able to recognise a form and employ the appropriate interpretative strategy successfully.

We can illustrate the Law of the Text using the example of Expressionist theatre. The most familiar form of Expressionist theatre has a number of striking features: warped and architecturally impossible sets; lighting that casts deep, atmospheric shadow; little colour, with everything in black, white and grey – or else violent, garish colour; exaggerated and emotionally charged acting, with large, melodramatic gestures and *in extremis* facial expressions; a theme of liberation from parents, state or bourgeois respectability; a drifting, fragmentary narrative that slips from location to location and from one time to another.

Individually each of these elements might be interpreted in a number of ways. However, there is much less potential for diverse interpretation when we address them *en masse*, as parts of a single text. The semic potentials of the different signifiers meet upon the image of an extreme and idiosyncratic subjectivity, a para-logical and grotesquely distorted view of the world as seen by one 'tortured' consciousness. This, broadly, was the view of Expressionism, for it regarded the modern inner self as at war with the 'respectable', stultifying social world. This view was informed by certain of the discourses influential upon early modernism – psychoanalysis, Nietzschean philosophy and so on

– which enabled the spectator to read the theatrical text. If we as modern spectators can derive this meaning from Expressionist theatre it is because such theatre or such ideas are still a part of our cultural subjectivity. If we cannot, it is because those ideas are not available, cannot be mobilised as a Law of the Text, and we will effect a different interpretation or not be able to read the text at all.

THE ABSTRACT AND THE CONCRETE

The Law of the Text enables a theatrical event to function as a symbolic unity. This symbolic register was the focus of work undertaken in the 1930s by the Prague Formalists, who were arguably the first to turn an informed semiotic eye upon the stage. Terming their work 'the semiotization of the object', Keir Elam gives an account of their conclusions:

> The very fact of [the object's] appearance onstage suppresses the practical function of phenomena in favour of a symbolic or signifying role. ... A table deployed in dramatic representation will not usually differ in any material or structural fashion from the item of furniture that the members of the audience eat at, and yet it is in some sense transformed: it acquires, as it were, a set of quotation marks. It is tempting to see the stage table as bearing a direct relationship to its dramatic equivalent – the fictional table that it represents – but this is not strictly the case; the material object becomes, rather, a semiotic unit standing not directly for another (imaginary) table but for the intermediary signified 'table', i.e. for the *class of objects* of which it is a member.

(Elam 1980: 8)

This accurately restates the Prague Formalists' view; in Jindrich Honzl's words, 'Everything that makes up reality on the stage ... stands for other things' (see Matejka and Titunik 1976: 74). Nevertheless the explanation is incomplete because it describes only one of theatre's registers.

Pavis points out that mime implicates two kinds of movement, the gestural universe of the mime itself and the world of ordinary gestures that is drawn into the spectator's interpretative consideration as a comparison. In this he describes a situation unique to live performance. No artform truly constructs an 'illusion', for when reading a novel or watching a film we remain aware that we are experiencing fiction. But this is relative. In reading a novel we engage solely with language, while with a mainstream film our attention, our interpretative activity, is always bounded by the edge of the screen. When we are confronted with the real physical presence of the actor, however, we are reminded of the outside of the fiction. We are reminded of *artifice*; the 'author' is present and the event we see is a product of his or her authorial contrivances. Theatre is an 'uncomfortable' artform because its symbolic register is continually threatened by another, one in which theatre's fictionality, its meaning-*making*, remains overt.

It is these two registers that Robert Weimann examines in his book *Shakespeare and the Popular Tradition*. Even in its earliest form, the 'seasonal ceremonial', Weimann argues, theatre functioned in two ways, both as a mimetic representation of reality and as a ritual which was dance-like, offering no such illusion. Theatre continued to employ these two registers even in medieval plays like the mysteries and the moralities, but by that time they had devolved to two separate spaces. Illusionistic performance took place in the *locus*, a platform which was often raised on a scaffold, and which represented a hypothetical location, an other-place/time. This was the space of high-born characters and serious issues, and its mode of signification reflected that. Describing a stage direction that required a character to draw a curtain, Weimann explains,

> in the medieval drama it is the symbolic functioning of the various *loca* that tended to distance them from the audience. Herod, sitting atop his scaffold, physically objectified his high rank and manner by means of a spatial distance that also facilitated the kind of representational *mimesis* implicit in the drawing of the curtain because of the illusiory need to 'rest'.
>
> (Weimann 1978: 80)

For Weimann the features of the locus – its symbolic, illusionistic quality, the status of its themes, its real distance from the spectator and also its *conceptual* distance – operate together to effect a specific kind of signification. Raising the stage on a scaffold metaphorically separates the drama from the world of the audience and its everyday concerns. Being thus 'elevated', the stage is able to deal with the 'higher' issues of religion and morality. Because such issues are abstract they cannot be represented directly, only by symbols; that is, the world is represented not in its everyday form, but in the terms of its theological Law of the Text, the categories and conceptual entities offered by its dominant discourse/sign system. Functioning symbolically in this way, characters, actions and props must therefore be translated into something else, with the result that the whole space becomes 'illusionistic'. Indeed, it is precisely this illusionistic and symbolic status which allows *realistic* depiction to flourish, because it permits one human being to represent another and the drawing of a curtain to indicate a motive. Theatrical 'illusion', therefore, does not involve any hallucination; the event signals that its elements are to be read symbolically, as parts of an other-place, and the audience does so in order to understand, to *interpret*, the text.

But Weimann also describes how a different register of theatrical signification was effected in the *platea*, the undifferentiated 'place' in which comedy was performed. This platea was an entirely 'non-representational' and 'unlocalized' setting, sited down among the onlookers. The platea dealt with the audience's everyday concerns, which could therefore be represented in their ordinary form, requiring no symbolic translation. Like modern stand-up comedy, then, the platea was not concerned to conjure an illusion. In close proximity to spectators and occupying no hypothetical other-place, the fools and clowns who played there did not need to maintain a coherent character. They could therefore step in and out of role and even address the audience directly, for with no illusion of place or character it was not necessary to hide the mechanics of meaning-making, the artifice, of the performance.

Historically the locus, the symbolic space, has often been signified by spatial and architectural arrangements. Raised scaffolds and platforms, picture frames and proscenium arches straddling the playing area, empty zones between spectators and the stage – these serve to indicate that the time/space of the performance should be regarded as separate from the ordinary social space of the audience. Like the plinth on which a statue is placed or the literal frame surrounding a painting, such 'framing signifiers' signal that the event thus isolated is special, the bearer of symbolic meaning, and therefore to be decoded. Signifiers of this kind are not always necessary, for, as we saw, the Pavisian coherence of a performance is often enough to signal a 'gap' between it and the everyday world. But whether achieved through coherence, framing signifiers, or simply the conceptual 'frames' we bring to the event, the kind of space or register the production employs grants it a status, construing its utterances either as immediate and concrete (platea) or abstract and symbolic (locus).

Weimann's study ends with the Renaissance but his distinction is useful for conceptualising modern theatre, and we can illustrate this with the work of French playwright Jean Genet. With the 'ritual' form he develops in his plays *The Balcony* (1957) and *The Blacks* (1959), Genet walks an 'uncomfortable' line between the two kinds of theatre. *The Balcony* constructs a locus, an other-place where the plot occurs. This, however, is a brothel where characters act out their sexual fantasies, creating symbolic worlds within the playworld. We see them taking on roles, acting, and this reminds us of the real actors' presence. The play's 'illusion' is periodically punctured by references to how that illusion is created, so the spectators are made conscious of *The Balcony*'s own theatrical sleight of hand, the mechanics with which it conjures its illusion. The audience becomes aware of both actors and characters, real place and other-place, and is required to adopt two contradictory postures towards the stage, to view it as both a symbolic locus and a concrete platea.

Theatre, then, operates in two registers. The first we shall call the *Abstract* register. In Elam's words, this 'suppresses the practical function of phenomena in favour of a symbolic or signifying role' and it is therefore bound up with the other-place of the locus. Being conceptually distanced from the audience, it functions on a symbolic level. It deals with abstractions – not the tangible and equivocal social world we experience, but a world already quantified, categorised, by the discourse the locus encodes. Thus it construes reality in terms of that discourse's symbolic entities: the stage table represents a general class of objects, 'Tables', the character of theatrical realism becomes a 'fully rounded individual', and the world of Expressionism is seen through the distorting eye of the repressed, subjective self. It is this very quality of symbolic transposition that enables it to be illusionistic. The stage becomes an other-place and its

19

objects become things of the playworld – the person is not an actor but King Lear – and this applies not only to realistic theatre but to all forms that foster an illusion, operating primarily in the Abstract register. But to support this illusion the Abstract must efface its own mechanics. The discourse of its Law of the Text must be the only interpretative logic, and the Abstract register must elide or reinterpret all signs that it is a product of artifice, a fiction.

The second we shall call the *Concrete* register. Here the person onstage is recognised as an actor and the table as *that* table. This register does not function symbolically, as its stage is not differentiated from the real, social space/time of the audience. Consequently its utterances have the same status of *provisionality* as any ordinary utterance, a result of our recognition that its meanings have been *made*. Thus it deals not in systematised symbolic categories but in the real material stage and the multiplicity of discourses found there. Its views are not abstract but partisan, told by a discernible teller. Manufacturing no illusion, its mechanics and fictionality can be admitted within the performance. That is, artifice must be accounted for in our interpretation of the text; we must make-sense not merely of the told but also the telling.

In most theatrical forms these two registers function side by side. They are antithetical, however, for the Abstract's illusion is threatened by the Concrete's overt artifice, just as illusion can potentially redefine signs of contrivance, give them other significance, within its Law of the Text. In privileging one or the other, or juxtaposing them as Genet does, a theatrical form determines how we address what it says.

THE DIALOGIC SPACE

All that we have examined makes it apparent that we cannot speak unguardedly of a production's meaning. Meaning in the theatre is always *made*, and one of its makers is the audience. This is true of any artform, but it is especially important in the theatre because there the audience is also in a sense 'created'. In its programme for Trevor Griffiths' play *Real Dreams* staged in the Pit at the Barbican, London, in 1986, Britain's Royal Shakespeare Company made explicit what is usually taken as read:

Please do not smoke or use cameras or tape recorders in the auditorium. And please remember that noise such as coughing, rustling programmes and the bleeping of digital watches can be distracting to performers and also spoil the performances for other members of the audience.

These proscriptions for audience behaviour are part of a larger protocol that most of us know. We are not permitted to eat or drink in the auditorium, particularly during the performance. Talking or making noise generally is frowned upon unless in response to the performers, and then only in sanctioned forms and at sanctioned times: laughter after a joke, applause at the performance's end. Movement is to be minimised, if not entirely eradicated. A particular position is to be adopted, and it is not acceptable, for example, to kneel up in your seat. One must face forward so that the eyes remain more or less fixed on the stage.

There are rules for behaviour in any communal area (and also for private areas, often legally enforced) and some of those listed also pertain elsewhere. There are practical reasons for all of them but, being social, such 'practicality' is always shot through with relations of power. The prohibition of non-theatrical activities, the alignment of the body and the gaze, the eradication of anything that might detract from stage utterance – together these work to determine our relationship with the stage. At the very least they indicate that we must view it as something with considerable cultural prestige, a space which demands uninterrupted interpretative scrutiny.

Such uniformity of behaviour, however, is always to some degree also a uniformity of response. Sitting quietly, still and in darkness, for example, we effectively remove ourselves from the readable whole of the event. That does not mean we overlook our own and our fellows' presence; rather, our behaviour *signifies* that the audience is *non*-signifying, excludes the spectator from the frame of what is interpretable so that the text consists solely of the fiction being enacted on the stage. Thus theatre's decorum of behaviour itself fosters an illusionistic locus, and a reading in the Abstract register. The effect perhaps becomes more obvious when we remember that until the nineteenth century the lights in the auditorium would have remained as bright as those on the stage, and spectators would have talked, walked

21

around, bought and eaten meals, and greeted friends while the performance was taking place. In adopting the appropriate *literal* 'position' required in the modern theatre, however, we have already performed an interpretative act, one derived from our culture and common to all members of the audience.

This emphatic uniformity of behaviour/response is exclusive to live performance. Viewers at an exhibition of paintings wander around at their own pace and read or overlook works largely as they will, while novel-reading is a solitary activity. Even in a cinema we are not constrained to the same degree because there are only other members of the audience to observe us. But in the theatre are live performers able to discern and judge our responses. The watchers are also watched and social pressure to sit silently, or laugh or applaud at the appropriate points, is very great. Theatre therefore provides a mechanism for group discipline and unified interpretation whose efficacy outstrips that of any other artform. Theatre may not lend itself to detailed consideration – one cannot turn back the page – but it excels at prompting audiences to adopt its viewpoint, because its behavioural decorum brings with it a decorum of interpretation.

The meanings offered by a particular theatrical event, then, are produced in the interaction between auditorium and stage. Theatre governs its own reading by establishing relationships, ways of viewing that enable the audience to make-sense of the theatrical text, and in doing so determine the kinds of sense that can be made. We can now use this and the other analytical instruments we have examined to understand theatre's distinctive signifying regime in total.

The theatrical experience is sometimes conceived as a kind of hallucination, with the audience actually believing that what takes place onstage is real. As we have seen, this is inaccurate. The audience of course remains aware that it is in a theatre, and so is able to appreciate technique, recognise the respected actor, and demonstrate group unity with laughter and applause. Theatre does not deal in 'belief' but in signification, creates not delusions but responses and interpretations. It achieves this by manufacturing relationships between the audience and the stage. The precise terms of any such relationship depend on the form of theatre involved, for each form requires the spectator to respond with its own juxtaposition of Abstract and Concrete registers, and its own Law of the Text.

The relationship between the stage and the auditorium is one we may term *dialogic*. By this we mean that the roles of both partners in the exchange are defined relative to each other. The nature of the utterance from one dictates its mode of reception, dictates the range of responses appropriate to the other. Despite overstated claims for 'feedback', however, the power to dictate this relationship lies largely in the hands of the stage. In practice, a particular form of theatre signals to its audience how it must be interpreted, the kinds of interpretative strategies that must be used in its own reading, and so 'creates' its audience as interpreter. Different theatrical forms will therefore manufacture different audiences. Each form can be regarded as a distinct *interlocutor*, one partner in an exchange, whose 'identity' automatically offers a complementary role to its audience. The audience's role consists of adopting an interpretative strategy appropriate to that kind of theatre, a logic written into the form itself.

This indicates the *active* role played by the audience in decoding the text. Theatre does not *impose* a reading, any more than discourse imposes its view of the world. Rather, each form 'hails' the spectator, offers a position from which the text is readable. The identity of the stage as discursive partner determines the dialogic relations, and these relations include the appropriate interpretative strategies – collectively comprising the *interpretative posture*. The audience is willing and able to adopt that posture; making-sense of the production is, after all, what we go to the theatre for. It is not that highly illusionistic forms, for example, banish awareness of the actor's presence or of theatre's contrivances. Rather, these questions are outside the posited relations, beyond those reading strategies that have been signalled as appropriate. The audience, then, has to recognise, accept and put into practice the interpretative codes, and in doing so operates within semic parameters encoded in the event itself. Every form of theatre predicts a limited range of audiences as 'answer' to its proposal. To enter into these dialogic relations is to accept those parameters, to act in unison with other spectators, and so to become a member of an audience.

1

STANISLAVSKI'S 'SYSTEM'

SPIRITUAL REALISM

The term 'realistic' is often used as an ordinary adjective, as if the quality it ascribed to the novel, painting and acting performance were unproblematic, purely a matter of their corresponding to reality. Realism is thus seen as the style without a style, simulating what is real without altering it or adding any meaning it does not already possess. This is a misconception. 'Realism' more accurately describes a number of artistic movements that arose at particular points in our cultural history, where they paralleled other kinds of discourse, political, scientific and philosophical. Realism is always material – built of words, paint on a canvas or bodies speaking and moving through space – and so is always a *fabrication* of reality. In any of its historical incarnations, realism reveals a repertoire of themes and images which, far from being neutral, reproduce constructions of the human subject and the world it inhabits. But one thing that all forms of realism share is the misassumption that they demand of their reader/spectator that they merely simulate the real.

Constantin Sergeyevich Alexeyev, known as Stanislavski (1863–1938), is generally considered the founder of modern, realistic acting, not because he was the first to pursue realism on the stage but because he organised his techniques into a coherent, usable system. The international success of his ideas is due in part to their availability in written form. Although his autobiographical work *My Life in Art* (1924) contained descriptions of his theatrecraft, it was in 1936 that the first book designed specifically to teach his theories, *An Actor Prepares*, emerged in print. This was followed by two companion volumes,

Building a Character (1950) and *Creating a Role* (1957), both published posthumously. Together these three texts detail the praxis Stanislavski himself termed 'Spiritual Realism', but which is generally known simply as 'The System'. Much of Stanislavski's own work as a director and actor differed significantly from the techniques detailed in these texts. Indeed, he ultimately found certain of his published ideas obstructive to the process of acting, and his practice underwent a fundamental change (see Coger 1964). Nevertheless it is the principles described in these three books that have historically proved most influential, doing more to shape realistic acting in Europe and America than any other practice, and it is therefore this written System which we shall focus upon.

Champions of the System tend to be fierce in their defence of its neutrality, asserting that it does not lead to a particular style of performance but is simply a practical means of creating characters suitable to any theatrical form. But while it is true that System-atic acting is varied, its variety is not infinite and it does display consistent characteristics. Behavioural detail, 'plausibility', a sense of profound psychological depth, a marked linearity or smoothness to the performance as a whole – these are the hallmarks of Stanislavskian work, and if we view them as the signs of 'good acting' *per se* it is largely because the System has been at the heart of orthodox western performance training for a substantial part of the twentieth century. Stanislavski's ideas have become the accepted 'common sense' in performance, seeming 'self-evident', so that actors not infrequently employ the Russian's basic concepts without knowing that they do so. Thus for examples of this mode of acting we need not look far. Performances of the classics in national institutions almost invariably employ Stanislavskian ideas at a fundamental level, and so provide accessible examples of his techniques in action.

THE PSYCHO-TECHNIQUE

Near the beginning of his first teaching text, *An Actor Prepares*, Stanislavski describes the other modes of acting then employed on the Russian stage. 'Mechanical Acting', for instance, uses an existing repertoire of conventional stage gestures, which Stanislavski calls 'stencils' or 'rubber stamps': 'spreading your hand over your heart to express love ... shaking one's fist in revenge' (Stanislavski 1980: 24). In contrast, another mode, the 'Art of Representation', entails the painstaking reconstruction of the character's external qualities (posture, voice, movement, dress) with detailed research followed by long and repetitious rehearsal. Stanislavski is quick to dismiss both modes, but also rejects what he calls 'Naturalistic' acting, described by one chronicler of his work as the 'indiscriminate reproduction of the surface of life' (Benedetti 1982: 11). For Stanislavski these three very different forms all prove inadequate not because they fail to simulate real life convincingly, but because they concentrate on appearance. The characters created by these methods are all surface, drafted and executed for gratuitous effect, and so offer 'prettiness in place of beauty, theatrical effect in place of expressiveness' (Stanislavski 1980: 26).

Stanislavski's rejection of these styles is not simply a matter of aesthetic preference, it reflects the humanist assumptions that inform his work. Although humanism is a broad church, all its variants hold to an essentialist vision of the human subject; humankind, it asserts, is characterised by a fundamental core, a transcendent 'human nature' common to all individuals, which links them more profoundly than any differences may separate them. Thus the function of art for humanism is to express what is universal, meaningful to all people regardless of cultural, social or historical differences, so prompting for the viewer a recognition of our shared humanity. It is on this basis that Stanislavski rejects all acting that concentrates on exteriors. 'Realism' in Stanislavski's sense is the form which expresses what is typically human – not the stereotypical, but that which is representative of humankind *per se*, its essence. Thus to be counted a 'true art', he asserts, acting must go beyond the superficial, external self and focus upon what is profound and universal, the character's 'inner life'. Stanislavski tells the actor,

> To play truly means to be right, logical, coherent, to think, strive, feel and act in unison with your role . . . we call that living the part. . . . You must live it by actually experiencing feelings that are analogous to it, each and every time you repeat the process of creating it.
>
> (Stanislavski 1980: 14)

Stanislavski's goal, then, is first of all an *internal* realism, and internal preparation is the basis of the System as it appears in his teaching texts. Thus actors are forbidden to use a mirror when creating their characters because 'it teaches an actor to watch the outside rather than the inside of his soul' (Stanislavski 1980: 36). Unlike the Art of Representation or Naturalism, System-atic Acting aims not to simulate real behaviour but in a sense to re-produce it, to conjure within the actor's mind the thoughts and feelings which *cause* observable, physical behaviour to occur. Thus Stanislavski tells his actors that they must never aim for 'results', never attempt to portray sadness or jealousy *per se*, but to evoke those internal forces which motivate one to behave in that way.

The ultimate aim of such practices is to build a complete hypothetical consciousness for the character, to stage in the actor's mind a stream of thoughts and feelings that correspond to the character's own 'experiences'. This stream must above all be continuous. For Stanislavski the self is not a static thing but a process, consisting of what he terms an 'unbroken line' of mental operations and sensations. The key term he uses to describe this is 'action'. On one level 'action' refers to the individual words and deeds (and thoughts; 'action' need not be physical) the actor undertakes in performance. But these are parts of that larger 'action' which is the individual's, and so the realistic character's, unceasing inner life. To create a viable character the actor must reproduce this mental continuum: 'On the stage you must always be enacting something; action, motion, is the basis of the art followed by the actor' (Stanislavski 1980: 36).

But not all mental states can be evoked at will. Much of our daily life occurs at a level which Stanislavski calls 'subconscious'; we walk, talk, gesture without planning these activities, and feel emotions in a similarly unpremeditated way. While the 'inspired' actor may be able to induce emotions, most performers can only approach a role at a conscious level, where emotions, among the most important causes for behaviour, remain inaccessible. This for Stanislavski is the central predicament of all acting: 'we are supposed to create under inspiration; only our subconscious gives us inspiration; yet we apparently can only use this subconscious through our consciousness, which kills it' (Stanislavski 1980: 13).

Thus for Stanislavski what is required is some way to tap the actor's subconscious, and this is provided by what he terms the 'Psycho-Technique'. This Psycho-Technique is at the heart of a variety of practices, of which the 'Magic If' is the simplest. The Magic If describes the ordinary human ability to place oneself in a fictional situation and extrapolate the consequences. During an exercise in which his pupils are to imagine them- selves as trees, Stanislavski asks, 'I am I; but *if* I were an old oak ... what would I do?' (Stanislavski 1980: 65). A similar approach is to be used in preparing for a role. In a scene from a Shakespearean drama, for example, where a character visits the court of the king, the actor might imagine a whole series of sensory details (the time of day and year, the weather. What does the court look like? What happened on the journey there? Does the king inspire fear, love, mistrust?). In doing so the actor provides himself/herself with a set of 'inner circumstances' in the absence of real, external ones.

This very crude example nevertheless serves to illustrate the principle at work. By imagining a series of 'inner circumstances' that correspond to the role, Stanislavski asserts, the actor provides baits to 'lure' out their subconscious. The imaginary details are to act as 'challenges to action', stimuli which provoke genuine responses. At the same time the actor's concentration on these imaginary 'facts' is to focus attention away from emotion itself, so that it is not drawn into conscious considera- tion and remains automatic, 'subconscious'. In effect, the actor must recreate something resembling the conditions of everyday life, wherein thoughts and emotions are born non-consciously in response to situations, so that the Psycho-Technique seeks what amounts to a reproduction of behaviour onstage. By creating an 'unbroken line' of such imaginary details, the basis for a System-atic character's inner life is established.

The ultimate goal of the Psycho-Technique in all its many forms is to gain access to the actor's 'Emotion Memory', a concept Stanislavski adapted from the work of the early psychologist, Théodule Ribot (1839–1916). According to Ribot, individuals retain a subconscious record of emotional experiences accumu- lated over the span of their lives. These are not stored in isola- tion, however, but are always associated with the physical and sensory circumstances that accompanied their first occurrence. In Stanislavski's view, by re-evoking those circumstances imagina- tively with the Psycho-Technique the actor is able to summon the associated feelings. Using techniques such as the Magic If, the actor simply finds a moment in their life when the required emotion was experienced and imagines the occasion in detail, thus summoning the feelings associated with it.

An important consequence of this is that the character's hypothetical psyche will always be based on the actor's, since it is the actor's emotions, experiences and responses that provide the bricks out of which a role is built. This does not invalidate the performance in Stanislavski's view. The humanistic System aims to evoke what is universal to humankind, seeks to depict those facets of existence which, he asserts, are common to all. Thus a character's emotions are equally well represented by the actor's and, rather than try to imitate a character's external life, Stanislavski instructs actors 'always [to] act in your own person'. By the same logic, the actor's own psyche is to be the benchmark by which the character is judged true or false. 'Nature', in the form of the actor's mind, should prevent him or her from 'going down the wrong path' (Stanislavski 1980: 16), and if the general shape of the character's psyche accords with the actor's, the creation will be 'true'.

Once the right internal states have been established, Stanislavski maintains, these will shape the physical performance automatically; just as in everyday life our thoughts and feelings automatically appear as words and actions, so the 'physical materialisation of a character to be created emerges of its own accord once the right inner values have been established' (Stanislavski 1968: 5). In fact Stanislavski does have an ideal of voice and movement in mind: actors must stand with erect spines, must correct any unpleasing body shapes, and so on. But these, he asserts, are simply a means of honing the actor's bodily 'instrument' to allow internal states a clearer expression. The raw signifying material of the performance is provided by thoughts, emotions and imaginary 'facts', none of which will require codification but will surface on the physical body (as intonation, gesture, facial expression and so on) in a form which is, Stanislavski assumes, innately understandable.

As we have seen, the model of the psyche underlying Stanislavski's techhniques is in part drawn from Ribot. However, at least as great an impact was effected by the school of psychology known as Behaviourism, for Stanislavski read the work of its most important Russian theorist, Ivan Pavlov (1849–1936), extensively. Pavlov maintained that behaviour is in large part built of 'conditioned reflexes', responses to stimuli already imprinted into the nervous system by previous experiences. In his famous experiments with dogs, a bell was rung each time they were to be fed. Eventually the dogs came to associate the bell with food and would salivate at the sound of it, even when no food was forthcoming. Pavlov thus postulated a general explanation of behaviour as produced in the movement *External Stimulus* → *Conditioned Reflex* → *Physical Response*, with the external world triggering actions via the nervous system directly, without intervention from the will.

Whereas Ribot provided the principle of Emotion Memory, it is Behaviourism that underpins the actual practice of the Psycho-Technique, and the parallels are not difficult to discern. Just as Behaviourism asserts that stimuli can evoke physical responses directly via the nervous system, without wilful choice, so the Psycho-Technique is presumed to enable emotions to find physical expression not consciously but precisely by *bypassing* consciousness. Moreover, emotions are to be evoked using a false stimulus. Pavlov's dogs were made to salivate by a bell, and Stanislavski's actors are similarly supposed to induce physical responses to emotion using imaginary 'inner circumstances'. The main difference is that there is no place for will or intention in Pavlov's account, for both the initial external regime and the stimuli were provided for his dogs by their keepers. In contrast, Stanislavski's actors must provide their own trick stimuli, consciously fabricate lures for their unconscious selves in order to induce emotional responses – as Stanislavski states: 'our cardinal principle; Through conscious means we reach the subconscious' (Stanislavski 1980: 176).

The techniques described so far may appear to be neutral, merely practical. But when one examines the precepts on which those choices are based it becomes apparent that these obliquely determine the nature of the System-atic performance. In doing so they also dictate what meanings it is possible to proffer in this style of acting.

As we have seen, Stanislavskian actors model and judge their characters' psyches on their own – or rather, on what they *deem* their own to be. This is a crucial distinction. In the Introduction we noted that, from an Althusserian viewpoint, subjectivity is composed of a number of positions offered the social subject in discourse. The subject is actually fragmented, consisting of a variety of different discursive placements. We rarely experience this fragmentation because, in order to operate as a competent social individual, it is necessary to adopt the posture of a coherent, unified subjectivity, albeit that this is illusory. Actors too are social subjects and view themselves as such a coherency. By definition, then, they base their characters' psyches on an inaccurate model.

The consequences of this only become apparent when we see how it interacts with another of the System's assumptions. As we noted, Stanislavski sees behaviour as innately understandable, as a transcultural mode of communication that does not require any 'language'. Thoughts and feelings, he assumes, are not read, simply *recognised* in the actor's behaviour, but this is not so. Just as human beings are 'hailed' by a variety of discourses, they are born into a world of existing behavioural codes, and part of the process of socialisation, of becoming a social subject, is learning how to behave in given situations. This is not to say there is only one way to behave. Rather, in a given culture any one situation will have a limited range of codes appropriate to it: postures, ways of moving, gesturing, types of eye contact, ways of speaking and kinds of discourse. Other situations will have different ranges, so that one might act in a certain way in the presence of one's peers but quite differently with one's parents, a lover or a High Court judge. What we regard as politeness or decorum is actually our negotiation of given social structures by the adoption of appropriate behavioural personae.

These behavioural practices are not merely functional, they signify. Socio-political relations provide perhaps the most obvious example. As we noted in the Introduction, when in the presence of someone with greater authority than oneself, greater social *power*, a whole set of codes come into play regarding proximity, stance, tone of voice and so on, all of which constitute signs and are eminently 'readable' to both parties. This becomes evident when one refuses the established codes; throw your arm around a judge and tell a joke, and the judge will immediately be able to read your implicit rejection of his or her superior status. Sociality signifies, and behavioural codes are legible to all who are competent in their use.

Stanislavskian actors, then, do not 'express' their psyches in a universal language. They select from the available codes, albeit in a non-conscious way, choosing elements of behaviour from the existing cultural pool that best convey their characters' inner characteristics. However, they do so on the assumption that characters are coherent, unitary identities, whereas in real social life we all adopt a multiplicity of discursive and behavioural personae. So System-atic acting specifically avoids discontinuous, heterogeneous selections, choosing instead elements of behaviour which fit neatly together.

System-atic acting is consequently characterised by a smoothness, an absence of discord and disjuncture. Being composed of gestures, postures, regimes of movement, intonations and facial expressions which accord with that narrow and unitary conception of the character's psyche – which are chosen precisely because they signify it – the Stanislavskian performance text offers an image of the illusory coherent self no matter what character is being portrayed or which text staged, and this is the result of the very practices employed. It is this continuity (or, more accurately, lack of discontinuity) which allows the elements of the performance to form a pre-eminent Pavisian coherence, to achieve a systematicity that is potentially meaningful, able to encode discourse – presenting not just a simulation of human behaviour but a construction of it. To discern the nature of that construction, we need to examine Stanislavski's techniques further.

UNITS AND OBJECTIVES

These techniques are not to be practised in a vacuum, for when working on a text, Stanislavski explains, the actor must take a range of other factors into account. The play's historical setting, the social milieu it depicts, the production's overall style, any themes the director chooses to emphasise – these are what he terms the 'given circumstances', which, because they detail the work's basic situation, are the framework in which *inner* circumstances are to be imagined; '*if* gives the push to dormant imagination, whereas the *given circumstances* build the basis for the *if* itself' (Stanislavski 1980: 51). The most important 'given' factor is the playtext, which for the actor means the words and deeds he/she must perform. To work with these the System offers what are perhaps its most famous conceptual tools, Units and Objectives.

The Stanislavskian actor begins by plotting the role's overall trajectory. The important experiences and turning points that the character undergoes are used as milestones to plot its 'Through-Line of Action', the general shape of the path this hypothetical individual will travel, changing and evolving *en route*. At this preparatory stage the actor must also decide upon the character's primary motivating force, the goal which consciously or unconsciously drives it through the play's events, its 'Super-Objective'.

Such general plans are, Stanislavski argues, of too large a scale for the actor to work with in their entirety. Nor is this necessary; just as one day of real life is composed of separate periods of activity, so the 'unbroken line' of the character's inner life should be built of a sequence of smaller 'lines'. The role must therefore be divided into sections which are dramatically complete but small enough to be manageable, called 'Units'. Taking each Unit individually, the actor then considers what causes the character to behave in the way specified by that fragment of text, what desire lies at the heart of its actions, the Unit's 'Objective'. It is the Objective that actually shapes the performance, for the actor must genuinely try to achieve his/her character's desire, even if the playtext dooms that attempt to failure. Thus Objectives tell the actor how the drama's given words and deeds are to be played, how the text is to be interpreted.

For Stanislavski the most critical stage in this process is naming the Objective. The right name, he asserts, will 'crystallise' a unit's 'essence', clarify the character's motive and thus the actor's task, making for sharp, uncluttered playing. Moreover, the name must always conceptualise the Objective as *active*. As we have seen, for Stanislavski the self is a process, ceaselessly in mental motion, continually feeling and thinking, and its Objectives must therefore be conceived in terms of 'action'. Consequently the Objective should not be envisaged as an image or state of mind ('Suffering' or 'A Mother's Love'), for these are merely the visible *results* of action. To *cause* those results – to reproduce behaviour onstage – Objectives must take the form of goals or desires able to provoke action. Thus Objectives should be named with the infinitive of a verb, as in 'I wish to seduce X' or 'I want to convince Y'.

In insisting that Objectives be named in this fashion, Stanislavski implicitly conceptualises the human subject as a kind of desiring machine, actually consisting of the process of trying to achieve its aims. But in performance there is a more tangible result. Required to attempt the satisfaction of his/her Objective, the actor is placed within that process, not viewing the action from outside but partaking of it, so that all his/her resources are bent to that task. The result is a flawless super-imposition of actor and role, with the audience seeing only a person trying to achieve their goals.

When all Units have been dealt with in this way they are reassembled into the complete role, and then compared with the large-scale designs with which the actor began, the Super-Objective and Through-Line of Action. Any mistakes in choosing individual Objectives will stand out as deviations from these and may be altered. The immediate consequence is a more emphatic signification of that illusory, unified self that we examined in the previous section. Made to conform to the linear Super-Objective and Through-Line of Action, the performance becomes smoother, more discord-free.

This is only the first step in the System-atic process of creating a role, for Units and Objectives render no more than a rough outline for a character. Plays, Stanislavski observes, give the actor little information to work with; 'the dramatist is often a miser in commentary . . . even characteristics are given in laconic form' (Stanislavski 1980: 55). Most plays offer only dialogue, the occasional stage direction, some indications of how certain lines are to be spoken, and perhaps a potted description in the dramatis personae. For the bulk of the time the actor is onstage the text gives no detailed information about what the character is doing, thinking or feeling, and it is therefore necessary to add a great deal to achieve realistic breadth.

This additional material is to come from the actors themselves. Stanislavski describes a number of techniques and we can put them into two broad categories. In the first the actor works in a deliberate, intellectual fashion, expanding the given circum-stances by drafting for the character a 'life' that extends beyond the limits of the play. Biographies may be contrived, or accounts of what characters were doing in the moments before a scene begins. Images of the character's life, or which are imagistically associated with it, are to be played across the mind's eye during performance like an 'imaginary moving picture show'. These practices are to have two effects, to create a corresponding 'mood', and 'arouse emotions', while at the same time holding the actor within the 'limits of the play'; summoning forth genuine responses via imaginary 'inner circumstances', and creating a hypothetical world for the actor to work within.

The second category of techniques demands a more subjective approach, requiring the actor to inject his/her own personality and experiential history into the work. Events from the actor's past that are analogous to something undergone by the character, images, objects, people – all these are to be called to mind to add depth and substance to the role. As with the techniques of the first category, the desired effect is twofold: evoking the Psycho-Technique, calling up 'moods' and 'emotions' that can find a physical expression in the performance, while at the same time building a network of images and associations that actors can focus upon during performance, an internal 'reality' to hold them within the 'limits' of the drama. Stanislavski states,

> You have to invent a whole film of inner pictures, a running subtext consisting of all kinds of settings and circumstances. . . . [This] is necessary for our own creative natures, our subconscious. For them we must have truth, if only the truth of the imagination, in which they can believe, in which they can live.

(Stanislavski 1968: 119)

For Stanislavski the aim of all these practices is to create the 'life of a human spirit'. From a semiotic perspective, however, such claims are of less importance than the real effects of such techniques on the material performance text. For our purposes three of these are especially significant.

Viewed objectively, most roles consist of little more than some dialogue and the description of a few physical actions. The realistic actor's practical task is to perform these in such a way as to render them credible. That is, he or she must design and execute a character able to function as the plausible author of not some but all areas of the role.

The play presents the situations the character encounters; these are 'given'. Also given are the character's responses to these. Units and Objectives are a tool for designing a hypothetical persona which, when confronted with the play's events, may plausibly 'react' with the play's responses. Objectives approach scenes rather like an equation to be answered; given the situation, what motive would cause someone to say this, to act in this way? When all the small fragments, the Units, of a role have been dealt with and assembled into a whole, the actor has a scaffolding of motives/aims/desires on which to build. All other claims aside, then, Units and Objectives are a practical method of satisfying the play's requirements in performance, of designing a hypothetical psyche capable of functioning as the originator of all the required deeds and utterances.

The second effect is a filling-out of the performance text with the actor's personal input. In crude terms, this provides a vast number of performance signs to occupy the 'gaps' between the text's sparse instructions, a constant but subtle stream of minutiae which signifies that the character is ceaselessly thinking, feeling, responding.

This extra signification is important because, as we have noted, the character must signify psychological depth, indicate that it has an independent inner life, and so is capable of acting as the 'author' of the deeds and dialogue assigned it by the playtext. Stanislavski asserts that, by employing the Psycho-Technique, the actor's personal input fills the performance with legible expressions of specific thoughts and feelings. This claim must be viewed with some scepticism. Even if such behavioural details did relate in a direct way to the actor's internal experiences, it is unlikely that an audience would be able to decode them, to read their precise psychic content; although we are capable of recognising behavioural postures, since we do so in everyday life, we are less adept at reading minds. But such minutiae do not go to waste, for the added performance signs collectively signify psychological complexity *per se*.

The third effect comes about obliquely, via the actor's own experience of Systematically working on the role. Having established parallels between his/her own psyche and the character's, Stanislavski argues, the actor will develop what he terms a 'sense of faith'. This sense of faith consists of the belief that, since the character is based upon the actor's self and experiences, it is true to the nature of humanity, a viable blueprint for a real individual. Stanislavski explains:

> Once you have established this contact between your life and your part, you will find that inner push or stimulus. Add a whole series of contingencies based on your own experience in life, and you will see how easy it will be for

you to believe in the possibility of what you are called to
do on the stage.

(Stanislavski 1980: 49)

Despite the metaphysical descriptions Stanislavski gives of his
work there is nothing magical about the System, for it requires
only those skills employed in ordinary social life, albeit that they
must be used with greater dexterity. In effect, his 'sense of faith'
describes the actor's successful adoption of what is for all
practical purposes a behavioural persona. In everyday social
exchange we employ behavioural codes appropriate to given
situations, weaving these into a coherent regime to represent
ourselves within those given rules. While we may be self-
conscious in unfamiliar situations – conscious of the gap between
our 'real' selves and the ones we signify – in time we learn to
exploit the new structures and assume an appropriate role.
Similarly, the System-atic actor constructs a regime of thoughts,
feelings, images, movements, the whole apparatus of the
Stanislavskian character, appropriate to the given situation of the
play. Once he/she has confidence in this construct, a 'sense of
faith', the actor performs more fluidly, 'behaves' within the
play's established parameters. The fragments of the role, created
by diverse means, cohere into a linear performance as the acting
becomes less deliberate, more automatic, more habitual and 'subconscious'. It even becomes possible to improvise 'spontaneous'
actions. Once the structures and limits of the character are
successfully internalised, these will guide even impromptu playing, ensuring that the actor stays within role. The ultimate result
is a marked coherence to the acting, with all signs disciplined
to stay within set limits, signifying the single, defined character.

As we noted, the System has so suffused our culture's view of
acting that often it seems merely the obvious and 'common-sense'
way of creating and performing a role. At the very least, its basic
assumptions that one must 'get inside' the character, and exploit
one's own experiences, seem self-evident. Therefore it is perhaps
necessary to state what is usually accepted without comment:
inner life, inner circumstances, the Magic If, the Psycho-
Technique, the imaginary moving picture show, Objectives –
all these are *psychological* in colouring. Indeed, the majority of
determinants on behaviour admitted within the System are

psychological ones. Stanislavskian performances thus offer psychological explanations of human behaviour, and do so by establishing the appropriate Law of the Text.

We saw in the Introduction that the Law of the Text is that logic which determines the meaning of all the signs presented. Any single sign – this gesture, that intonation – is likely to have a number of potential interpretations available to it in culture, but because we view that network of signs that is the *text* (the novel, film, painting, theatre production) as having one organised meaning, we seek out a discourse able to subsume all its parts, able to contain its interpretation.

How is this Law of the Text signified in practice? Putting all Stanislavski's claims aside, let us consider what the visible, material performance text consists of. To begin with, we have two streams of signs stemming from different sources. One stream originates in the playtext but comes to us via the use of Units and Objectives. As we saw, Objectives enable the actor to design a hypothetical self to function as the origin of the role's deeds and utterances. But they do so by ascribing to those 'effects' exclusively *psychological* causes. Objectives by definition conceive of a character's actions as psychologically determined, and require the actor to interpret the play's given deeds and dialogue in a psychological way. Although the playtext provides the words, an Objective such as 'I wish to seduce X' tells you how to speak them, and how to move, gesture, compose your facial expression and engage with X in a way that complements your speech – or rather, in a way that complements, *signifies*, the psychological motive that is deemed to lie *beneath* your speech. In this way Objectives automatically *interpret* the playtext, translating its story into a tale of its characters' desires.

The second stream of performance signs stems from the actor's personal input and consists of a mass of behavioural minutiae which serves to credit the character with psychological complexity. But the audience is in no position to distinguish between the two streams, for the actor's 'sense of faith' enables them to weave all signs into a fluid, coherent persona. The audience therefore sees *one complex* psychology, a psychologically profound individual (actor's input) pursuing their desires (Objectives); mind dictating actions according to their will. The audience is presented not with a character but with that *particular* character, the unique individual who feels, thinks and so acts in that singular way. All signs emanating from the actor are ascribed to this individual, signify it and, simultaneously, are semically contained by its logic. This individual thus becomes the basic, given unit that the audience must use in its sense-making, and so the discourse of 'Individualism' which it encodes becomes the interpretative logic governing the play, the Stanislavskian performance's preferred Law of the Text. In this way the System's techniques mobilise the play's narrative, words and actions to present the spectator not with any generalised human subject, but with a unique, autonomous, self-motivating Individual.

This conception of the human subject is usually termed the humanist or bourgeois individual and, far from being 'universal', it emerges at a particular point in history. We shall examine its historical position later, for it is now more important to note what it excludes. According to Marxist theory, human behaviour is in large part determined by the social and economic circumstances in which the individual exists, while Feminism asserts the impact of social constructions of gender. Within a Freudian framework, factors of which the individual is not aware (the drives of the unconscious, inaugural experiences of infancy such as the Oedipal rite of passage) are able to form, channel and repress desires and so determine actions. Sociology acknowledges that behaviour is shaped by the need to conform to established social roles, while Marxism, Feminism, Post-structuralism and most species of Structuralism all see human subjectivity and the behaviour derived from it as a function of the subject positions offered in discourse/ideology. In all these instances behaviour is shaped by forces acting *upon* the human subject's consciousness. But in the System human beings are represented as desiring machines, constantly in pursuit of their own aims, their actions dictated by forces within their psyches, so that the sole author of human action, consciously or subconsciously, is the individual self.

Stanislavski did demand that his actors consider such factors as class and historical context. However, in practice any elements of the performance that arise from these are redefined by a discourse of humanist individualism, the social content of those signs contained within that Law of the Text, and they instead become manifestations of the character's uniqueness, a testament to its singularity. Edward Braun observes that, although Stanislavski achieved

A seemingly effortless realism in performance, a perfect illusion of life . . . [nevertheless] the danger remained that for all the perception of behavioural detail, the playwright's overall design, what he was saying *through* the medium of the character's actions, could easily be overlooked.

(Braun 1982: 27)

This result was evident in Stanislavski's own work. After he directed Chekhov's *The Seagull*, the author complained that Stanislavski had turned what was a humorous piece into a tragedy, misconstruing the play's intentions. This kind of 'misinterpretation' is as much a product of the System's practices as any decision on the part of director or actor. Stanislavski had built the production around what he deemed to be the characters' own internal experiences, from which perspective their plights did not seem at all comic, and as a result the production was suffused with melancholy. But the consequences are actually more serious, for in interpreting all playtexts humanistically, the System disseminates a conception of the subject which is politically charged.

COMMUNION

Stanislavski was acutely aware of the problems caused by stage fright, and his System as a whole can be seen as a means of combating it. Describing the disorientating effect of 'the abyss of the proscenium arch' upon the actor, he states,

In ordinary life you walk and sit and talk and look, but on the stage you lose all these faculties . . . all of our acts, even the simplest, which are familiar to us in everyday life, become strained when we appear behind the footlights before a public of a thousand people.

(Stanislavski 1980: 77)

What does stage fright entail? We can best describe it using the concept of *defamiliarisation*, a term coined by the Russian Formalist aesthetician Viktor Shklovsky (see Jefferson and Robey 1982: 27–31). In attempting to define the distinctive 'literariness' of literary language, Shklovsky explained that language is ordinarily used in an habitual and automatic fashion. We usually view it as the mere vehicle of ideas, a transparent window onto meaning, and so overlook its materiality, its existence as a concrete thing separate from those thoughts it is used to convey. But in literary usage – most of all in poetry – language is rendered visible once again by the introduction of formal elements as obstacles to our habitual use, making language 'difficult'. Poetical devices such as rhyme, rhythm and the practice of setting the words out in lines – these force us to become aware of language itself, so that it is thrown into relief, 'foregrounded'.

A similar effect is produced by stage fright, for the audience's gaze defamiliarises the actor's behaviour, making deliberate what is usually 'subconscious'. With the knowledge that our every movement is being scrutinised, ordinarily habitual actions become the subject of conscious attention, and hence of conscious control. But conscious volition is not able to govern the complex balance of muscles used in walking (or speech, gesture, facial expression) with anything like the same proficiency. The fluidity of habitual movement is replaced by an observably fragmented sequence of distinct actions performed in a premeditated fashion (singly and with an observable 'change of gear' between each). Onstage this serves as signification of an undesirable kind, as signs of the actor acting rather than the character behaving; that is, as signs of theatrical artifice.

Stanislavski therefore aimed to eradicate stage fright and restore the actor's natural ability to act (or perhaps 'behave') onstage. This is in part achieved as a side-effect of some of the practices we have explored already: by encouraging the actor's 'sense of faith' in his or her creation, the resulting persona – what Stanislavski calls a 'mask' – shields the actor from the audience, so that it is the character's words and actions that are subject to the spectator's gaze, not the actor's. However, a second category of techniques blocks the disruptive gaze in a more direct way, and those exercises termed the 'Circle of Attention' and 'Object of Attention' are exemplary.

Training for the Circle of Attention begins with the actor on a darkened stage. A lamp is then turned on to illuminate a circle of light around the actor, beyond which nothing is visible:

> In a circle of light, in the midst of darkness, you have the sensation of being alone . . . it is what we call Solitude in Public. You are in public because we are all here. It is

solitude because you are divided from us by a small circle of attention.

(Stanislavski 1980: 82)

During an actor's training the size of the circle is to be varied but always kept within the limits of the stage area. With practice, Stanislavski asserts, the actor will learn to imagine a circle without the aid of a lamp, and do so during a performance. The aim is to marginalise the actor's awareness of the audience's presence, allowing the actor to act as if unwatched.

This is an example of what Stanislavski calls 'external attention', where the actor focuses upon the real, physical circumstances of the stage. The next stage of 'inner attention' requires a more personal and imaginative response, and this is to be nurtured with the more advanced 'Object of Attention' exercise. Here a real object, a prop or piece of set, is chosen for the performer's focus. Again the actor begins with external attention, working upon the object's physical characteristics: 'Look at this antique chandelier. It dates back to the days of the Emperor. How many branches has it? What is its form, its design?' Then inner attention is employed to evoke an imaginative and emotional response: 'Do you like it? If so, what is it that especially attracts you? . . . This chandelier may have been in the house of some Field Marshal when he received Napoleon' (Stanislavski 1980: 89). In both cases the desired effect is that the audience's presence be removed from the actor's immediate sphere of awareness, with the result that he/she are is no longer self-conscious of their actions. In this way the conditions of everyday behaviour – actions freed from conscious control – are to be re-established, allowing the actor to perform fluidly.

But inner attention goes beyond combating stage fright, for the Object of Attention exercise is also part of the Stanislavski's Psycho-Technique, a means of imagistically building a character and holding it in one's mind. By focusing on a chair, for example, and relating its characteristics to the character (does its design relate to the character's occupation? its social position? the colour to its personality, or some event in its past?), the actor is to use it to anchor the character's qualities during performance, employing the chair in a similar way to the 'magic picture show' of mental images. In fact all these techniques are based upon Stanislavski's theory of 'Communion', a term which describes actors' relationships with any object of their attention. Stanislavski lists the forms of Communion which are acceptable: with oneself in a dialogue between intellect and emotions (soliloquy); with another 'soul' (actor); with a real object; with an imaginary object (for example, the dagger in *Macbeth*); with a mass object (a crowd scene).

The System's means of combating stage fright thus merge into the Psycho-Technique, for 'Communion' with an object not only serves to limit the actor's attention to the confines of the stage, it is also a tool for evoking character. The character's 'unbroken line' of thoughts and feelings must relate not just to Objectives and inner circumstances, but also to the other 'objects' of the playworld, including set, props, other characters and even, according to Stanislavski, lighting. Moreover, in Stanislavski's view it is this continuity which makes for an 'unbroken line' in the audience's relationship with the event. He writes:

> Can you imagine a valuable necklace in which, after every three golden links, there is one of tin, and then two golden links tied together with string? And who would want a constantly breaking line of communication on the stage? ... If actors really mean to hold the attention of a large audience they must make every effort to maintain an uninterrupted exchange of feelings, thoughts and actions among themselves.
>
> (Stanislavski 1980: 196)

To maintain character one must 'commune' with the other actors and objects on the stage, and this also establishes an unbroken line of 'communion' with the audience.

Here, then, Stanislavski acknowledges that the Systematic performance creates a specific kind of relationship with the auditorium. But 'communion', with its metaphysical connotations, is a misleading term. The stage is a material place, and it commnicates via concrete means. 'Communion' in all its forms produces observable signs, and it is these which will enable us to understand the dialogic relationship which the Stanislavskian performance text proffers.

The Circle and Object of Attention exercises and Communion all limit performers' attention to the stage, while demanding at the same time that they engage imaginatively and intellectually with everything that falls within that compass. This means that touch, gestures, words and even glances will connect only with those objects and individuals that occupy the playworld – set, props, other characters and imaginary daggers – but *will* connect with those continually and emphatically. Everything the actor does will visibly describe a link between himself/herself and the playworld's other elements, signalling to the audience that all are part of the same fictional reality. The elements of the production are thereby woven into a single whole, a fabric or 'necklace' of objects/characters sewn together by the thread of deeds, utterances and all the minutiae of behaviour, so that the performances themselves 'act' the production into a unified text, a unified *locus*.

What exactly is the locus? To describe it as the play's setting is too crude for our purpose here. More accurately, the locus is a notional 'space' in which everything functions symbolically, in the Abstract register, so that the actor becomes Hamlet and the actual stage another, hypothetical place. The locus is distinct from the real, social space of the audience because it demands that its elements be interpreted differently. The audience is capable of doing this; all it requires is some indication that the locus is separate. As we noted in the Introduction, a metaphorical 'frame' must be drawn around the event, including all the production's parts and excluding all else.

It is precisely this 'framing' that the System effects most efficiently, and it does so by two means. First, the Circle and Object of Attention exercises, and Communion, visibly weave all the production's elements into a single whole, creating a symbolic space separate from that of the audience. At the same time the System banishes signs of artifice by eradicating stage fright and by having the actor acknowledge *only* those things that fall within the symbolic space, the locus. In fact, the two effects are symbiotic, for, just as eradicating signs of the actor (social space) means that the subject will be read solely as a character (symbolic space), so the establishment of a symbolic space will redefine signs of artifice (actor) as signs from the locus (character).

Thus with the System we have the most firmly framed locus possible, and, as a consequence, Stanislavskian performances diminish the Concrete register while preferring the Abstract. As we saw, the Concrete register reveals its own artifice, displays the process by which its meanings are constructed; in exhibiting its 'authors', it shows its meanings to be authored. Conversely,

44

by concealing artifice the Abstract presents its meanings as non-constructed, author-free; they are not a construction, they simply *are*, have an unquestioned existence in the world. Thus in the Abstract register the object on stage stands not for a particular object but a general order of objects, of which it is the symbolic representative; not *that* table (chosen by the designer, placed on the stage) but 'Tables' *per se*.

This indicates the relatively passive dialogic relationship System-atic performances offer their audiences. As we have seen, Stanislavskian acting presents a particular ideological construction of the human subject. However, it simultaneously informs us that this is not 'constructed' at all, for, by eradicating all signs of the stage's meaning-making process, it construes those meanings as non-constructed, as neutral, 'natural' and non-partisan. Thus the System presents us with humanist individuals and tells us that they are representative of human beings *per se*. That which is historically and ideologically determined it offers as 'universal' by both containing our interpretation of the characters within its humanist Law of the Text, and by offering an interpretative stance which demands that we accept such conceptions uncritically.

THE HISTORY OF THE SYSTEM

A society's aesthetics are of course part of its culture and so are shaped by, and reproduce, the meanings that circulate in that culture. This is equally true of the aesthetics of performance. That is not to say that acting must 'reflect' the social order in some direct fashion. Rather, forms of social organisation, culture and ideology are all part of the same interacting complex, and the ideas, the discourses, of that complex both provide the basis for meaning and limit the kinds of meaning possible – provide the materials out of which meaning may be *made*. To both 'write' and be 'read', acting must deal in notions that circulate in society, and will bear the traces of such. Far from being 'universal', we may therefore expect System-atic acting to encode contemporary discursive formations, and two of these prove particularly significant.

The first is that of the bourgeois subject, and the ideology of which it is a part, humanism, has a long history. Very briefly, in the sixteenth and seventeenth centuries western society underwent a fundamental historical change, as the remains of the old feudal order gave ground to the economic mode which we now call 'capitalism'. Capitalism led to the formation of new social structures, giving birth to a new ruling class which, because of its association with mercantile centres in towns and cities, came to be called the burghers or 'bourgeoisie'. Although it would be many years before this class gained political power commensurate with its wealth, the ideas it promoted achieved dominance more quickly, cohering into that ideological discursive formation which came to be termed 'humanism'.

The ideology that dominated the prior, feudal world envisaged society as an organic whole, a finely graded hierarchy shaped according to God's plan, in which everyone was allotted a fixed place. But humanism was built upon discourses that had not God, but the human subject, at their centre. The new economic logic saw people as independent vendors in the 'free market', owning and selling property or, if they possessed nothing else, their labour. Political writings conjured the image of the free, autonomous 'citizen', while legal discourse developed the concept of the individual who enters freely into contracts, *creating* socio-economic relationships rather than adhering to those handed down from above. Protestantism argued that each Christian had access to God and His truth directly, requiring no mediation from church or saints, while Rationalism and Empirical Science both predicated a subject whose view and understanding of phenomena was objective and reliable, who could elicit truth independent of any external agency. In their various ways, these component discourses of bourgeois ideology all have the autonomous individual as their prerequisite, take as their starting point the subject who is self-contained and self-determining, the possessor of free will and a capacity for objective knowledge. While it may appear liberating, however, this concept had under capitalism a crucial ideological dimension. In imaging the social subject as autonomous and free, the discourse of bourgeois individualism concealed the real material circumstances that governed people's lives; although part of a free market, most individuals lack the means to exploit that freedom.

It was not until the nineteenth century that a fully fledged aesthetic of literary and theatrical realism developed, providing a formal means of disseminating humanist principles. Realism and the bourgeois individual are symbiotic concepts. Realism presents itself as a 'slice of life' as seen by a stable, autonomous subject, while the very existence of that which we term 'the individual' is itself continuously restated by realism's imaging of its viewpoint, so that, whatever their content, the novels of Zola, Dickens, Dostoevsky and Tolstoy, and, later, the naturalist plays of Ibsen, Strindberg, Chekhov and Hauptmann, all restate the concept of the individual implicitly.

This conception of the human subject was not seriously challenged until the late nineteenth and early twentieth centuries, when a number of theories and discourses that were to prove crucial in the formation of *modernism* gained cultural currency. Many of these offered new views of human subjectivity: Marx argued that consciousness was shaped by systems of ideas, 'ideologies'; the new sociology described the way identity was moulded by one's assumption of given social roles; Saussure stated that all human perception was a product of cultural sign systems. In their different ways, these opposed the notion of the stable subject, complete unto itself.

Most significant for our purposes are those of the new discourses which focus on the human psyche, as this is the second trace borne by the System. The most important figure in this respect is Freud, for psychoanalytic theory revolutionised the way the self was viewed. Freud is representative, however, of a more widespread cultural shift towards notions of internality. The philosopher Henri Bergson argued for two conceptions of time, one which was external and objectively measurable, and another which reflected one's subjective experience. The American pragmatist philosopher William James imaged the mind as a 'stream of consciousness', a ceaseless and multi-levelled flow of sensation, and this term was taken up and used to describe the experiments with interior monologue characteristic of the novels of Virginia Woolf, James Joyce, Marcel Proust, William Faulkner and Dorothy Richardson. In the visual arts, Impressionism focused on the individual act of perception, the effect of light on the retina to produce a momentary, subjective image; subsequent movements such as Expressionism and Surrealism represented specifically subjective, sub-social realities. All these theories and movements evidence a new concern with the interior self, and it is as part of this general tide that we can view Stanislavski's work. With the System we see a blending of the basic figure of the bourgeois individual with the new emphasis on psychology, an ideological construct, born in the seventeenth and eighteenth centuries, concretised into an aesthetic with nineteenth-century realism, and finally modified and informed by modernist discourses that explored the realm of interiority.

The significance of an aesthetic is never fixed, however, never limited to that granted it by the culture from which it originated. Aesthetics can be re-used, given new meanings; classical Greek and Roman art and ideas, for example, have been variously employed in different phases of neo-classicism. The System-atic character embodies the humanist individual, certainly, but this ideological construct has been mobilised to more specific political ends, and two instances prove especially revealing.

Stanislavski and his collaborator, the teacher and dramatist Vladimir Nemirov-Danchenko, founded the Moscow Art Theatre in 1897, providing a platform for this new form of realism and ultimately establishing the System as a dominant acting style. In the aftermath of the Russian Revolution of 1917, however, there was an explosion of theatrical experiment, particularly in Moscow. Formal experiment entails a search for new modes of seeing/representing, and theatrical innovation thus complemented the Revolution's rejection of the old order. But by the late 1930s experiment in the Soviet Union was entirely suppressed. The project of the Soviet state was no longer the overthrow of the old regime but the consolidation of a new one, and this entailed, among other things, the creation of new social and cultural norms. The cultural norms favoured by the new ruling elite were those of Socialist Realism, an aesthetic which employed nineteenth-century realist techniques to depict heroic, idealised individuals in an optimistic light.

Socialist Realism was used to paint a positive, and largely false, picture of the Soviet Union for its people, so harnessing their efforts in building the new state. Its imposition required the banishment of the USSR's revolutionary diversity of artistic views, for experiment, the *interrogation* of existing modes of seeing, was now antithetical to the state's project, being condemned as 'formalism' and 'bourgeois decadence'. The political urgency of this suppression is suggested by the very emphatic form it could take; Stanislavski's former pupil, Vsevelod Meyerhold, was imprisoned and executed. System-atic realism, however, reproduced the old view of the bourgeois subject now being re-employed by the Soviet state, and so was not incompatible with the new line. While experimental theatre dwindled, Stanislavskian acting – with its obscuring of real, material determinants, and the uncritical posture it demands of its audience – thrived.

This is not to say that Stanislavski supported Stalinist policies, for he did not. Rather, this example illustrates the way in which acting styles are inevitably a part of the ideological conflict that takes place within representation of any kind. A similar process is revealed in an examination of the System's history in the West. At the end of the nineteenth century industrial production in the developed world entered a more complex phase. New technology needed new kinds of skilled workers to operate it, and a minimal superstructure of education, health provision, transport and so on was put in place to service their needs. Being more complex, production and the systems that supported it were also vulnerable to disruption, so that a compliant and consensual society was required to ensure their continuance, a culture with widely shared values able to minimise differences and mobilise all to the task of its maintenance.

All these features began to develop gradually over the first third of the twentieth century, but the task became infinitely more urgent during the 1930s with world-wide economic depression, and later, with the social upheaval that resulted from the Second World War. In response the societies of Western Europe and North America developed means of 'husbanding' industry and commerce, so that with Roosevelt's New Deal policies and Britain's adoption of the socio-economic theories of John Maynard Keynes (a path to be followed by other European nation states), governments began to intervene directly in economic life on a greater scale than ever before. At the same time, an expansion of health and welfare services minimised social dissent by giving the populace reasons to support the *status quo*. Most significant for our purposes, however, are the cultural changes that took place, for the same period saw the creation of large, publicly funded arts, media and education establishments. The main thrust of culture and education in the post-war period represented an attempt to inculcate the populace with the moral and cultural standards of an educated middle class. By such means western states sought in earnest to establish that shared consensus of values upon which society could be unified. Describing the period from a British perspective, Alan Sinfield writes:

> Historically and currently, in most of the world, human societies have been and are generally controlled by force. ... [But] Since what people of my generation call 'the war', meaning 1939–45, a distinctive attempt has been made in Britain and other parts of Europe to arrange things differently. The idea has been that we will all, or almost all, be persuaded to acquiesce in the prevailing order because we see that it is working generally to our benefit. ... To win the war, people were encouraged to believe that there would not be a widespread return to injustice and poverty. The war exemplified (though not without contest) a pattern of state intervention and popular cooperation to organize production for a common purpose. ... Full employment and the welfare state created, for a while, the sense of a society moving towards fairness.
>
> (Sinfield 1989: 1)

These changes resulted in an increasingly corporatised society where the state guaranteed many basic services for the populace, and in which public consent was courted as never before. This means of ordering society is usually termed 'welfare capitalism' and it is validated by the political ideology of Social Democracy – an ideology to which, for a time, all 'legitimate' political parties and governments of western Europe and North America subscribed, albeit with modifications. Broadly, Social Democracy views society as a single whole, an organised structure that operates only with the integration of its parts. Thus over the post-war period we see a sequence of previously marginalised social groups – ethnic communities, women, gays, and disabled, elderly, homeless and unemployed people – all being offered some limited recognition and inclusion within the social whole. Social Democracy is, however, humanist in its assumptions. It is geared towards the elision of, for example, class difference, not its recognition and eradication; that which is shared by all human beings is more profound than that which divides them.

In parallel with their social and economic husbandry, then, western states intervened on a cultural, ideological level with the aim of ensuring the acquiescent society necessary to maintain the *status quo*. Although we should not overlook the many real differences, in this respect the West's project bears marked similarities to that of the Eastern bloc nations, and it is in a comparable light that we must view western theatre's adoption of the System and its rise to become the legitimised orthodoxy in acting. As we have seen, the System can depict the full range of social subjects yet construe each as representative of the universal humanist individual. That is, it can incorporate signs of a character's class, historical and social position, and so on – determinants imposed upon the self from outside – while rendering such factors subordinate to the character's essential humanity; can display real, material differences while construing these as trivial compared to what is shared and the same. It therefore aligns itself with the state's desire for a discord-free society, contributing to the creation of a cultural consensus and hence to social stability.

These are specific examples, but realism is always caught up in such struggles for power. As we noted at the beginning of this chapter, realism presents itself as a simulation of the real. By shaping our conception of the real world, ideology controls our ability to act upon that world, so that realism inevitably becomes a focus for ideological intervention.

2

STRASBERG'S 'METHOD'

THE NEW REALISM

Lee Strasberg (1901–82) turned to the stage in the 1920s, that decade in which the foundations of modern American theatre were laid with the work of such companies as the Provincetown Players and the Theatre Guild, and with the early plays of formative US dramatists such as Eugene O'Neill and Susan Glaspell. Dissatisfied with indigenous schools of actor training, Strasberg studied under one of Stanislavski's Moscow Art Theatre performers, Richard Boleslavsky. Boleslavsky had travelled the United States as part of an MAT tour but stayed to deliver a series of lectures (see Boleslavsky 1975), finally joining with another of Stanislavski's actors, Maria Ouspenskaya, to found America's first System-based academy, the Laboratory. Fired by the desire to create a 'truly American theater', Strasberg and another Laboratory graduate, the director Harold Clurman, joined with young Broadway producer Cheryl Crawford to found the now legendary Group Theatre. Over the ten years of its existence the Group specialised in grittily realistic, socially orientated drama, producing directors Elia Kazan, Robert Lewis and Arthur Penn, the playwright Clifford Odets, and actors such as Lee J. Cobb, Van Heflin, Frances Farmer, Stella and Luther Adler, and Franchot Tone.

The Group disbanded in 1941 but six years later Crawford, Kazan and Lewis founded an academy in New York where trained actors could 'sharpen' their skills, naming it the Actors' Studio. Strasberg was eventually made the Studio's artistic director, and from 1951 it became for all practical purposes his school. Equally, although Clurman, Kazan and others must be credited with influence, the style of acting that was developed in embryo with the Group Theatre, and refined at the Actors' Studio, is generally acknowledged to be Strasberg's creation. This came to be known as 'The Method'. As a style, the Method has exerted a greater influence on American acting than any other practice, an impact which in recent years has become international. Accessible examples of Method work may be found in the film performances of Studio actors such as Marlon Brando, Ellen Burstyn, Jill Clayburgh, James Dean, Robert De Niro, Sandy Dennis, Bruce Dern, Robert Duvall, Jane Fonda, Dustin Hoffman, Dennis Hopper, Paul Newman, Al Pacino, Geraldine Page, Estelle Parsons, Mickey Rourke, Eva Marie Saint, Rod Steiger, Christopher Walken, Shelley Winters and Joanne Woodward.

Although the young Strasberg considered himself an heir to Stanislavski, when questioned by Stella Adler the Russian proved sceptical of the American's practices (see Garfield 1980: 33; or Hirsch 1984: 78). Indeed, the Method produces very distinct performance texts, constituting a separate school. Above all else, it was conceived as a pre-eminently *realistic* style of acting, a realism which, in Strasberg's view, derived from its approach to character, the Method actor's uncompromising search for 'truth' and 'authenticity'. But that is to see it from the practitioner's subjective viewpoint. Objectively, acting is a material practice and presents its audience with concrete signs. All acting styles are composed of a characteristic repertoire of such signs, an *iconography*: types of movement, posture and speech, ways of combining them and so on. That is not to say that all actors of a particular school perform in precisely the same way. Rather, it is from this iconography, this pool of performance signs, that the actor selects, either adopting the style consciously or doing so unconsciously by employing its techniques.

For a style of acting to be considered realistic, however, a second quality is required. As we have seen, realism is not an inherent feature of a performance but derives from the way that performance is received. Realistic acting is the mode *deemed* realistic by its viewing culture, the style whose distinct repertoire of conventional signs – whose particular kind of artificiality – is agreed to signify the 'real'. The Method's realism must therefore derive from its distinctive iconographic components. For our purposes, four of these prove particularly significant.

The first component was a new 'ease' or naturalness onstage. Group actors would use their bodies freely, employ gestures which were expressive but familiar, non-symbolic, use ordinary cadences and demotic speech patterns. This was partly the fruit of Strasberg's use of relaxation techniques and exercises to acclimatise the actor to the stage. Freed of defamiliarising tension and its resulting self-consciousness, actors were able to fall back upon the behavioural regimes of ordinary life – not necessarily to use its behavioural codes, but to act without the overriding requirement to be communicative, intelligible for an audience.

The Group's emphasis on naturalness was a reaction to the theatre of the time. The American stage of the 1930s was insecure in its own cultural status, and acting deferred to European models, especially a British style termed 'heroic' or 'aristocratic'. Although less stylised than nineteenth-century modes, aristo-cratic acting was mannered by modern standards, favouring crisp, sharply articulated diction and emblematic movement, gesture and posture to produce performances that were both clear and, according to the aesthetics of the time, 'beautiful'. By effectively signalling their own conventionality, however, such qualities subverted any claims to modern realism. From the out-set Strasberg and his colleagues were opposed to all convention, and their new 'system' was conceived as a revolt against exist-ing mannered styles. This was not solely an aesthetic preference, for they believed that convention *per se* automatically stifled 'truth'. Describing the Group Theatre's view, Clurman wrote:

> The aim of the system is to enable the actor to use himself more consciously for the attainment of truth on the stage. . . . We are not satisfied with most of even the best previous productions, which seemed to us to show more competent stagecraft than humanity or authenticity of feeling. With few exceptions, what we saw was 'performance', fabrication, artifice.
>
> (Clurman 1983: 43)

Aristocratic acting not only appeared artificial, then, it also produced artificial meanings. It moulded the actor's 'truth' into conventional forms, rendering it 'inauthentic', no longer the genuine expression of his or her intentions.

This moulding of performance was perceived to parallel the theatrical establishment's casting practices. In the 1930s the milieu of non-establishment theatre was suffused with radical ideas and rhetoric, and Strasberg's reading of *Das Kapital* led him to formulate a supposedly 'Marxist' analysis of acting. In commercially orientated Broadway, he believed, a system of type-casting wherein non-star actors would only be cast in roles for which their (mainly physical) attributes suited them. The actor was thereby industrialised and the role made a commodity, a product manufactured by the theatrical machine and alienated from its producer and their creativity. Thus one of the Group's functions was to provide actors with roles they would not otherwise be offered, while its convention-free acting technique was similarly to enable them to achieve authentic expression. It was to be, in Strasberg's terms, a 'proletarian' style. If aristocrats are formal and mannered, masters of the stage's artificial conventions, proletarians lack such mastery and are rough and awkward. But by avoiding established formulas, they remain free, capable of genuine expression.

Thus the very informality of Group performances operated as a sign, signifying their realism, and did so by implicit comparison with other styles. Just as the conventionality of aristocratic acting inadvertently acknowledged the audience's presence – indicated that it was *acting* – so the absence of convention functioned as a sign of the natural; when we see actors acting in a markedly casual way, unconcerned whether their words/actions are clear, we read this as an indication that they are 'behaving' within the play's world rather than striving to engage with ours. But whereas 'naturalness' was a characteristic of Group work, at the Studio it developed into a fashion for masking the process of performance. As Arthur Penn observed, *'Not* to act (in a particular way) continues to charm Studio actors. . . . The cult of being real, which floods the place, can encourage vehement displays of *hiding* craft' (Hirsch 1984: 221). By concealing any possible indication of artifice, adopting a stridently casual persona, Group and Studio performers presented their work as 'authentic'.

The second iconographic component was an enhanced signification of the character's 'inner life'. This was a by-product of Strasberg's conception of acting *per se*. For Strasberg, the actor's essential task was to create and maintain an imaginary reality so profound and detailed that it could provoke him or her to real responses. To this end he insisted on lengthy and varied improvisations both in training and in rehearsals. When working on a play, actors would create hypothetical scenes that extended the character's life, its 'inner circumstances', far beyond the playwright's story. More importantly, he employed techniques designed to enhance the actor's powers of concentration. 'Analytical memory' exercises involved the handling of imaginary objects, developing the actors' ability to immerse themselves in imaginary worlds. Similarly, real objects were used to evoke imagistic associations of the character, anchoring it in the actor's mind.

Some of these techniques were, as we saw, a part of the System, but they played a more central role in Strasberg's practice. The result was a stream of behavioural minutiae far denser than that produced by Stanislavskian work. Method performances abound with subtle detail, nuances of gesture, vocal inflection and facial expression, which function as signs of the character's internality, indicating that it is constantly thinking, feeling and experiencing. In addition, the Method actor's enhanced concentration tends to surface in performance itself, where it is ascribed to the character and read as psychological 'intensity'. When this is allied with dense minutiae, Method performances present their audiences with characters who signify a complex inner life. The image offered is of individuals possessing great psychological 'depth'.

The Method's third distinctive iconographic component is heightened emotionalism. Indeed, Strasberg's emphasis on the character's inner life is in practice a concern with its *emotional* life, a focus evident from his early days as a practitioner. Praising Strasberg's achievements with the Group, Clurman wrote:

> Here at last was a key to that elusive ingredient of the stage, true emotion. And Strasberg was a fanatic on the subject of true emotion. Everything was secondary to it. He sought it with the patience of an inquisitor, he was outraged by trick substitutes, and when he succeeded in stimulating it, he husbanded it, fed it, protected it.
>
> (Clurman 1983: 45)

Strasburg's preoccupation with the expression of emotion is sometimes explained anecdotally: Boleslavsky left the Moscow Art Theatre when Stanislavski's interest in emotional psychology was at its height, and exaggerated this emphasis because of his own preference for emotional work, conferring upon America a lopsided System. But in fact Strasberg was always predisposed towards this emphasis (see Hirsch 1984: 75). In his view the key task of acting throughout history, and the problem it has never entirely solved, is how to obtain 'true emotion'.

The technique Strasberg terms the 'Emotion Memory exercise' is the cornerstone of the Method, and to explain it he, like Stanislavski, drew upon the theories of the early clinical psychologist Théodule Ribot. There are, Strasberg argues, three forms of memory: mental (remembering a fact), physical (remembering how to walk or tie shoelaces) and affective. Affective memory is of two kinds. The first, 'Analytic' or 'Sense Memory', deals solely in physical sensations, and, as we noted, was employed by Strasberg in the 'handling' of imaginary objects, a technique designed to enhance actors' ability to create imaginary worlds. The other area of affective memory is that which enables actors to summon genuine feelings from their past and use them in performance. This Strasberg refers to as 'Emotion Memory'.

The actor begins the Emotion Memory exercise by choosing a moment from their past when a particular emotion was experienced in a potent form. Strasberg insisted that the memory be at least seven years old, since only feelings whose traces remain for so long are entrenched enough to be reinvoked. The actor then recalls all the sensory information from that moment in precise and far-reaching detail: temperature, sounds, smells, textures of clothes – everything that impinged upon the senses. The memories are not to be recalled *as* information, such as 'It was cold', but as *experiences*; 'my hands felt cold'. According to the exercise's Pavlovian logic, recalling these sensory experiences will cause the emotion associated with them to manifest itself automatically. Over the period of training the actor should practise evoking six to ten emotions so that these can be recalled easily in performance. Deciding where in a play a given feeling is required, the actor can then summon it from their emotional 'paintbox', Strasberg maintaining that 'after sufficient exercise, the recall can be accomplished in one minute' (Strasberg 1988: 112).

Although it derives from Stanislavski's ideas, the Emotion Memory exercise was Strasberg's own creation, a modification of Boleslavsky's teachings. For our purposes it has several discernible results. First, Method performances tend to deal not merely in emotions but in emotions of an extreme kind. In selecting an experience from the past to employ onstage, few actors will choose a moment when they were relatively happy or moderately sad. Indeed, for such feelings to be retained after seven years, the initial experience must be a potent one. As a consequence Method performances are usually marked by displays of highly charged feeling, expressions of sublime pleasure or, more often, trauma and emotional distress.

In addition, these highly charged emotional displays tend to be discontinuous with the emotional tenor of the rest of the performance. Stanislavski's System produces very coherent character, an 'unbroken line' in which all elements interweave smoothly to form a unity. By choosing homogeneous behavioural codes based upon their own illusory unity, and eradicating discordant elements according to the logic of the 'Through-Line of Action', Stanislavskian actors build performances which are markedly even. But the Method thrusts highly charged expressions of emotion into the performance without integrating them. Emotion erupts in explosive flashes, so that performances are characterised by drastic swings in feeling.

It may be assumed that Method performances will therefore appear psychologically implausible, but in fact the opposite is true. Emotion, and particularly unpredictable emotion, implies spontaneity. It infers an inner space of the psyche whose workings cannot adequately be judged by external expression. As spectators, we more readily assume an *inner* self as the author of fragmented emotional display, so that the very discontinuity of Method acting supports a psychological reading.

Combined with other Method techniques, however, Emotion Memory also produces an effect of quite a different order, for it nurtures actors with idiosyncratic performance personae. Emotion Memory brings to the stage a behavioural regime that derives from the performer himself/herself, not from the playtext. It is the *actor's* emotions, or, more precisely, their extreme expression of them, that shape the character. Consequently, the Studio has produced many actors – De Niro, Dennis, Pacino, Duvall, Winters, Steiger and so on – who consistently construct character from their own unique expressive mannerisms, 'act themselves' in a variety of roles. Reflecting on his observations of Studio work, Foster Hirsch recalls:

> I was sometimes bothered that the distance between the actor and the character – the inevitable gap between simply

being and giving a performance – was not clarified, as if to be yourself in a believable way was enough. ... it seemed to me that the actor would often stop at a point where he was loose enough to uncover his own wounds and blemishes. When it's arrested there the process can become one where the *actor's* insides are revealed rather than the character's.

(Hirsch 1984: 221)

Behavioural informality or 'casualness', psychological intensity, heightened and discontinuous emotional display – these are three consistent features of the Method performance. They form the core of its iconography, for although Strasbergian actors often employ their own unique performance personae, their mannerisms nevertheless fall into predictable categories, proffering the same orders of meaning. There is, however, a fourth iconographic component, and it is the most important, for it mediates the audience's perception of all the others, altering the meanings offered by the Method performance text.

UNBLOCKING EMOTIONS

Underlying all Strasberg's ideas, implicit rather than explicit, is a model of the human psyche. It forms the unspoken conceptual basis for his practices, and is the ultimate source of the Method's distinctive features. To explain the Method's fourth iconographic component, we must first examine the model of the self which underpins it.

As we noted, Strasberg placed considerable emphasis upon preparatory training in relaxation. The aim of his relaxation techniques was not simply the elimination of nervousness, for they were also designed to enhance what was, for Strasberg, the actor's most important tool, his or her ability to express emotion. In one such exercise the actor would be asked to sit in a hard chair and find a way to be comfortable in it, the purpose being to train him or her to feel 'comfortable' onstage. Seated, the actor is instructed to check and consciously relax the major muscle groups in turn, especially those associated with tension. According to Strasberg's account, the seated actor will often feel some 'emotion' welling up unexpectedly and, surprised, will initially resist it. The actor is directed to overcome that resistance by emitting 'evenly vibrated sound' from deep within the chest. If this fails to remove the resistance, the sound should be made 'sharp', 'fully committed' and 'explosive', for this, Strasberg asserts, will clear a passage for even the strongest of emotions.

Despite the arcane imagery, it is possible to discern the underlying shape of the problem such exercises are designed to address. The above technique pictures emotions emerging from the inner self to seek natural, physical expression. They meet resistance, however, in the shape of an outer, 'uncomfortable' self. Such resistance is created by 'tension', described by Strasberg as 'the presence of unnecessary or excess energy which inhibits the flow of thought or sensation to the required area' (Strasberg 1988: 125). Tension, then, physically constricts the outer self like an uncomfortable chair, preventing natural emotional flow. The obstacle is overcome by the passage of 'sounds' – primal, pre-rational and emphatically physical – from deep inside, which free the body from tension and allow emotions to pass unhindered.

In his very techniques, then, Strasberg images a discord between the experience of emotions and their physical *significa-tion*. Speaking of when he became artistic director of the Actors' Studio, Strasberg explained how he 'came to realize more and more that an actor could experience and yet not be able to express an emotion. . . . This difficulty is true not only for actors, but for all human beings' (Strasberg 1988: 94). Although techniques such as the Emotion Memory exercise enable one to evoke and experience feelings, the problem of how to communicate them to an audience remains. With a group of techniques called 'Exercises for Unblocking Emotion', Strasberg addressed this problem directly. The most interesting of these, known variously as 'Song and Dance' or 'Singing the Words', was developed by Strasberg for use with dancers and singers, but he subsequently employed it to deal with the expressive problems of Studio actors.

The actor begins the Song and Dance exercise by facing and making eye contact with the class, establishing that it is he or she, not some hypothetical character, who is the source of expression. At this point the actor must strive for awareness of 'tensions and feelings'. In the technique's first phase the actor sings a song. While retaining the melody, however, they must break with its given structure and speak each syllable separately, giving each equal weight and emphasis. In the second phase the actor again performs the song but this time in short, staccato bursts of syllables. In addition, they must match the bursts to spontaneous movements. These, it was stressed, should be unplanned and irregular, not formalised or dance-like. The class chair or 'moderator' then calls for the movement and sound to be repeated. If the actor is 'blocked' they will display uncontrollable muscular contractions such as tics, tremblings and spasms. By this means the Song and Dance exercise seeks to eradicate the discord between the inner and outer self directly. By progressively eliminating the various curbs on physical expression – inhibitions of movement or those arising from self-consciousness before an audience, the song's metre, even the shaping of syllable sounds into words – the actor's tensions are purged in the form of muscular spasms. He or she is therefore theoretically free to respond in a natural way – not with intellectual concepts as expressed by words, but with unstructured movement and subsocial 'sounds'.

For Strasberg the inability to express feelings is an affliction peculiar to the modern world. If in some past, prelapsarian era emotions could be freely expressed, there is, Strasberg asserts, a 'peculiar, divided, dual quality [to] modern man' (Strasberg 1988: 20). Modernity has caused a 'fall' to occur, separating emotion from its means of external expression, the essential, inner self from the signifying outer. Relaxation and Unblocking exercises thus aim to re-establish this lost unity, and realign the emotional and physical selves so that feeling can flow in a natural, unmediated way.

For Strasberg this discord has a specific origin. He states:

> Whatever capacities the human being is born with, it is by means of training and conditioning that he learns to use them. ... He is conditioned to express his feelings and emotions not by the nature, character and strength of his own emotional responses, but by what society and his environment will permit. ... Often he does so in ways which become so limited that we call them 'mannerisms'. Since to the individual these are his natural expressions, he thinks of them as being real and true and does not perceive that they are mannered. At the Actors' Studio I

had to find ways of dealing with an actor's mannerisms that obscured the truth of expression that involves the relationship between intensity of feeling and emotion.

(Strasberg 1988: 95)

The subject's natural ability to emote and express, then, is repressed by the modern world's 'conditioning'. For Strasberg such conditioning may result from personal experiences such as traumatic events in an individual's past, or shared ones such as learning codes of behaviour, but it always occurs as a result of the self's encounter with the external, man-made world. It is this which channels impulses, preventing their expression or moulding them into 'inauthentic', socially acceptable forms, so that they no longer represent the subject's 'true emotion'. Regardless of the particular mechanism by which it is effected – behavioural codes, personal inhibitions, stage fright, culturally determined 'mannerisms' of expression, or the conventions of aristocratic acting – the division of the modern self and its resulting inability to express feelings ultimately originates in the individual's absorption into the social order. It is caused, that is, by socialisation.

This conception of the psyche – an inner essence stifled by the outer, its impulses repressed by social conditioning – has little in common with Stanislavski's, but is one that has long held a privileged place in American culture. Historically, most of the discourses and ideologies that have dominated American thought have been without a substantial social-determinist component, a thoroughgoing conception of the subject as *constructed* – not merely repressed – by social environment. Political discourse of both the Left and Right, for example, tends to gravitate about concepts of liberty and individualism, not the remodelling of social structures but the *escape* from them, into a realisation of one's natural self. As a consequence American culture has produced an array of artefacts and ideas which image an inner, essential self under threat of suppression from a socialised outer. The United States has traditionally viewed itself as the land of freedom, where personal opinions may be voiced without interference. Indeed, freedom of expression is at the core of its own myths of origin, both the Founding Fathers' search for a land in which to pursue their religious beliefs, and the nation's liberation from the yoke of British imperialism by revolution. American culture both valorises individualism and promotes suspicion of state intervention, defining the self in opposition to society. Indeed, the 'American Dream' itself focuses upon the liberation and satisfaction of individual potential, both economic and personal.

Such concepts are reproduced in day-to-day cultural artefacts. The legend of the civilising of the West depicts the lone pioneer imposing their mark upon the land, out of reach of the social, while the 'Man with No Name' figure – so called after its appearance in Clint Eastwood films, but actually evident in earlier westerns – offers as its central image a human subject defined, 'named', by no one but himself. But the principle extends far beyond such orthodox, mass-cultural forms. The late modernist (or perhaps early postmodernist) school of American performance, the work of such as John Cage and Merce Cunningham, operates under the assumption that semically charged codes, images and cultural fragments (the ordinary environmental sounds employed in Cage's compositions, the everyday movements used in Cunningham's dance) can be lifted out of their former context and used within a new text as if virginal, with none of their prior cultural freight attached; assumes, that is, that they can be freed from their existing cultural codification. Even the politically motivated theatrical avant-garde of Beck and Malina's Living Theatre eschewed all determinist views of the subject, focusing upon humankind's liberation from society's rule.

Far from being informed by a Marxist, social-determinist perspective, then, Strasberg's view entails a conception of the human subject not as constructed by the social but enchained by it. The Method shares with many of these other practices and artefacts an underlying vision of the individual as divided between an 'authentic' inner and a potentially repressed/repressive outer self – and shares also a desire to elude the latter and return to a state of Rousseau-like freedom. The Method, moreover, offers a means of achieving this. Both with the Group Theatre and at the Actors' Studio, Strasberg employed a series of what we may call 'para-linguistic' exercises. In the 'Gibberish Exercise', created by Boleslavsky, a group of actors would be asked to perform a scene from a play, but do so speaking only nonsense words. Similarly, in the 'Recitation Exercise' a lone actor would recite a speech or poem while physically performing a number of other, quite unconnected tasks dictated by the class moderator. In both cases the performer's goal was to make the physicalised scene entirely comprehensible to those watching; Robert Lewis playing a clerk taking a shower while reciting 'I Sing the Body Electric' became part of Studio legend.

It was intended that diverse benefits accrue from such exercises. By dispensing with meaningful language, for example, they are to sharpen the actors' tonal, inflective and mimic skills, enhance their ability to represent a character's hypothetical life without the supporting framework of textual dialogue. Equally, they are to train actors to perform a number of tasks concurrently, for onstage one must consider blocking, gesture, dialogue and the director's instructions simultaneously. But these techniques also produce a different, more oblique result. Both the Recitation and Gibberish Exercises require actors to perform not just in the absence of a linguistic text but in *opposition* to it. They train performers to create and express physical texts, coherent regimes of performance signs, which contradict – indeed, overcome – the words they are given. Para-linguistic work of this kind, then, demands that actors treat playtexts and language in general as blocks to expression, as a part of that repressive sociality which is to be vanquished by other means.

If the playtext is a block, what does it obstruct? As we have noted, both with the Group and at the Studio, Strasberg insisted on substantial improvisation in order to build for the character a detailed inner life. When rehearsing a play, for example, actors would immerse themselves in their roles by improvising scenes, acting their characters in situations that were not a part of the playtext and so building more extensive 'inner circumstances'. Improvisation played an equally large part in general training, and a Studio practice called 'the Scene' is exemplary.

The Scene offered a kind of laboratory situation in which actors who were working on roles could present work-in-progress to an audience of their peers. The Scene was relatively short, and entailed actors performing often very ordinary, everyday tasks, but doing so in character. It was stressed that the piece was not to be in a stage-ready state, and Strasberg would sometimes berate actors who produced a polished performance. Rather, Scenes were to be an exploration of the character's inner reality, an opportunity for actors to immerse themselves in a role completely, under performance conditions. David Garfield observed how, in a Scene where an actress peeled carrots in a sink, she accidentally dropped one and then retrieved and washed it without hesitation (Garfield 1980: 142). She was warmly congratulated for this, for it was taken as evidence of her absolute absorption into the character's imaginary life. Actors were encouraged to go to great lengths to create this reality, so that a Scene might justifiably last half an hour if that amount of time was required to conjure up the character's inner world.

Improvisation is common to many modern schools of acting, but in the Method it occupies a central and distinct position. The Scene enables the actor to build for the character a detailed inner life, but does so in disregard of the play from which that character is taken. As with Strasberg's other improvisational techniques, the Scene was sometimes the focus of more creative activity than the playtext itself – indeed, improvisation was usually undertaken before practical work on the playtext was begun; as Ellen Burstyn noted, 'The words are the last thing we come to' (Hirsch 1984: 210). This places the actor in a particular relationship to the play, regardless of his or her attitude towards it. Although Strasberg demanded that his actors root their work in the text, at a *procedural* level his techniques required them to regard the playtext's conception of the character as an obstacle; to address it, that is, like language, sociality and so on, as an obstacle to the expression of what the Method considers most important, 'true emotion'. In Stanislavski's System characters are created to satisfy the play's requirements: in the Method they are constructed *despite* those requirements, for the Strasbergian actor's notion of the character's internal reality takes precedence over the play.

Text and dialogue, then, become potential obstacles to the expression of the actor's preformed image of character, their vision of its 'truth'. This was evident in Studio work, for with plays by Shakespeare, Shaw and Coward, where dialogue has priority over, or is the medium of, the character's inner life, Studio actors sometimes proved unable to sustain a synthesis between their own image of the role and the one inferred by the playtext. Having observed an actress perform a scene from Dylan Thomas's *Under Milk Wood*, Hirsch noted:

> . . . words – the playwright's text – are often treated like the enemy, an obstacle to the actor's expressiveness. The inner

work that is emphasised at the Studio is a way of helping to make the author's words real to the actor; the inner monologue that the actor creates, his personal excavation of the material, in effect turns him into a co-author. But I wonder if this stress on inner work always 'feeds' the words and is equally useful for all kinds and styles of language. . . . Will concentrating on props and creating a detailed physical and psychological reality that precedes and underlies the language help her to *express* the language?

(Hirsch 1984: 191)

The Studio often faced criticism for the difficulty its actors experienced with dialogue. But value judgements of that kind are of less importance than the concrete effect on performances. The techniques described so far nurture a conflict between the actor's conception of the character's inner life and all other elements, and in performance this conflict becomes a readable sign.

THE ICONOGRAPHY OF NEUROSIS

Strasberg sought to free the actor from the distortions and repressions of society and culture. Once liberated, actors will, he argued, be able to express their emotions and meanings in their 'authentic' form, present audiences with their own individual and genuine 'truth'. The Method's aim was therefore to eradicate cultural blocks, permitting inner experiences to manifest themselves naturally in the actor's outer, physical actions.

This view of the human subject, and its implied model of human communication, however, is open to question. As we noted in the Introduction, subjectivity consists of a matrix of positions offered in representation. The subject therefore cannot escape sociality, for it is built of socially derived components. Strasberg presumes a self which pre-dates our entrance into the social, but the self is a social creature.

This impacts upon Strasberg's notion of human expression. We often conceive of 'emotion' as something natural and universal, and hence acultural. But even if this is so, the *expression* of emotion is a different matter. Television has provided western audiences with the opportunity to see how people from other cultures behave, and in viewing filmed footage of, say, Middle Eastern women experiencing grief or Japanese businessmen enjoying an informal evening's entertainment, it becomes evident that the forms in which even potent emotions are expressed are culturally specific. This does not make them any less authentic; although we may not realise it, our own emotional expressions are equally culturally shaped. Whatever an adult individual's feelings, those feelings can only manifest themselves via a body which is already culturally programmed, and only be communicated to other individuals via given codes. Even if the actor has internal experiences which defy the given mechanisms of expression, those mechanisms are the only means available.

Since Strasberg's view of subjectivity and communication is flawed, his goal of liberating the actor's expression is destined to fail. But this very failure has a crucial effect upon the performance. As we saw, the Method's massive emphasis on the construction of an inner life for the character nurtures a conflict between what the actor wishes to convey and the mechanisms available to him or her to do so. The actor creates and internalises a hypothetical psyche, but then finds it in discord with the words and actions of the play, and the communicative conventions both of the stage and of society in general. This is due not to the way actors view their characters but is a result of the techniques used to *construct* them. By developing a notion of the character as antagonistic to behavioural codes, theatre's conventions, the text and, most importantly, language itself, Method practices manufacture performances whose most distinctive feature is a spectacular failure of communication.

On the stage that failure becomes a readable sign. Presented with the spectacle of actors struggling to express their roles, the audience attributes that struggle not to the performers but to the characters. When we see characters wrestling with language, fighting to communicate their emotions and *failing*, we read this as indication that language is inadequate to convey them, that their thoughts and feelings run deeper than words can express. In inferring the *existence* of 'blocked' feelings, then, the failed attempt at expression signals to spectators that the character possesses dimensions which cannot be seen. The Strasbergian actor's very inability to communicate signifies the character's profound psychological depth.

Thus, although Strasberg's stated aim was to liberate expression, his practices actually achieve the opposite. Far from eradicating difficulties of communication, the Method makes them a key feature of its performances, employs them as signs of the character's psyche. The psyche is by definition immaterial, and so cannot be expressed directly with material signs. The Method overcomes this by signifying it in – or more accurately, *by* – its absence. The very fact that a character cannot express its inner self indicates to those watching that its inner self exists; when we observe something failing to be communicated, that failure effectively acts as a sign of the 'something'. In the early years of the Studio, critics made much of Method actors' inability to communicate clearly – Brando's indecorous and inexplicable gestures, Dean's enigmatic squint, and the tendency of both actors to mumble indecipherable vowel sounds and leave their sentences unfinished. Once the Method style gained a more secure place in American and international culture, however, such difficulties were readable as a lack of expressive skills on the part of the *characters*, signalling their psychological profundity.

This failure of expression is the definitive feature of the Method performance, and emerges in a variety of forms. It is perhaps most obvious in the way actors employ language. Robert De Niro, Al Pacino, Sandy Dennis, Shelley Winters, Dennis Hopper and a host of others 'distort' dialogue by delivering conventional lines in unconventional ways. They use odd inflections and rhythms, defamiliarising language to suggest other, unknown meanings. Similarly, they emphasise words that are not central to the sentence's apparent, conventional meaning, suggesting that the true meaning that characters wish to convey is not quite encompassed by the language they are obliged to use.

Many Method actors also emphatically signify an 'outside' to language, a realm of meaning that lies beyond the concepts it makes available. De Niro, Brando, Christopher Walken, Mickey Rourke and especially Sandy Dennis will appear to search for a word mentally, signifying an internal self in pursuit of a means to communicate its thoughts via an inadequate medium. All the above performers, as well as others such as Jill Clayburgh, Brando and Dean, employ numerous breaks in speech and hesitant pauses, inferring a self that lies beyond its linguistic inscription. They indulge in indistinct vowel sounds and cut off words half-spoken, suggesting that the dialogue channels meaning in directions other than those they desire. In moments of excitement, De Niro, Pacino, Walken and Robert Duvall will persistently repeat words or phrases, indicating that their true significance cannot be communicated with only one utterance. All these devices signify the presence of meanings beyond language, originating in the character's inner self.

The social self is not of course inscribed via language alone, and linguistic failure may be accompanied by a whole battery of physical mannerisms. Sandy Dennis, who, like De Niro, is practically an index of Method gestures, will undergo facial distortions and may twist her arms and hands as she speaks, physically figuring her character's expressive struggle. When discoursing with another, Method actors will often deliver signs that are outside the one-to-one channel; De Niro, Dustin Hoffman, Christopher Walken and especially Al Pacino will stare off at an angle to their interlocutor and employ a faint but sustained nodding, as if seeking to elude that social positioning. Rod Steiger, Mickey Rourke, Dennis Hopper and Robert Duvall will smile at seemingly inappropriate moments, as if their true internalities were erupting into a false and alien externality. Clayburgh, Jane Fonda, Hoffman and Eli Wallach will use an all-purpose 'social smile'. The smile signifies insincerity or uncertainty, and so argues for a disparity between inner processes and the role imposed on the character. Duvall, Steve McQueen and Rip Torn adopt personae of impenetrable impassivity. They may avoid eye contact, use pensive silences, stillness and blank expressions to suggest a more active internality lying behind what is so obviously a controlled mask. The performances of De Niro, Pacino, Fonda, Hopper, Dean and Dennis abound with signs of anxiety, agitation and hyperactivity, symptomatic of their alienation from the social world in which they find themselves.

Any catalogue of this kind must be crude and incomplete, for the domain of such signs is vast, subtle and complex. Yet all the above signify the psyche via its very failure to signify itself. This is the fourth distinctive iconographic component of the Method. Combined with casualness, intensity and heightened and discontinuous emotional display, expressive failure proffers an image of the human subject as possessing a deep psychology, one more profound than they can express. Moreover, it is a psychology of a particular kind. The Strasbergian character is fractured and schismatic, its inner self observably dislocated from its outer, figuring that 'peculiar, divided, dual quality' Strasberg considered characteristic of the modern subject. Method performances therefore tend to represent characters as troubled, afflicted. In extreme cases this leads to depictions of psychosis, as in De Niro's performance in Martin Scorsese's *Taxi Driver* (1976). But most often it takes a milder form. By producing a plethora of signs of the psychological and combining these with the image of psychic fracture, Method techniques inscribe their characters within what we may term an iconography of neurosis.

These four components, and the logic of psychic fracture they collectively signify, provide the Method's *interpretative* logic, its Law of the Text. By weaving all signs into a single semic whole, this Law of the Text governs our reading of the Strasbergian performance. We can illustrate its effect using the example of Robert De Niro's performance in Michael Cimino's *The Deer Hunter* (1978).

The Deer Hunter tells the story of three small-town, working-class men who are conscripted to fight in the Vietnam war, and subsequently endure enormous physical and mental suffering. The film's early sections are set in America, where the three and their friends embark on a final, valedictory deer hunt in the mountains. While there, however, the character played by De Niro becomes irritated with the drunken horseplay of one of his friends, played by the late John Cazale. When Cazale's character reveals he hasn't brought the proper clothes and asks to borrow De Niro's spare boots, De Niro becomes exasperated. He holds up a single bullet and shouts angrily, 'You see this Stanley? This is *this*. It isn't something else. This is *this*.' In performance the lines were accompanied by a full battery of Studio mannerisms, De Niro grimacing and gesturing, and giving every indication of extreme agitation.

The scene is quite mesmerising and De Niro's performance was justly valorised. Yet it is never entirely certain what is taking place. Clearly the character is experiencing great emotional distress, but outside of De Niro's acting itself, neither dialogue, narrative nor scenography offer any definitive explanation for the extremity of the trauma or its physical manifestations. We appreciate why De Niro's character might be irritated, but not why the event should give rise to such violent psychic disturbance. The reaction of the character in De Niro's playing suggests an emotional cause, but one that is never specified.

This is not a problem for spectators, however, for the dense stream of signs De Niro produces – gestures, facial expressions, vocal intonations and so on – provides fertile ground upon which they can perform their act of sense-making. The signs remain ambiguous because they are alien to established behavioural codes, and so defiant of customary strategies of reading. They are therefore potentially overdetermined, able to bear any of a wide variety of interpretations; but the one interpretative logic they all defer to is that of psychic disorder. As a consequence the acting does not *need* to explain itself. Within the logic of the fractured psyche, all behavioural peculiarities can be read as products of a mind whose relationship to the real, external world is idiosyncratic, super-individualistic. Actions and utterances do not have to be explained because the schismatic psyche renders the implausible plausible, the unique response of an indecipherable inner self.

Despite Strasberg's famous demands for 'motivation' and 'precision', then, Studio acting rarely deals in *definable* motives, and is anything but precise. Indeed, it is its very imprecision that enables spectators to ascribe its behavioural minutiae a meaning. The Method actor produces a rich mist of generalised signs of the psyche, a cascade with vast but unspecified potential for meaning, whose parts are then turned into semic units in the spectator's interpretative gaze. But the spectator's meaning-making activity must take place within the parameters of the Method's Law of the Text. This governs the interpretation of the performance, determines what causes and meanings we may ascribe to characters' actions, and therefore effectively determines what meanings we may confer upon the story as a whole. By virtue of their volume and intensity, the Method actor's behavioural minutiae swamp all else so that practically the only reading possible is one contained within a discourse of psychic disturbance.

This is apparent in *The Deer Hunter*. In the second half of the film De Niro's character, now a Green Beret, returns home from Vietnam. Finding that a welcoming party has been arranged in his honour, he hides, crouching in the rear of his cab, and has the driver continue past his house and take him to a motel. In his motel room he drops into a foetal crouch, backed defensively against a wall, and rocks on his heels like an infant. He holds one palm over his temple and eye as if to cradle an inner pain, glances anxiously before him and generally signifies his agitation. Such gestures suggest an emphatically *internal* anguish, and these are the signs we must use to make-sense of this crucial scene in which the war's effects are depicted – to ascribe a significance not only to De Niro's character, but also to the film as a whole. The Vietnam war is thus represented as a psychological trauma suffered by the film's central protagonists, and perhaps by America as a nation. With meaning contained by those signs' shared interpretative potential, their Law of the Text, all other, more analytical explanations of the war are rendered extraneous. Economic, political and ideological analyses are marginalised, for none are shown as having any purchase upon the psyche. Even conventional psychological readings of the kind Stanislavski's System offered – characters motivated by love, jealousy, guilt – are overpowered by an image of the modern subject as fraught, fractured and ultimately indecipherable.

THE FRACTURED SELF

The actor most often hailed as the greatest and most influential exponent of the Method is Marlon Brando, his position only recently challenged by the likes of Al Pacino and, particularly, Robert De Niro. Interestingly, however, Brando was already a 'star' at the Studio's inception. In 1947 he was in the process of establishing his distinctive acting persona in the role of Stanley Kowalski in Kazan's production of Tennessee Williams' *A Streetcar Named Desire*. Since Elia Kazan was a Group member and Studio co-founder, it might be assumed that he introduced Brando to Method techniques during rehearsal. Brando himself, however, claimed his most formative teacher to have been Stella Adler, who, although a member of the Group, was an adherent of Stanislavski's techniques and had emerged as a fierce critic of Strasberg's practice (see Garfield 1980: 33).

This is not an isolated case. Many of the most noted and apparently exemplary Method actors, including De Niro, Fonda, Paul Newman, Rod Steiger and Montgomery Clift, joined the Studio only after their careers were established, whereas others like Dean rarely attended Studio sessions. This suggests that, rather than creating a style, Strasberg's techniques reproduced one which already existed. In seeking out a means for recreating that 'peculiar, dual, divided quality' of the modern subject, he condensed and refined for the stage an iconography already granted significance in American culture at the time. To understand the Method's socio-historical position, we must therefore look beyond Strasberg's theories to the society which favoured them.

Although Method actors were traditionally accounted 'rebels', the Studio style rapidly gained both popular and establishment recognition. Its swift success was due in part to its association with 'youth culture'. Albeit ubiquitous today, youth culture only became a significant cultural phenomenon in the 1950s, when popular music, fashion, film and so on disseminated the notion of teenagers/young adults as a distinct social group. Studio actors Brando and Dean – and to a lesser degree, Newman and Clift – were adopted as icons of the new youth movement, their public personae becoming inextricably associated with its key themes of rebellion against established values, and psychic distress borne of youth's inability to conform to social and parental norms.

These ideas found important echoes in the period. America in the 1950s displayed a growing interest in psychological matters, and particularly psychic fracture. Psychoanalysis blossomed as a middle-class pursuit, and became a common theme on stage, film and television. Alfred Kinsey's *Sexual Behaviour in the Human Male/Female* (1948–53), the so-called 'Kinsey Report', revealed a gaping disparity between publicly sanctioned conceptions of 'decent' sexual behaviour and people's private desires and activities. Equally, the 'Beat' movement both reproduced the image of psychic discord in its semi-existentialist depiction of *Angst*, and represented individuals in revolt against a repressively conformist society.

Such concerns gradually seeped into the wider cultural landscape, and the breadth of their impact is illustrated by that most American of film genres, the western. Traditionally, westerns dealt primarily with ethical issues, and with characters who conformed to, or were variations of, established generic stereotypes; even when straddling the line between good and bad, they usually reinforced the distinction. In the 1950s and early 1960s, however, the genre began to be remodelled. Kazan's *Viva*

Zapata! (1952), Penn's *The Left-Handed Gun* (1958) and Brando's own *One Eyed Jacks* (1961) (the second starring Newman, the first and last starring Brando) took a different slant. Their protagonists were antisocial and displayed aberrant psychological traits, and yet clearly demanded the viewers' sympathy, for they lived in societies which were corrupt and stultifying. In new westerns of this kind, the old legal/moral terms on which characters were defined gave way to the discordantly psychological, with society both the cause of the hero's disorder and the legitimate target of his resentment.

These movements were the leading edge of what was to become a more fundamental historical shift. In the 1960s, America's view of itself fragmented, its old consensus of ideas and values – those of moral rectitude, the 'American Dream', the American Way and so on – coming under scrutiny. At the same time there was a marked and almost instantaneous move in focus away from the 'average' citizen and towards recognition of American society's supreme heterogeneity. Francis Fitzgerald makes the point succinctly:

> In the fifties our textbooks, like our television commercials, pictured the United States as a more or less homogeneous society: a nation of happy families, white and middle class, or, on the other hand, a nation of individuals with a common understanding of good citizenship and common virtues. ... In the sixties this picture changed. ... In the textbooks of the late sixties and seventies, the United States was not a 'melting pot' as it had been until then in their pages, it was a 'stew' or 'salad' of different groups: it was 'multiracial, multicultural and pluralistic'.
>
> (Fitzgerald 1987: 15)

Such cultural change was lent added force by a series of historical events. The Vietnam war and the protest that surrounded it, the 'sexual revolution', campus disruption, the emergence of a militantly 'alternative' youth culture and lifestyle, and of ethnic, gay and women's politics – all these fostered disillusionment with, and rebellion against, the old order. Moreover, many of these movements were promoted not by culturally disenfranchised groups but by the white middle classes, precisely those who had once been taken to represent the image of American normality. With the questioning of a society now deemed conformist came an interrogation of the very images with which that conformism had been depicted.

One result of this was a profound recasting of the visions of America that America itself produced. In US cinema from the 1950s to the 1970s, images of the socially 'normal' and symbolically central gave way to those of the peripheral and eccentric, so that films increasingly featured members of ethnic communities, women, the emphatically working class and those who had fallen out of society altogether (notably law-breakers, who had always featured large but who now were allowed to triumph over law, were the heroes) as their central protagonists. Similarly, romanticised representations of the 'outsider' became common, graduating from Brando's 'Wild One' to Clint Eastwood's 'Man with No Name'. Psychic disorder came to be depicted not as a disease of society's fringes but of the white, middle-class family; a tradition begun, perhaps, in 1955 with Nicholas Ray's *Rebel Without a Cause*. Overall, the period was marked by more and more images of ethnic and cultural diversity, social and psychic schism, and a behavioural idiosyncrasy representative of a new, nonconformist America.

These changes in representation did not alter the basic, distinctively American model of the human subject; as we have noted, even radical political discourse concerned itself with liberation from social constraints. Rather, the two elements – asocial individualism and social diversity/psychic fracture – combined in a way which favoured the Method performance, and was partly responsible for its later, great success. The Methodist character is the super-individual, oppressed by society's impositions and always struggling to escape from them. Strasberg's 'proletarian' actor is at once ordinary and extraordinary, the common man and yet the individual, a status that made him both ideologically and commercially successful.

The same was not true, however, of the representation of women. Until the late 1970s and 1980s only one Studio actress was in the front rank of the Hollywood star system. Some Method actresses like Sandy Dennis, Eva Marie Saint and Joanne Woodward were perceived as possessing skills surpassing those of other Hollywood actresses, but were nevertheless passed over for the most desirable roles in favour of performers of a more traditional cast. This is remarkable, given the success of male Studio actors, but it is not inexplicable. The iconography of neurosis quickly became an acceptable way of representing men because extreme individuality is traditionally a male preserve. The range of acceptable images of women has always been narrower and stricter, in tandem with conventions of female beauty. Indeed, the neurotic woman was so demonised a figure that she could appear only as victim or villainess, effectively banning the majority of Studio actresses from most leading roles in mainstream Hollywood cinema; the Method actress could not be 'normal' enough.

The one exception confirms this. Until the 1980s Jane Fonda was the only Studio actress to be consistently offered leading, high-profile roles. This was partly because she was part of a Hollywood dynasty, of course, and because she began her career in the 1960s as one of the so-called 'bikini girls', a label whose sexual connotations perhaps continued to make her bankable. But Fonda's success was also due to the particular form the Method iconography takes in her performances. Typically, Fonda presents an exterior which is controlled and self-possessed. But psychic schism – emerging in uncertain glances aside, quick, nervous gestures and smiles, a rising vocal pitch; images of urgency and doubt – makes this exterior seem insubstantial, precarious. Such precariousness, those cracks in her tough exterior, infer a different, inner self, one that is fragile and needy. They suggest the kind of vulnerability which is traditionally ascribed to women, an insecure, emotional centre masked by the façade of severity. This is characteristic of Fonda's performances in a sequence of films such as *Klute* (1971), *Julia* (1977), *Coming Home* (1978), *The California Suite* (1978), *Comes a Horseman* (1978), *Rollover* (1981) and *The Morning After* (1986), each reiterating the usual, ideological conception of women, inferring an emotional dependency beneath any 'modern' appearance of self-containedness.

Thus the Method performance keyed into American culture by presenting an image of the subject which paralleled dominant cultural trends. So influential is the Method that non-Strasbergian actors now regularly reproduce Strasbergian effects, not just in the United States but in Europe too, and particularly Britain. But our reading of such effects does not remain static. As we saw when examining the history of the System's reception, cultural artefacts never have finished meanings. The significance of a given object is derived from the cultural context in which it is placed; it is a sign in the wider semiotic system. When that context undergoes radical change the meaning may alter, for it can draw upon – be mobilised within – different discourses.

This is the case with the Method. We have seen how the ideology of Social Democracy dominated political and cultural thought in the West for a substantial part of the twentieth century. Recently, however, a new collection of concepts have taken centre-stage. We may group these together under the title Neo-conservatism. Rejecting Social Democracy's focus on the interdependency of the individual and the social whole, Neo-conservatism in its various forms venerates the individual to the exclusion of all else. Indeed, it views the relationship between the individual and society as inescapably antagonistic. Articles of Neo-conservative faith include freeing the individual's economic potential from taxation, bureaucracy and legal constraint, granting it responsibility for its actions by reducing health care and welfare provision, and by demanding more punitive sentences for law-breakers, promoting freedom of choice in the market place by the reduction or elimination of funding for the arts, education and nationalised industries, and so on.

Collectively, these and other principles image the social subject as inherently oppressed by society, the state, and all rules and governance. In doing so, however, it masks the actual social forces that impact upon individual actions. In practice we are not all the free individuals, able to make our own choices, of the kind Neo-conservatism conceives us to be. But in construing us in this manner, it masks the real, material differences between us; between those who have material and economic power and those who do not, between individuals who begin the 'race' with advantages and others whose freedom to choose will always be limited by necessity – between the ruling elites in whose interests this profoundly reactionary ideology operates, and those they effectively rule.

Neo-conservative ideas have nevertheless gradually but substantially changed the discursive landscape in Europe and the United States over the last fifteen to twenty years. It is not that all views have altered, but that the context in which utterances and representations occur is now composed of different terms. Thus some cultural artefacts are redefined; objects, images and ideas may carry different associations because the objects/images/ideas they now relate to are different. This redefinition is, in the Method's case, sadly ironic. Strasberg was concerned with repression in the widest sense, and, if not actually radical, his views were those of a committed liberal. Moreover, at its best the Method led to highly detailed performances which eschewed all simplistic, generic pigeonholes, demanding that spectators view characters critically and intelligently. But 'proletarian', Strasbergian acting depicts individuals as repressed by the social, at war with it. In the new discursive milieu the Method therefore imagistically reproduces the central principle of Neo-conservatism, so that the acting itself seems to validate and confirm that ideology's founding premise, to construe it as 'real'.

3

BRECHT AND EPIC THEATRE

THEATRE FOR THE SCIENTIFIC AGE

The theatre of Bertolt Brecht (1898–1956) conformed to no single style, for style, he argued, should always be dictated by the work's polemical purpose. Over the span of his career he experimented with a variety of theatrical modes. His early plays employed an Expressionist-like form, perhaps evidencing the influence of dramatists Frank Wedekind and, more obliquely, Georg Kaiser. His collaborations with Erwin Piscator at the Berlin *Volksbühne* or 'People's Stage' were drawn on a large, spectacular scale, in contrast to his simple *Lehrstücke* or 'instruction pieces'. For the latter Brecht drew upon the model of Japanese *Nôh* theatre, just as the so-called 'new playing style' of his production of *Antigone* at Chur, Switzerland, featured elements adapted from the classical Greek stage. Best known of all, perhaps, are his late, more traditionally crafted productions, the 1947 American staging of his *Life of Galileo* starring Charles Laughton or the Berliner Ensemble's 1954 *The Caucasian Chalk Circle*. Equally, Brecht's critical writings reveal a wealth of borrowings and influences, ranging from the traditional German popular theatre such as could still be seen in fairgrounds in Brecht's youth, to Chinese acting, English and Spanish Renaissance theatre, and contemporary agitprop groups like Russia's 'Blue Blouse' companies, as well as canonical authors such as Shakespeare and Büchner, and even cabaret (see Calandra 1974).

The continuity of Brecht's work, then, lies not in its style. His was a continuity of purpose, for throughout his professional life Brecht sought to create a theatre which was analytical, one which opposed existing theatrical orthodoxies and was committed to the political Left; in his words, a 'Theatre for the Scientific Age'.

In his essay 'A Short Organum for the Theatre' (1949, in Brecht 1964), Brecht argued that the development of scientific reason had been the central project of western society since the Renaissance. While in previous epochs the world had been explained largely in metaphysical terms, during the historical modern period – beginning in the sixteenth century and reaching full flow with the eighteenth century's 'Age of Reason' – intellectual enquiry proceeded along increasingly rationalist lines. But although there had been great success in turning this scientific, analytical focus upon the natural world, the ruling class, the bourgeoisie, had prevented any comparable examination of the social world. A scientific understanding of human society was required, and a theory was already available in the form of Marxism, which Brecht began studying in the 1920s in an effort to understand the complexities of social reality. His theatre was to present a Marxist-based analysis of social relations. It was to be a 'theatre for instruction'.

For Marxism society is an ongoing process in which all parts interact and determine one another. Society comprises a number of different forces or 'moments' which are in 'contradiction', pulling the social whole in different directions, pushing towards different outcomes. This general process in which disparate forces collide and struggle against one another is termed in Marxist theory a *dialectic*, and it is this which determines the shape of society and all its component parts, determines *history*. Things we customarily regard as given – the individual, common sense, morality, human nature – are themselves seen as products of this dialectical process; not 'natural' but man-made, borne out of their society/historical period, and so specific to it.

The most important determining factor in the social whole is economic power. Within Marxism each phase of human history is characterised by a 'mode of production', a particular social arrangement for producing goods; our own society's arrangement is termed *capitalism*. Upon this mode of production are erected social structures (classes and class relations) and political forms (laws, institutions, modes of government) which complement and maintain it. In doing so, however, they also maintain the reign of that class which rules by virtue of its ownership of the 'means of production', the materials and technological apparatus for producing goods.

The reign of the ruling class is also supported by a social product of quite a different order, a system of ideas or 'ideology'. Ideology both reproduces the discourses necessary for that society's continuance – necessary for the ruling class's continued reign – and makes that social system appear natural, simply 'common sense' or 'the way of the world'. Consequently there will be considerable disparity between a society's own *ideological* conception of itself and a Marxist view. It will therefore be the task of any Marxist theatre to point up that difference; to describe the forces which actually shape social life – in Brecht's terms, to reveal 'society's causal network' – and show the ideological view to be constructed, borne out of its historical time and place. This is indeed the case with the Marxist theatre of Brecht. His work was 'propagandist' to the extent that it sought to depict what he believed to be the real relations of power that lay beneath the patina of appearance, to show his audiences the true nature of society, thereby empowering them to change it.

The first problem confronting Brecht's theatre was one of *scale*, for 'man, flesh and blood man, can only be embraced through those processes by which and in [the] course of which he exists' (Brecht 1964: 46). Naturalism and realism, still the dominant theatrical forms in Europe in the early twentieth century, represented life on the scale of individual personalities, the single location and the extended family. They were therefore unable to depict those larger social, economic and ideological forces which impact upon human existence. Using the example of the then relatively new petrochemical industry, Brecht explains:

> Petroleum resists the five act form ... fate is no longer a single coherent power; rather there are fields of force which can be seen radiating in opposite directions; the power groups themselves comprise movements not only against one another but in themselves etc., etc. Even to dramatise a single newspaper article needs something more than the dramatic technique of a Hebbel or an Ibsen.
>
> (Brecht 1964: 30)

Social reality is determined, 'fated', by a multiplicity of forces, beyond the power of realism or naturalism's narrow frame to represent. A new form was required, one able to depict forces of a larger scale, and this was to be what Brecht termed *Epic theatre*.

One component of this new form was a narrative structure made up of 'episodic scenes', for which Brecht drew upon such diverse sources as Elizabethan and Expressionist theatre, and the work of the early nineteenth-century German playwright Georg Büchner. Episodic scenes are complete in themselves, set in one location with a single collection of characters, and essentially deal with one issue and event. As such they are subject to broadly the same kind of limitations as naturalism; although they may cover broad socio-political themes, we read them within their own dramatic confines.

It is in the leap between scenes, however, that those limits are overcome. If one scene is set in a scientist's workshop and another in a prince's palace, as in *Life of Galileo*, the audience's reading must make the connection between them. This will require an interpretative logic which encompasses both, one possessing a broader perspective than any single scene; by showing the Sun to be at the centre of the heavens (workshop), Galileo's new cosmology threatens the old ideological vision of 'crystal spheres' that underpins princely power (palace). The audience, then, must use a Law of the Text that is of a socio-historical scale, and this becomes the discourse within which the political content of the scenes is read. By using scenes which are far apart in terms of time, location or the social position of its characters, Brecht necessitates a socio-political reading of each scene's events; Galileo's life is no longer a story of merely personal achievement and tragedy, but a tale of his historical conflict with the political order of his time.

The principle at work here is one of *montage*. Montage was a key concept in many areas of early twentieth-century art (particularly those involving mechanical reproduction: film, photography, printing) and entails juxtaposing disparate images so that each informs and qualifies the other. Film directors such as D. W. Griffiths in the United States, and Dziga Vertov, Lev Kuleshov and, most importantly, Sergei Eisenstein in the USSR employed the principle to theorise their editing techniques, the cutting together of different shots to form a narrative. During the middle period of Cubism, Picasso and others incorporated printed materials in collage or *papier collé*, posing graphical representation against their own painting techniques, while the Berlin Dada group developed *photomontage* for political caricature. Brecht employs montage techniques at many levels of his practice, but his work differs from most of the above in that it seeks to provoke a dialectic; by showing ideas/images in *contradiction*, Brecht attempts to represent the collision and interaction of forces in society itself. This is a feature even of Epic theatre's narrative structure. Whereas in realism the story develops linearly according to a notion of dramatic 'growth', in Epic theatre it was to proceed in montage-like leaps, juxtaposing this scene against the next, one 'moment' against its opposite.

The model which Brecht found in Elizabethan and Expressionist drama, however, brought problems. Dramatic conflict in those theatres was created by a 'friction' between the individual and society, so that it was the character's personality which powered the drama. Rather than individual psychology, the Marxist Brecht saw human action as determined by the social and economic environment. He states:

> The extraction and refinement of petroleum spirit represents a new complex of subjects, and when one studies them carefully one becomes struck by quite new forms of human relationship. A particular mode of behaviour can be observed both in the individual and in the mass, and it is clearly peculiar to the petroleum complex. But it wasn't the new mode of behaviour that created this particular way of creating petroleum. The petroleum complex came first, and the new relationships are secondary ... petroleum creates new relationships.
>
> (Brecht 1964: 29)

Whereas Elizabethan and Expressionist dramas privilege psychology, for Brecht it is *social* relationships which shape behaviour. Working with like-minded producer Erwin Piscator at the Volksbühne, Brecht's initial response was to dispense with psychologically detailed character altogether, in the late 1920s creating stage subjects that were devoid of individuality, merely cursors to trace material forces. Equally, Brecht praised the early silent films because, as he saw it, they rejected 'bourgeois' psychology as a basis for motivation, concentrating instead on external action; Chaplin's tramp was a 'document' of social processes and laudable because 'as soon as the human being appears as an object the causal connections become decisive' (Brecht 1964: 50). 'Action' showed behaviour as determined by society at large, not individual personality.

Such treatment of character enlarged theatre's vision, and practitioners outside Germany attempted similar expansions of scale. The experimental theatres of post-revolutionary Russia tried various means of bringing history to the stage, directors such as Nikolai Petrov organising vast open-air productions with huge casts. Eisenstein, in his pre-cinema role as theatre director, staged Georg Kaiser's Expressionist play *Gas* (1917–20) in a real gasworks, foregrounding the industrial situation that created its social relationships. At the Volkesbühne Brecht and Piscator also used large casts, in conjunction with genuine pieces of machinery that could be seen at the workface. In this way the focus was shifted from individuals to the forces which shaped them.

This use of real objects itself contributed to the enlargement of Epic theatre's socio-historical compass. In later productions Brecht was to insist that props should be real and bear signs of use. Clothing and elements of set were manufactured with great historical accuracy, some costumes ending their lives in museums. From a Marxist perspective, even such inert objects can have meaningful socio-historical content. The aesthetics of clothes design and architecture both key into a society/epoch's ideology: power relations can be signified in the grandeur of an arch, and repression in a Chinese woman's bound feet. Similarly a pot which is battered and grimy bears the inscription of the productive processes of which it has been a part. Of course, few spectators would glean such intelligence in a naturalistic set, but in Brecht's theatre these fragments would appear on a stage that was otherwise bare. Isolated in a non-signifying field, they would be subject to immense interpretative focus from the audience; like the statue placed in the open space of a museum or the painting hung on a bare gallery wall, they are offered up for intense scrutiny. Being made aware that such scrutiny is demanded – aware that such signification is *offered* – the spectator seeks out a more detailed reading.

Perhaps the most interesting of the Volksbühne techniques, however, was the use of projection screens suspended over the stage or hung on the rear flat. Onto this a film sequence, photograph or cartoon would be projected, once again using the principle of montage. The projection – a written commentary or statistics, or a picture of some historical-scale event – would inform the audience's reading of the onstage action and vice versa; onstage we might see characters starving while the screen shows a list of stock exchange prices. In reading the two together, the audience must find and employ a Law of the Text that encompasses both. The anguish of the starving characters is no longer a personal tragedy but becomes part of the greater economic picture, just as the list of prices is itself contextualised by its cost in human terms. Later in his career Brecht did not have the Volksbühne's resources available to him, but he achieved a similar effect with MCs, choruses and storytellers and placards bearing scene-titles, all of which served to situate local actions in an informing context.

Although Brecht referred to his own work as Critical Realism, he used 'realism' in his own specific sense. If realism proper attempts to show the world as it appears, Epic theatre was to depict it as, according to Brecht, it really was. In fact Epic theatre and one form of theatrical realism, naturalism, do share a common discursive ancestor. In the nineteenth-century, Determinism, the view that human behaviour was a result of environmental and hereditary factors, gained considerable cultural currency, supported as it was by the growing acceptance of Darwin's deterministic theory of Natural Selection. Naturalism was the theatrical embodiment of Determinism, seeking to place human actions in their shaping environment. Epic theatre can be seen as an extension of the same project, showing those forces of the *socio-historical* environment that determine human lives.

For Brecht, however, this did not mean reproducing that environment realistically: the very opposite. Since our usual view of the world is sculpted by ideology, orthodox realism will by definition be ideological, and any successful escape from ideological representation must always be non-realistic. As we noted, Brecht sought the most appropriate means to convey a play's message, the content dictating the form, and pressed a great variety of formal devices into service in order to proffer an alternative, radical view.

Nevertheless the key social, economic and ideological moments of a society did have to be depicted, for Marxism, or 'dialectical materialism', requires that society be recognised as historically and culturally specific:

> The field [of human relationships] has to be defined in historically relative terms. In other words we must drop our habit of taking the different social structures of past

periods, then stripping them of everything that makes them different; so that they all look more or less like our own, which then acquires from this process a certain air of having been there all along, in other words of permanence pure and simple. Instead we must leave them their distinguishing marks and keep their impermanence always before our eyes, so that our own period can be seen to be impermanent too.

(Brecht 1964: 190)

If notions of a universal 'human nature' are ideological, a means of inferring that the current *status quo* is the natural order and unchangeable, then Epic theatre was to show human beings as the product of their specific socio-historical circumstances. This required the use of detailed characters, but Brecht's dismissal of individualised character at the Volksbühne was only a temporary move and he soon returned to the issue. Epic theatre's characters, however, were not to be defined psychologically. For Brecht psychology was a bourgeois science which, by focusing on internal forces, effectively denied external ones. Characters were instead to be inscribed via *social actions*.

This was to be achieved by Brecht's acting theory, *Gestus*, which entailed finding performance signs capable of indicating social positions and relationships. Following John Willett's formulation (see Willett 1964), we can best describe the individual 'gest' as an amalgam of gesture and gist: in the *gesture*, the actor's action is encoded the *gist* of the social relationships in which the character is enmeshed. The gest can vary widely in scale and kind, can be a single movement or an entire mode of behaviour, each corresponding to the overview of social relations of the world depicted, the play's 'basic gest' or *Grundgestus*. The most obvious examples of gests might include simple behavioural codes; bowing or taking off one's hat to a superior, altering one's proximity or tone of voice, and so on. In practice, however, Gestic acting was more subtle, capable of conveying detailed information to an audience.

Brecht's own model book for the production describes Helene Weigel's gestic performance in the title role of *Mother Courage* in 1949 (for an accessible and interesting account, see Jones 1986). Mother Courage is the definitive *petit bourgeois* businesswoman, who continues to praise war for the trading opportunities it offers even as it destroys her family and her life. The play is full of business deals and even personal relationships are conducted as contracts. In Weigel's performance, each time Courage concluded a transaction she would close her purse with an audible snap, signifying her satisfaction, so that the sound came to represent her entire view of life. When her last child is killed by the war, Courage pays for the burial; she counts out the coins, keeping only one for herself, returning it to her purse and snapping it closed. The snap of the purse reminds us of all the other deals; business, supposedly the means of her survival, is actually the means of her destruction, but Courage is so immersed in capitalist ideology that she cannot see this. Her careful saving of one coin tells us that she has learned nothing and remains the thrifty businesswoman even at her daughter's death: the lone coin tells us that, nevertheless, she is reduced to a state of poverty and despair, and reminds us why.

Even in this single gest we can see intimations of both Courage's class and ideological position and the social and economic circumstances which shape her actions. In practice a gestic performance would be built of a multitude of such signs. The gestic actor would break every scene into sections and find for each a gest which conveyed the character's social location/ relations at that point. Each gest would be performed distinctly and with clarity so that its meaning was easily apparent.

Gestus is sometimes viewed as a kind of archetyping or stylisation, but in practice gestic acting varied greatly from production to production, the plays' different settings, styles and polemical projects demanding different forms. Perhaps in some productions gests of the order of 'capitalists stand like this' were used, resulting in stereotyped, foreshortened portrayals, while others appeared almost Stanislavskian in their realism. But, whatever their form, from a materialist viewpoint gestures are always social. The behavioural codes characteristic of a specific social group constitute a sign-pool that the individual draws upon. As we have noted, the social subject is both the passive recipient of discourses and behavioural codes, and their active reproducer in his or her actions and utterances. The subject's use of codes is only 'individual' in so far as it is a particular selection from a given repertoire. The same is true for gestic actors; they do not employ a formal system of signs but select from an existing pool of socially derived gestural conventions. Gestus operates at that point where the distinction between the individual and the social dissolves.

The sequence of gests that make up a performance are thus to be read by the audience as signs of the character's social position, historical situation and so on – as clues inferring those forces which shape the character's life. With Gestus as so far described, however, this is doubtful. We have seen how Stanislavski's System, for example, redefines all indications of class and epoch as signs of individuality, mobilising them within a discourse of the humanist subject. With more realistic forms of Gestus, where a 'rounded' character is created, we can expect the audience to adopt a similar interpretative logic. Indeed, any theatrical form will tend to offer its own interpretative rationale, and even the more stylised or foreshortened kinds of Gestus will prompt the audience to search for the discourse able to subsume all its signs; to assume, and find, a Law of the Text. While this may not be a logic of humanist psychology, it will probably be one which views the character as author of its own deeds and utterances – whereas Brecht desired the character to be seen as *authored-by* society. While the techniques discussed in this section enlarged theatre's vision to accommodate a Marxist view, the auditorium's dialogic relations, the interpretative activities demanded of the audience, go unchanged.

This calls the 'democratic' status Brecht claimed for his work into question. As we have seen, Epic theatre offers a critique of the world as it is 'naturally', ideologically perceived. But the strategies we have examined merely replace the old perspective with a different, Marxist one, with the audience still subjected to an authorial *fait accompli* as regards meaning. To address this question it is necessary to look more closely at Brecht's theories and the kind of theatre to which he was opposed.

THE *GESAMTKUNSTWERK*

Brecht described the theatre to which he was opposed variously as bourgeois theatre, dramatic theatre, Aristotelian drama, and the *Gesamtkunstwerk*, the 'integrated' or 'total[ised]-artwork'. The latter term derives from Wagner and refers to his plan for a theatre in which all elements and media work in unison towards a single expression. It is this term, *g-werk*, that we shall employ, since it expresses what is for our purposes that theatre's key quality.

The g-werk displays three interdependent features, the first of which is that it effaces its own status as fiction, its artificiality. The priority of this theatre, Brecht argues, is the 'engendering of illusion', and to render that illusion seamless it must remove any sign that the performance is a representation under construction, thus making it appear powered by forces within the playworld rather than the efforts of theatre workers. Deluded, the spectator's role is therefore a passive one, so that 'their relations are those of a lot of sleepers, though of such that dream restlessly because, as is popularly said of those who have nightmares, they are lying on their backs' (Brecht 1964: 187).

For Brecht, then, the g-werk effects a kind of hallucination, and 'illusion' and 'dream' are his favourite metaphors in this respect. Clearly they are inaccurate, and their misformulation led Brecht into dubious claims. If the g-werk fosters 'illusion', Epic theatre must seek to emulate those forms which subvert it. Brecht therefore praised the theatres of China, the Spanish and English Renaissance, classical Greece and the medieval period for their use of non-realistic conventions and mannerisms. These, he believed, made their artifice obvious and so denied illusion.

This must be questioned. The distinction between realistic and conventional, 'mannered' acting, for example, is often a difficult one to make in practice. Realism was a *concern* even for the Elizabethan stage. One of Shakespeare's players, Richard Burbage, was noted for his realistic performances, which commentators contrasted with the more oratorical style of another lauded actor, Edward Alleyne (see Holland 1984). But there is a difference between such 'philosophical' concern and the actual performance signs with which realism was deemed to have been achieved. The 'realistic' in this sense proves to be shifting ground, a new iconography of images developing, superseding the old, and being superseded in their turn. The shift in what is considered realistic results from such factors as altering behavioural codes, new concepts of the human subject, and changing class structures, all of which are interrelated. But these work at one remove, the remove of disparity, altering not what *is* realistic but what is culturally *construed* as such.

Once one recognises that realism is conventional, the bald distinction between it and other forms breaks down. The realistic is that form of convention *deemed* realistic by its viewing culture. Even the most accurate naturalistic productions require their audiences to accept conventional devices, to overlook their fiction-signifying power. Audiences are quite able to do this as long as those devices are familiar, their interpretative requirements understood. In all likelihood a new and unfamiliar theatrical form does signify its own artificiality, but the effect fades once it becomes readily recognisable. Just as the audience accepts a conventional mode of realism as empirically 'true', so it overlooks the fiction-signifying power of convention *per se*. Brecht confuses the reception of Spanish classical theatre, medieval theatre and so on in their own time/culture with their reception in his.

Convention *per se*, then, does not necessarily signify artifice, and this has implications for Brecht's dubious terminology of 'dreams' and 'illusions'. If we accept that the g-werk's audience experiences a hallucination, then it follows that this will be best effected by the most complete eradication of evidence of artifice; hence the assumption that convention *per se* subverts the g-werk. But we have seen that the power of any sign to indicate artifice or not is determined by the theatrical form in which it appears. Burbage was considered pre-eminently realistic, non-artificial, on his own stage, but would almost certainly appear mannered on ours.

Rather than the inactivity of Brecht's sleeper, then, we have a dialogic relationship, an auditorium culturally complicit with the stage. The spectator brings to the theatre a knowledge of how things are to be read, so that the most blatant conventions need not signify artifice. It is by this means rather than total illusion that the g-werk renders its audience passive, for their passivity consists of using only those interpretative strategies acknowledged to be appropriate to the form. We can therefore reformulate Brecht's ideas; the g-werk does not need to 'hide' potential signs of artifice, merely govern their reading; achieves not a seamless illusion but a seamless containment of interpretation.

This leads us to the second key feature of the g-werk. In 'A Short Organum for the Theatre', Brecht uses the analogy of a child on a carousel horse to describe how the g-werk effects its illusion, noting that 'the degree to which its wooden seat resembles a horse counts little, nor does it matter that the ride is confined to a small circle'. A simulation of reality, then, is not required. Brecht explains:

The pleasures given by representations of different sorts hardly ever depended on the representation's likeness to the thing portrayed. Incorrectness, or considered improbability even, was hardly or not at all disturbing, so long as the incorrectness had a certain consistency and the improbability remained of a constant kind.

(Brecht 1964: 182)

This is a perceptive observation, for here Brecht recognises that convention and stylisation *per se* need not signify artifice. The g-werk's playworld need not be realistic, only 'consistent', and it can represent reality in any way as long as that representation coheres into a single whole. The second feature of the g-werk is its organic *unity*, the integration of its parts to construct a coherent reality. But from what does this unity, this 'consistency' derive? All theatrical forms use a variety of media: movement, set, lights, words and so on. Since these are qualitatively different and cannot 'resemble' one another, their consistency must reside in a quality ascribed *to* them; it must result from their *interpretation*, that containment of potential meaning effected by the audience's culturally derived Law of the Text. In controlling the decoding of signs, the Law of the Text makes the theatrical event's parts cohere into an organic whole, rendering them all 'of a constant kind'.

This unity was a particularly prominent feature of those forms of theatre which dominated the late nineteenth- and early twentieth-century stages of Europe. The influential Richard Wagner theorised it as *synaesthesia*, the purposeful integration of all senses/media to achieve aesthetic harmony, a principle taken up by his theatrical successors Adolph Appia and Edward Gordon Craig. Although less obvious, it is equally central to naturalism. In seeking to contrive a perfect simulation of life onstage, pioneering naturalist practitioners such as August Strindberg and André Antoine tried to ensure that all stage elements were subsumed within a realistic vision, even removing disruptive scene breaks and intermissions, and plunging the auditorium into total darkness so that nothing might impinge on the reality of the playworld.

But although Brecht was heir to a theatre particularly concerned with aesthetic unity, we have seen that such unity is effected equally well by the spectator. The audience automatically

91

assumes that the stage proffers a unified text, and so seeks a single logic for its reading. Stanislavski's Psycho-Technique was designed to enable actors to maintain the 'unbroken line' of a character's life, but its effect was to discipline performance signs to indicate a single psyche, thus making the unitary humanist self the source of all signs and meanings. Stanislavski's example illustrates the relationship between the g-werk's elision of artifice and its organic unity, for the unbroken line *is* the eradication of signs of performance. Making humanist individualism the text's interpretative discourse effectively redefines all potential signs of artifice as signs of the character, the resulting coherence creating a closed system of interpretation.

This leads us to the third and perhaps the most important feature of the g-werk: the status of the stage event as offered to its dialogic partner, the audience. For all signs to cohere into a unity they must be placed in a special space where their Law of the Text can reign exclusively. They must be 'framed', conceptually separated from the social space of the audience and the interpretative 'rules' that pertain there, and enclosed in a space free of all rules except those of the theatrical form which occupies it. The g-werk most often achieves this by constructing a locus. Most literally, the locus is the hypothetical place/time where the play's events occur. It is a slice of an entire, fictional world through whose transparent boundaries the audience sees the story unfold, governed by that world's causal logic. Although those boundaries often correspond to the perimeter of the playing area, the frame is not a material thing, of course, but conceptual, separating the symbolic from the non-symbolic.

It is by constructing a locus that the g-werk privileges the stage's Abstract register over the Concrete, the told over the telling; the action takes place not here and now but there and then. In this register the object – be it actual (a table) or conceptual (morality) – stands in for a class of objects rather than a particular one: 'Tables' instead of *that* table on the stage; 'Morality' rather than a particular moral system. It presents the world as quantified by the form's interpretative discourse, its reality already categorised, made-sense of, by the logic of its Law of the Text. The Abstract register presents these categories not as constructs but as (symbols of) essences with a real, objective existence in the world. As a result, its particular conception of reality is offered as given; Stanislavski's system presents the audience not with human subjects but with the Individual, a particular *construction* of the human subject presented as universal, eternal. It is by this means that the g-werk credits its conceptual entities with the authority of *Logos*.

Logos is a term employed in theology and classical philosophy, but its current usage derives from the work of the seminal post-structuralist philosopher Jacques Derrida (see Culler 1982: 89–110). According to Derrida, within any discourse or ideology there is one founding principle that is deemed beyond interrogation. It is from this, the Logos, that all the discourse's other claims and formulations derive their status as 'truth'. In the discourse of Christian theology, for example, the concept of God is the authority underpinning all claims to meaning, all assertions about the world and existence. God is the one unassailable precept, and all other Christian truths – the Soul, Salvation, Grace – refer to Him in their claims for validity. Although the concept of God is itself constructed symbolically, in representation, by denying that construction it is able to act as a given truth. Thus while all other assertions must be argued, God's existence is unquestioned, thereby providing the basis for those arguments, the foundation from which they proceed.

It is this quality, this given-ness, that the g-werk credits to itself. In the Abstract register it offers its entities as author-free, symbolic of objects that objectively exist rather than objects constructed-out-of symbols; universals rather than the material product of human effort. Here we can see the interdependency of the g-werk's three features: elided artificiality excludes all evidence of the event's creation, and so offers its vision of the World as non-created, a given. Organic unity separates-off the locus so that the stage prefers the Abstract register, a prerequisite of its claim to truth. All three elements require one another and together form the g-werk.

The g-werk, then, is not a particular theatrical form, for its key qualities – a sharply defined locus, the eradication of artifice and a pre-eminent Pavisian coherence – are evident in a number of forms. Brecht opposed not just ideological constructions of the world, but also the means by which those constructions were represented. This is not esoteric, for form is itself an encoding of discourse, is 'readable', and, in offering spectators the usual ideological interpretative position, places them as subjects of that ideology. The spectator's relationship to a text, the dialogic position offered, can oppose ideological relations or reproduce them, empower spectators or render them passive. It is Brecht's attempt to create a radical form with radical relations that we shall now examine.

THE GESTIC SPLIT

The forms of theatre dominating the stage of Brecht's youth were not amenable to the expression of a Marxist perspective, for, as he notes, a 'technique which served to hide the causality at work in society can hardly be used to show it up' (Brecht 1964: 43). Moreover, such orthodox forms were linked to institutions. The 'great apparati' of ideological representation covertly control their works' content, 'impose their views as it were incognito'; plays that proved amenable to the apparatus were by definition 'good', whereas radical pieces were viewed as 'foreign bodies' and reworked into a form that rendered them politically palatable. But Brecht was equally dismissive of the supposedly progressive effect of experiment *per se*. Of certain avant-garde innovations in opera he wrote, 'The intention is to democratise but not to alter democracy's character, which consists in giving the people new rights but no chance to appreciate them' (Brecht 1964: 33). Thus Brecht's project was to create a theatrical *form* which offered its audience 'democratic' relations.

At certain points in his writing Brecht takes the surprising step of praising bad and amateur acting, claiming that it helped the work's 'educational effect'. Writing of the 'illusion' in which the traditional theatre's audience finds itself embroiled, he declares, 'This detached state, where [the spectators] seem to be given to vague but profound sensations, grows deeper the better the work of the actors, and so we, as we do not approve of this situation, should like them to be as bad as possible' (Brecht 1964: 187). In undermining illusion, then, bad acting pointed the way to an alternative to the g-werk.

The most comprehensive explanation of this is found in Brecht's essay 'The Street Scene' (1950, in Brecht 1964). Here he argues that a witness to an accident, recounting it to a group who did not see it, provides a basic prototype for Epic theatre. The situation has all the qualities Brecht requires. The recounting has a practical social purpose, explaining how the accident occurred and whose fault it was. This will determine what needs to be described and by what means – the content dictating the form – and the witness, like the amateur actor, needs no special skills. The street scene's most important feature, however, is that the witness does not seek to contrive an illusion, to transport his or her public from 'normality to higher realms'. The essay's key term is *demonstration,* for in this and Brecht's other theatrical prototypes – a witness in court and a director instructing an actor – the performer never hides the fact that he/she is performing. The sheer low-tech quality of the witness's demonstration will ensure that their opinion will be recognised *as* opinion, and 'If the scene in the theatre follows the street scene in this respect then the theatre will stop pretending not to be a theatre, just as the street corner demonstration admits it is a demonstration' (Brecht 1964: 122).

By *demonstrating* the role, then, gestic acting signifies its artificiality. Just as bad actors lack the skill to create seamless characters, the demonstrator never effaces their own presence as artificer. This is Brecht's first assault against the g-werk and it is found at all levels of his theatrical practice. Throughout his career he demanded that the orchestra, stage machinery and the whole technology of production remain visible to the audience. Unremittingly bright, white light was trained on the stage, discarding one means by which stage mechanics may be obscured and 'illusion' conjured, and half-curtains or no curtains at all allowed the moving of set and props between scenes to be seen. His plays employ storytellers (*The Caucasian Chalk Circle*) or narrator figures (*Galileo*) which, as well as enlarging the play's compass, signify its status as artifice, and titles, projections and even songs function in the same way. In his staging of *Antigone* in Chur, Switzerland, Brecht had the actors sit on benches in full view of the audience when not involved in the action. There they were to drop out of character, behave normally, again revealing the 'technology' of the production.

This unveiling of theatre's mechanics was also a priority of his scenic design. Brecht did not favour full naturalistic sets, and instead indicated locations with a single piece of stage property. In *Galileo,* for example, a prince's palace was signified by a doorway and portal with the rest of the stage bare. Isolated in a non-signifying field, the set fragment remains a blatant sign. Similarly, Brecht argued that even staging and blocking should be 'stylised or emphatically dramatic'. This, he claimed, was to sharpen meaning, but such paring down also effectively reveals the act of creating meaning. Indeed, Brecht writes of a 'definite gest of showing' that was to underpin all stage practice.

All these signal the text's fictionality, certainly, but there is a further consequence. While in Moscow in 1935, Brecht visited the Central Art Worker's Club and saw a performance by the Chinese actor Mei Lan-fang, hosted by Russian director Vsevelod Meyerhold. In writing of it, he focuses on the distinction between what is acted and the acting itself. Whereas the western 'psychological' actor strives for the seamless merging of himself/herself and the character, the traditional Chinese actor expresses *yuan*, the 'awareness of being watched':

> The artist observes himself. Thus if he is presenting a cloud, perhaps . . . he will occasionally look at the audience as if to say: isn't it just like that? At the same time he also observes his own arms and legs, adducing them, testing them and perhaps finally approving them. . . . In this way the artist separates mime (showing observation) from gesture (showing a cloud) but without distracting from the latter.
>
> (Brecht 1964: 92)

Here artifice is again flaunted, for advertising one's artistry for the spectator's appreciation necessitates their acknowledgement of the artificer. Such display is central to some strains of Epic experiment, and in the work of Meyerhold, for example, gymnastic and circus skills provided much of the spectacle. But Brecht's concern is slightly different, focusing instead on the separation between 'gesture' and 'mime'. Similarly, he argued that songs onstage should be delivered rather than performed, for the actor 'must not only sing but show a man singing' (Brecht 1964: 44). In both instances Brecht draws attention not just to overt artifice but to the resulting split between the act of telling and what is told – that is, between the actor and his/her role.

We shall term this separation of the character into actor and role the *gestic split*, and, after signs of social relations, it is the second essential feature of Gestus. The performance of that exemplary gestic actor, Peter Lorre, in the lead role of Brecht's 1931 revival of *A Man's a Man*, provides an illustration. To express terror at his character's imminent execution, Lorre turned his back on the audience, dusted his face in chalk dust, and then faced the auditorium again 'white-faced' in fear. The gest clearly indicates both the character's feelings and the act's fictionality; indeed, there is an obvious separation of the character who is fearful from the actor who is indicating that fear, to the extent that we might break the action down and ascribe its parts variously to the two 'persons' signified.

Brecht's instructions for would-be gestic actors are very general, because, as we have seen, Gestus is not a style but a set of goals to be achieved by whichever means are most appropriate to the message. He comes closest to a formula for the gestic split with his demand that the process of rehearsal be visible in the performance itself, so that the acting displays the signs of 'something rehearsed and rounded off'. Brecht suggests three practical means for achieving this: transposing the lines into the third person, transposing them into the past tense, and speaking the stage directions out loud. Although these techniques are to be used only in rehearsal, their separation effect is to last into the performance. In fact, the purpose of these practices is to enable actors to make their own feelings towards the characters evident. The gestic performance should be marked by a clear 'attitude', expressing the actor's approval, disgust and so on.

What began as the unveiling of artifice has now developed into something more complex. The effect of the above practices is to signal the distinction between role and actor, a distinction which is emphatic, since with 'attitude' performer and construc-ted character display differing views; the character may present himself/herself as the hero, champion of the play-world's moral values, while with smiles and vocal inflections the actor dissents from this opinion. In most forms of acting the performer presents the audience with a single coherency of signs, the character, which acts as the sole source of utterance. But with the gestic split we have signs emanating from two different coherencies, albeit that they occupy the same bodily space. Moreover, these function in different registers: the actor encompasses artifice and so is of the Concrete; the role exists only within the locus and is of the Abstract. The audience, then, is presented with two mutually exclusive ways of viewing the performance text.

The gestic split is Brecht's assault against that second quality of the g-werk, its organic unity, for it has consequences for the way we read the Epic text. In his essay 'On Brecht's Notion of

Gestus' (1978, in Pavis 1982), Patrice Pavis develops the point cogently and is worth quoting at length:

> In a dramatic form where the text is staged, the actor's gestures often only illustrate or punctuate the spoken word by creating the illusion that it is a perfectly integrated part of the enunciator, thus of his gestural universe. *Gestus*, on the contrary, approaches the text/gesture ensemble so as not to eliminate either of the two terms of the dichotomy. . . . So instead of fusing logos and gestuality in an illusion of reality, *Gestus* radically cleaves the performance into two blocks: the shown (the said) and the showing (the saying). . . . Gestus thus displaces the dialectic between ideas and actions: the dialectic no longer operates within the system of these ideas and actions, but at the point of intersection of the enunciating gesture and the enunciating discourse.
>
> (Pavis 1982: 44)

In the g-werk, a 'dramatic form where the *text* is staged', an organic unity is established. The Law of the Text ensures that all signs are interpreted according to a common logic, demarcating a space, a locus, where that logic reigns supreme. Meaning therefore derives solely from *within* that locus; from the 'friction' between, for example, a play's ethical values and a character's actions. In contrast, Gestus breaks the performance-text into telling and told, so that the audience must take the actor as well as the character into account. Meaning is therefore generated by the 'intersection' of role and actor, the interaction between signs that emanate from within the locus and those from without; between the Abstract and Concrete registers. These are fundamentally incompatible, requiring the spectator to view the stage in two different ways, and so cannot 'fuse' into one meaning. As a result the audience is offered two streams of signs, one of which originates outside the playworld and so is beyond its Law of the Text.

This is precisely the effect for which Brecht aimed. When viewing the work of a 'psychological actor', he states, the audience will tend to empathise with the character, to experience feelings sympathetic to those the character is experiencing; that is, the audience will conceive of the character in the locus's own terms. But with the work of the gestic actor, Brecht argues, there is not the same automatic emotional transfer, and the audience may respond with quite different feelings towards the events on the stage.

'Emotion' is an imprecise term, one which dogs much theatrical writing. If we see a character experiencing jealousy, we do not feel jealous ourselves; rather, if that character is presented as sympathetic, and if we view it in its own terms, we wish a positive resolution to its plight. The gestic split, however, enables us to take a different stance. It offers us a position outside of the character/locus's terms, one which puts those emotions in context, so that we need not empathise with them. We can take an 'attitude', approve or disapprove; on seeing distress we may feel joy, and seeing pleasure we may experience disgust. The context that Epic theatre offers is one of sociality. Epic theatre first involves a Marxist analysis of the social whole and so requires a theatre of socio-historical detail and scale. It also seeks to proffer a Marxist critique of the usual, *ideological* view of the world. By separating logos from gestuality – role from actor, the locus from its own mechanics – Epic theatre creates a position from which that critique can be voiced, that position being the Concrete register. This does not mean the actor takes time out to comment on his or her character; 'attitude' allows for little analytical detail. Rather, it is in the combination of Gestus's two features – signs of social identity and the gestic split – that this contextualisation is effected.

We noted previously that, although a gestic performance may be *built* of signs of sociality, it was unlikely to be *read* in that way, but would instead be interpreted via a logic that ascribes performance-signs to the *character*. But with the gestic split the situation is altered. The audience is now presented with two kinds of signification: signs emanating *from* the character and signs *of* the character from outside its world. Being incompatible, refusing to be 'fused', the audience must find separate means to interpret them. Signs of the Abstract register (character/locus) may be contained within a discourse of bourgeois individuality as before. But by the same general process, the audience will interpret signs from the Concrete register (actor/artifice) by finding a discourse able to encompass them all. What all these signs share is a social dimension, and sociality will therefore provide the basis for their interpretative logic *en masse*. Thus it is the gestic split which allows a social reading of the character; the Abstract register shows the character as author of its signs (gestures, words), but the Concrete depicts character as *authored-by* signs of the social. The character's actions and utterances are placed in the context of its social and historical position, while sociality is itself defined in personal terms, a montage effect in which each stream of signs informs the other.

This device is found in the full range of Brecht's practices. Indeed, once freed from the limitations of individual gests, much more detailed socio-historical intelligence can be communicated. In the guise of MCs, narrators and storytellers, actors do comment upon the locus from outside, while choruses and stories-within-stories produce utterances from separate spaces. As well as enlarging scale and signifying artifice, placards, scene-titles and projections offer alternate views of the events that take place within the playworld. Brecht termed this the 'literarisation of the theatre', juxtaposing theatrical representation with other kinds of cultural product – film, literature and newspapers – which, in his view, required less passive, more critical postures from their public. This is questionable but such literarisation does offer commentary from beyond the limits, and the interpretative logic, of the locus. A similar result emerges from all the Epic production's 'heteroglossia', its mixing of different forms, 'high' and 'low', literature and drama, fictional scenes and factual projections, the montage-like juxtaposition of different kinds of text demanding not necessarily 'better' but *different* modes of reading from the audience.

Once we extend the gestic split beyond acting and into these other practices, however, a problem emerges. Theatre is by nature polyphonic, employing different media. The audience rarely has difficulty integrating these media, subsuming them all within a single Law of the Text, and there is no reason why it should not do the same with, for instance, a placard and a dramatic scene. This is not a danger with gestic acting because the actor and character share the same bodily space and so are inherently contradictory; the stage body cannot be both real and a fiction, and so they separate, requiring two interpretative discourses. Paradoxically, it is with the *literal* separation between the origins of utterance (between stage and projection, locus and storyteller) that Epic theatre becomes vulnerable to the audience's act of sense-making unification.

It is with contradiction that Brecht avoids this, ensuring a conceptual split. On his stage the separate sources of utterance (narrative versus projection, placard versus dramatic scene) do not simply coexist but seek to define the same object/event. They are therefore in inherent interpretative conflict, for, having met on the same ground, their two interpretative registers demand mutually exclusive readings of the same sign. This was a key feature of Brecht's montage, the 'dialectic' he contrived between two warring visions of the world. In his instructions for the use of placards Brecht is explicit:

> The titles must include the social point, saying at the same time something about the kind of portrayal wanted, i.e. should copy the tone of a chronicle or ballad or newspaper or morality. For instance, a simple way of alienating something is that normally applied to customs and moral principles. A visit, the treatment of an enemy, a lover's meeting, agreements about politics or business, can be portrayed as if they were simply illustrations of general principles valid for the place in question. Shown thus, the particular and unrepeatable incident acquires a disconcerting look because it appears as something general, something that has become a principle.
>
> (Brecht 1964: 46)

The scene that is enacted onstage portrays particular individuals in an occurrence unique in their lives, an 'unrepeatable incident'. The title, however, is to construe the same scene in an 'anthropological' way, as illustrative of a general species of event characteristic of that society. The tension is between a view of the action from within the playworld and a view from without, an ideologically determined 'experience' versus a social analysis. In this way individual acts are posed against their sociohistorical context, each discourse informing the other. This is similar to the principle governing gests of social identity, for it regards the 'unrepeatable incident' as an event drawn from that society's characteristic pool, unique to the individuals who experience it, perhaps, but illustrative of their culture's modes of activity. As with Gestus, it is the split that enables the collision of discourses to take place, while it is simultaneously the contradiction of discursive views that ensures a genuine split.

It is this juxtaposition of discourses which distinguishes Brecht's work from that of other practitioners with whom he might otherwise be compared. While Eisenstein's theories of cinematic montage probably influenced the German, his practice was very different. Eisenstein's work is the forerunner of modern commercial cinema's editing techniques. The quick cutting between shots of different scale and location – from a long-distance crowd scene to a close-up of a face, for example, in the famous Odessa steps sequence of *Battleship Potemkin* (1925) – clearly implies specific connections for the audience to make, and so actually inhibits any plurality of views. But a feature of Brecht's practice was openly courted disjuncture between the different sources of signification, such that each informed and contextualised the other. As Brecht wrote of his collaboration with the cartoonist Caspar Neher,

> Neher's projections adopt an attitude towards the events on the stage; as when the real glutton sits in front of the glutton whom Neher has drawn. In the same way the stage unreels the events that are fixed on the screen.
>
> (Brecht 1964: 38)

ALIENATION OR THE *VERFREMDUNGSEFFEKT*

Brecht's breaking of the empathic link between actor and spectator, and the contradiction he effects between Concrete actor and Abstract character, are both part of the most controversial area of his theory, termed *distanciation* or more commonly *alienation* (not to be confused with Marx's use of the term). The *Verfremdungseffekt* or 'alienation effect' refers both to the separation of actor from character, or any of the Concrete/Abstract binaries, and to the audience's resulting disengagement with the locus. Brecht made its purpose explicit: 'The aim of this effect, known as the alienation-effect, was to make the spectator adopt an attitude of inquiry and criticism in his approach to the [play's] incident' (Brecht 1964: 136).

The first step towards alienation is to make the stage appear strange:

> Before familiarity can turn into awareness the familiar must be stripped of its inconspicuousness; we must give up assuming that the object in question needs no explanation. . . . A common use of the A-effect is when someone says: Have you ever really looked carefully at your watch? The

questioner knows that I've looked at it often enough, and now his question deprives me of the sight which I've grown used to and which accordingly has nothing more to say to me. I used to look at it to see the time, and now when he asks me in this importune way I realise that I've given up seeing the watch itself with an astonished eye.

(Brecht 1964: 144)

The alienation effect is Brecht's term for *defamiliarisation*, a concept we examined when looking at Stanislavski's means of dealing with stage fright. The very self-consciousness that Stanislavski sought to eradicate because it hampered the creation of unitary character, Brecht courts in order to fracture that character. Brecht met the Russian Formalist aesthetician Viktor Shklovsky in Russia in 1935, and was introduced to his theory of *priem ostranneniji* – literally 'strange-making'; the subversion of our customary, ideological view of an event/object, causing us to view it afresh.

This is the explanation that is usually accepted, and it is adequate for most purposes. Clearly, it complements Brecht's desire to undermine ideological constructions of reality. But as we have seen, the ideological g-werk need not be realistic, need not reproduce the real as ordinarily perceived. It can take many forms and its formal conventions, its unreality, need not subvert the representation, make it strange. We therefore require a more stringent definition.

Continuing with his explanation, Brecht states 'To see one's mother as a man's wife one needs an A-effect; this is provided, for instance, when one acquires a step-father' (Brecht 1964: 144). Rather than being 'stripped of her inconspicuousness', the woman is, as with the gestic split, the subject of contradictory definitions; as wife she is placed in a discourse of Sexuality, as mother in a discourse of the Family. It is this contradiction between at least two interpretative discourses that causes the alienation effect to occur, and occur in the gaze of the spectator. This second view accords more with our own theoretical perspective. We noted in the Introduction that subjectivity *consists* of a vast number of subject positions inscribed in discourse. There is therefore no possibility of 'escaping' discourse to reach a 'natural' or unmediated perception of the real, for that would be to escape subjectivity itself. What alienation actually does is juxtapose two contradictory discourses in the arena of the stage object. 'Making-strange' employs the plurality of available discourses in order to undermine the supremacy of dominant ideological perceptions.

This effect is attendant upon all Epic theatre's heteroglossia, its blending of different kinds of theatrical 'writing'. Many of Brecht's borrowings offer specific advantages: Greek theatre's chorus speaks from outside the narrative, Chinese acting is overtly artificial. But heteroglossia *per se* has a valuable consequence. In Gestic acting alone, broadly 'naturalistic' performance was mixed with stylised techniques drawn from Expressionism, cabaret, melodrama, *commedia dell'arte*, classical Greek oration and others, and such blending is evident in most areas of Brecht's theatre practice. While the actual semic contradiction between these may be open to question, any successful 'split' will tend to draw other elements of a production into the same fractured reading, creating what Brecht terms a 'radical *separation of the elements*' (Brecht 1964: 37).

There is, however, a possible flaw in this reasoning. During the interpretative process the Epic text's signs, styles and media will in effect fall into two categories. The first will consist of 'innocent', ideological utterance from the characters and locus – from inside the playworld. The second will include all other commentary upon it, signs from the platea, be they from the actor, placard or storyteller. Clearly the two sides of the split (actor versus character, placard versus dramatic scene) will not be equal in their power to provide an interpretation of all the production's parts. The Concrete register (actor, placard: platea) will dominate simply because it stands above the Abstract's 'naïvety'. As a view of events superior to the locus's own, explaining it, the Concrete register will simply become the site of a new unity, calling in the truth, a new Law of the Text, from the wings. Thus, we might argue, Brecht simply replaces one totalising discourse with another and Epic theatre is just another kind of g-werk.

To explain how Epic theatre avoids this we must address that last feature of the g-werk, the status it adopts as dialogic partner. We noted that the g-werk nominates the theatrical space as special, a symbolic realm which functions in the Abstract register. It is therefore conceptually separated from the audience's social space and the interpretative conventions that pertain there. In particular, it eludes that status of *provisionality* that is accorded ordinary utterance, the result of our recognition of a speaker, and therefore of his/her necessarily partisan viewpoint. The g-werk therefore presents itself as authorless and non-constructed, its meanings not provisional but a given truth; it proffers itself as the site of Logos.

Epic theatre in contrast advertises its own fictionality, for overt artifice reveals an author's hand at work behind the text's constructions. As a consequence, Epic theatre always shows itself in the act of telling, and its arguments are presented as manufactured. Whereas the g-werk is separated from the audience's social space, signs of artifice link the playworld to that space, show its meanings as produced within it. Those signs stem from the platea, a space undifferentiated from the spectator's, and so are ascribed that status of provisionality that is accorded any assertion that might come from the audience. Moreover, with the gestic split the signs of the author (Concrete) and signs of the locus (Abstract) are always in contradiction. The Concrete register takes an 'attitude' towards the Abstract, offers meanings which conflict with it. It is not just the *presence* of the author that is signified, but the author's partisanship; when the actor smiles knowingly in regard to the character he/she represents, or Caspar Neher's cartoon pig lampoons the capitalist glutton, we cannot but be aware that an *opinion* is being offered. The signs that operate in the Concrete register can never assume the status of Logos, can never offer themselves to the audience as an unmediated view of the world, because their bias is a part of the text.

It is for these reasons that signs from the Concrete register do not become the site of a new master discourse. Epic theatre does not merely reveal its artifice, it makes that artifice a part of the work that the audience must make-sense of; fictionality cannot be redefined as necessary 'convention', for the partisanship of the notional author must feature in any interpretative logic. The text's meanings are therefore proffered not as truth, but as, in Brecht's terminology, 'opinion', a construction of events as viewed from the position of an acknowledged, and subjective, 'demonstrator'. By this means he sought to create a theatre which, because it acknowledged its own position and bias, could act as a model for genuinely democratic social relations.

This then is the basis of Brecht's 'democratisation' of the auditorium. The effect the g-werk has on its audience is one of *univocality*; it shows us events and its all-subsuming Law of the Text tells us what they mean, how they should be read, so that spectators become unified into an audience in their reading of the text. In contrast, Epic theatre demands that we view its meanings critically, as products of an artificer's viewpoint. The dialogic role offered spectators does not 'allow' them to take a critical view, it *requires* them to do so in order to make sense of all the production's parts – the actor as well as the character, platea and locus. Epic theatre offers dialogic relations but no single dialogic position, meanings but no univocality, with the result that the audience is confronted with no settled inter-pretation, and the performance 'becomes a discussion (about social relations) with the audience [that the actor] is addressing' (Brecht 1964: 124). Defending his use of placard titles, Brecht explains:

> The orthodox playwright's objection to the title is that the dramatist ought to say everything that has to be said in the action, that the text must express everything within its own confines. The corresponding attitude for the spectator is that he should not think about a subject but within the confines of the subject. But this way of subordinating every-thing to a single idea, this passion for propelling the spec-tator along a single track where he can look neither right nor left, up nor down, is something that the new school of play-writing must reject. ... Some exercise in complex seeing is needed – though it is perhaps more important to be able to think above the stream than to think in the stream.
>
> (Brecht 1964: 44)

Having the audience think *of* the text's constructions of the world rather than *within* them is Epic theatre's ultimate goal. The so-called 'distance' that alienation puts between auditorium and stage is actually this critical posture that Epic theatre signi-fies as appropriate. In order to fulfil their dialogic role the spectator must take a position outside of all the performance's discourses, 'think *about* a subject', so that 'As he reads the projec-tions on the screen the spectator adopts an attitude of smoking-and-watching. ... By this means one would soon have a theatre full of experts, just as one has sporting arenas full of experts' (Brecht 1964: 44). On seeing a football player miss a goal, one would not accept it as inevitable, the 'natural order', but have an opinion on what the player did wrong, and how it might have been done better. Brecht sought a comparable response; his audiences were not to accept the story's events as inevitable but view them as choices made, by both the characters and the theatrical workers, and therefore form their own opinions about how things might be changed.

EPIC THEATRE AND MODERNISM

In his theoretical writings Brecht provided a critical vocabulary which is still in use today, and which has helped perpetuate his ideas. But although his work has proved the most successful and durable of its kind, he was not alone in his attempt to create a new socialist theatre. Erwin Piscator was already developing a socialist 'Documentary Theatre' when Brecht joined him, while in Britain in the 1930s practitioners such as Joan Littlewood and Ewan McColl were about similar projects; their 'Red Megaphones' company, out of which was to be born Littlewood's 'Theatre Workshop', was also experimental, analytical and committed to the political Left. In the USSR the director Vsevelod Meyerhold and his followers (including, significantly, the young Sergei Eisenstein) created a sequence of theatrical forms using devices based on ideas, and embodying aims, similar to Brecht's own. In the United States Hallie Flanagan worked under the auspices of the Federal Theatre Project, creating Documentary and Living Newspaper companies. Indeed, during the first half of the twentieth century Living Newspaper and agitprop companies, as well as playwrights and directors across Europe and North America, shared some or all of Brecht's aims, while new forms of arguably 'Brechtian' theatre are even today employed by practitioners whose goal is political dissent.

Such theatre, and Brecht's work specifically, is not difficult to place culturally, for his theories and practices stand at the meeting point of several historical trends. They are first a part of a Marxist tradition. It is not unusual for Brecht's politics to be distinguished from his drama, allowing him to be construed as a Great Man of the Theatre whose genius was obscured by well-meaning but naïve political rhetoric. But this view is untenable. The historical materialist explanation of human action, the pivotal role of contradiction, the assault on ideology and on the ideological relations of the auditorium, the construction of new anti-totalised relations – these constitute the informed translation of Marxist theory into theatrical practice.

But more than this, these qualities ally Brecht with a particular strand of Marxist thought. Marxism has always displayed a diversity of emphases and projects, and in the first half of this century these fell into two broad categories. For Lenin, Gramsci, Lukacs, Mao and others the urgent question was how to create a socialist society. As regards culture, this entailed finding a way to establish a community of views that could help bring about a revolution or, after a revolution, provide the consensual framework on which a new form of society could be built. Marxists of this stripe therefore concentrated on the opportunities culture offered for shaping ideas and opinions, for creating a cultural order that could help effect a social and political one.

The second tradition focused on Marxism as an analytical practice. It was concerned with the criticism (in the academic sense) of society, and particularly of culture. Walter Benjamin and the members of the Frankfurt School – notably Theodor Adorno, Max Horkheimer and Herbert Marcuse – Ernst Bloch and, arguably, Mikhail Bakhtin, analysed ideology, art, literature, language and representation in general, in their various ways seeking to theorise culture, to reveal and explain the mechanisms it employed. Rather than manipulate cultural media to socialist ends, they strove to produce a liberatory, social and historical understanding of them. It is in this second tradition that Brecht belongs. In both showing how human subjects are determined by their socio-historical environment, and offering new perceptual relations to the audience, Brecht sought to empower his spectators in the auditorium and in the world beyond.

However, Brecht and Marxism itself are arguably part of a wider phenomenon within modernism. Brecht's position as regards modernity is a multi-faceted one and requires detailed examination.

Two of the pivotal precepts of nineteenth-century thought were those of realism and the humanist subject. To a large extent these were symbiotic; realism was validated as the viewpoint of the stable individual, while the notion of the individual was continually reiterated by realism's imaging of that viewpoint. But as we noted, the late nineteenth and early twentieth centuries saw the emergence of a number of discourses to challenge that old consensus. Freud theorised human internality, while Marx and those other seminal theorists of what was to become sociology, Max Weber and Emile Durkheim, placed the human subject in an external, social context. J. G. Frazer's *The Golden Bough* (1890–1915) viewed religion – formerly discussed in metaphysical terms: Faith, the Soul – from an anthropological perspective, and Einstein's General Relativity explained the relationship between the observer and the phenomenon they observed, while Saussurean semiotics described the way 'reality' was constructed out of signs. All these proved crucial to the formation of modernist ideas.

Although these discourses address different topics there are qualities they share, and two are important for Brecht. First, they all offered a critique of the reliable viewing subject, such that reality was *by definition* other than it appeared. Marx described how ideology intervened in the act of perceiving the world, for Saussure perception consisted of the superimposition of sign systems, while in Einstein's schema one's position relative to phenomena dictated what one saw. The contemporary artistic field saw a parallel shift. If the humanist view of perception was incomplete, then the supposed recreation of that perception, realism, was no longer viable. From the end of the nineteenth century to the 1940s artistic production proffered a sequence of movements – Constructivism, Futurism, Supremicism, Dadaism, Cubism and so on – which together constitute a search for a new aesthetic language. Formal experiment became the norm, and Brecht's own innovations were a part of this. Epic theatre not only offered new visions of the individuals who populated its stage, it also provided its spectators with new subject positions. In seeing the traditional model of the human subject as insufficient, in adopting a new one and creating a form to express it, Brecht reflects the primary characteristics of modernist cultural production.

The second quality is allied to this. Regardless of their areas of study, many of the formative discourses of modernism had a rationalist, scientific colouring. As Brecht himself observed, scientific reason had been the primary project of western society since the Renaissance, but during the late nineteenth and twentieth century rational enquiry was increasingly focused not just upon the natural world but also upon humankind and its creations: Viktor Shklovsky and the Russian Formalists sought to elicit the 'literariness' of literature and the essences of other artistic media, Frederick Winslow Taylor developed Time and Motion Studies, the scientific quantification of human movement. Indeed, most of the theorists already mentioned strove to understand some element of human existence or society, to bring a scientific eye to the study of the human world.

This new rationalism had an important general impact. With the new scientific understanding of human artefacts – the mind, society, history and so on – allied with innovations in technology, it now seemed possible to remodel the human world, cure its ills. 'Progress' became a key motif and science and technology were often looked upon with great optimism, although this was muted by the results of new technology in the First World War. More specifically, the new scientific rationalism concentrated on several key areas. As we saw when looking at Stanislavski, one of these was human internality, the subjective and psychological, but a second and no less important rationalistic emphasis was on the social. Architects like Le Corbusier believed that by creating perfect environments they could create perfect lives. Constructivism raised functionality to the heights of a new aesthetic; houses became 'machines for living', stages 'working spaces for actors'. Pavlov theorised psychology as a function of social conditioning, and John Maynard Keynes developed a theory for the control of national economies.

Thus modernism instituted something of a renaissance for reason, a move from the older empirical rationalism, which asserted that the world was more or less as it appeared to the viewing subject, to a new critical rationalism which argued that by definition it was not. The consequences of this renaissance were not always positive. Discourse, representation, is inevitably bound up with relations of power, and modernist reason could itself be deployed to reactionary political ends: Time and Motion Studies enabled an even greater exploitation of industrial workers; Pavlovian Behaviourism fostered a mechanistic view of the human subject; Marx was rewritten to form the ideological basis of repressive states. Nevertheless critical rationalism, incorporating a reasoned understanding of the processes of sense-making, remains a potent instrument for countering such strategies of power, for it provides the means of analysing and subverting them.

Traditionally, this side of modernism has been somewhat marginalised by an Anglo-American critical orthodoxy within academia and society's cultural elites. It is this viewpoint, articulated in its various forms by such as Eliot, Pound, Woolf and by 'New Critics' such as Wimsatt, Beardsley and John Crowe Ransom, that we have inherited, and as a result our conception of modernism often tends to concentrate upon selected features: a concern with the internal, the subjective; a new rigorous and 'masculine' use of language by such as Eliot and Pound themselves; a disorientated flight from the modern world towards images of myth and a lost pastoral arcadia; dense classical references; an elitist pursuit of High Art. This, however, is only one side of modernism, and perhaps not the most significant, and it is to the other side, which we have outlined above, that Brecht belongs. His theatre is rationalistic, populist and socially orientated, experimental and politically committed to changing the existing order. As we noted, Brecht was not alone in trying to create a theatre of this kind, but he was the most successful, and for this reason the most influential upon the western stage.

4

BECKETT AND THE AVANT-GARDE

THE THEATRE OF ABSENCE

At the heart of the theatre of Samuel Beckett (1906–89) lies a critique of that most uniquely human of activities, the manufacture of meaning. Historically, different cultures have been dominated by distinct orders of meaning, different 'grand narratives'. Premodern western society held to a sacred world view; medieval culture assumed the universe to have been created by God, and therefore explained tangible, material reality in terms of His plan. Over the historical modern period this sacred paradigm gradually gave ground to one based on reason. Scientists explained physical phenomena rationalistically by postulating universal laws, while philosophers such as Descartes, Spinoza, Locke and Kant focused upon the mind's capacity for objective logic, its ability to discern the nature of reality by disinterested intellectual enquiry alone.

Despite their differences, sacred and rationalistic paradigms are both *teleological*, imputing a purposeful design to the universe, assuming that the material world conforms to an immaterial order and outcome. It is on this basis that they credit reality with meaning. In ascribing objects and events a place in their design (God's plan, the laws of nature) such paradigms grant them a 'higher', conceptual significance, one which transcends their identity as mere material things. In his 1931 essay 'Proust', however, Beckett challenged this principle (see Beckett 1965). Reality, he argued, is a 'perpetuum', a random continuum of phenomena, devoid of any meaningful design. Human beings usually obscure this fact, for to accept that reality is without order would be to acknowledge that human existence is without purpose or meaning; this would cause us to experience existential anguish, what Beckett calls the 'suffering of being'. Humankind therefore *projects* form and meaning onto reality, and does so as part of the very process of perceiving it. In Beckett's view we do not see the world objectively but 'annex' it, *make*-sense of experience to manufacture the illusion of a knowable universe. To this end we use shared conceptual paradigms such as those of religion and science, but effect a comparable ordering of our world in our ordinary, day-to-day actions, for we behave as if reality were purposeful, as if causes produced effects in a meaningful way, thus organising existence in the very process of living. By ordering and quantifying experience – ascribing to random reality a purpose, building structures of sense out of senseless events – we hold the unpalatable truth of a universe and existence without meaning at bay.

It is this proposition which lies at the core of Beckett's theatre. Science and religion – indeed, all such grand narratives – view the world as knowable. They address it as a realm of signs, interpreting its material objects/events as signifiers in order to elicit the immaterial meanings, the conceptual signifieds, that lie beneath. But the Beckettian universe is without any God or rational order from which such meanings might derive. His stage therefore offers a vision of reality which, lacking any conceptual dimension, any inherent order of abstract meaning, is composed of brute things; a universe in which all supposed 'meaning' is manufactured in the eyes of its beholders.

Perhaps the most distinctive feature of Beckett's dramatic craft is its utilisation of the theatrical medium itself. His instructions for the set of the first of his plays to be performed, *Waiting for Godot* (1955), are famously minimalist, for it is to depict only 'A country road. A tree. Evening.' The play is to be enacted on a stage which is for all practical purposes empty, devoid of the usual devices for representing place. Aside from a leafless tree, the only 'sign' used to indicate the play's hypothetical otherplace is the real place of the stage.

This is indicative of Beckett's drama in general, for his plays effect their signification using little more than the basic resources of theatre itself, the medium's own 'building materials' in their raw form. All his works employ bare or sparsely furnished stages; the fictional loci consist only of their spatial dimensions, which are represented by the *real* height, breadth and depth of the playing area, the space contained by wings, flies and rear flat or wall. Often, space is further shaped with light. In works such as *Krapp's Last Tape* (1958), *Rockaby* (1982) and *Footfalls* (1976) the action occurs in an illuminated area on a darkened stage. The 'known' world of the play, the domain of the character's 'annexation' of reality, is sculpted out of obscuring darkness with directional theatrical lighting. Even spotlights are employed in this fashion, the locus of *That Time* (1976) being comprised of an old man's spotlit face hanging in the air in a pitch-dark void, while in *Not I* (1973) the scene is further reduced to that of an illuminated mouth.

Theatre employs space and light of necessity, of course, but in most forms they, like all theatre's resources, are used to signify something other than themselves. Stages are frequently adorned with sets to represent not just spatial dimensions but a location. Although we know that the 'walls' of a realistically depicted drawing room are painted canvas, we read them as symbolic of real walls; the stage signifier represents a fictional signified, a concept of 'walls'. But in Beckett's work such materials signify nothing but what they actually are; the playing space of *Godot* indicates only the physical space of the playworld, while the area rendered visible to the audience by a spotlight in *That Time* depicts the space known, conceptually 'visible', to the character. Such materials do function in the Abstract register to signify a locus, but the locus consists only of those materials' fictional equivalents. As a consequence, the circumstances of the locus exactly parallel those of the performance itself. It is not that Beckett's stage lacks the resources adequately to depict a playworld; rather, his playworlds are comprised of no more than the stage.

This principle is evident at all levels of Beckett's stagecraft, for even the physical action of his plays is built of performance activities in their raw form. Much of the action of *Waiting for Godot* and *Krapp s Last Tape* is comprised of clowning and slapstick. In *Happy Days* (1961) the character of Winnie does no more than speak and emit behavioural minutiae, those details of gesture, facial expression and so on contrived by most styles of acting. In these plays, then, the characters themselves are acting, the action of the locus, the 'performed', paralleling that of the performance. Equally, blocking, the placement of performers about the stage, may be the core of fictional activity, the action of *Endgame* (1958) in large part consisting of its characters' movements and positions about the stage/room.

In later works Beckett employs basic theatrical materials in an even rawer, more economical fashion. Movement is often reduced to its core forms, comprised of no more than characters pacing, walking or rocking in a chair. The result is activity which is less mimetic, not the symbol of some more meaningful activity but walking or rocking *per se*; the acts themselves, nothing more. Similarly, dialogue may be stripped of syntax and grammar, the structures which enable it to express meaning, and so reduced to 'speaking' rather than an act of communication. Theatre's visual and audial elements are frequently pared down to essentials. *That Time*'s illuminated face is accompanied by disjointed, tape-recorded dialogue, and the spotlit mouth of *Not I* incessantly speaks disordered words; we are offered not 'characters' in the usual sense but those components of theatre used to *signify* character. In this respect perhaps the most interesting of Beckett's later plays is his 'dramaticule' *Come and Go* (1966), where each of the three characters exits the stage in turn, leaving the remaining two to talk, until finally all sit together, clasping each other's hands to form a 'Celtic knot'. The action of *Come and Go* is built of its characters' presence onstage and their bodily contact, parts of theatre so ordinary, so commonplace that they hardly seem 'materials' at all.

By such means Beckett depicts a world devoid of meaning, and does so at the level of signification itself. Theatre audiences customarily address all that appears on the stage as a sign. The physical object – set, prop, movement, spoken word – is assumed to be a signifier, and so scrutinised to elicit its concept, its signified. We therefore interrogate material objects for an immaterial meaning, read words for their speaker's thoughts and feelings, seek purpose in their movements and gestures, and so on. But our reading of Beckett's stage is not able to transcend the level of material things, for space signifies only space and movement symbolises movement alone. Although the components of Beckett's stage *do* demand to be read symbolically, for they are elements of a symbolised other-place, they lack precisely that 'higher' meaning which we expect; the *conceptual* signified of such signs is that they are *material*, they 'mean' only what they are. The audience therefore seeks transcendent meaning, only to find it missing, not from the stage but from the world it represents.

It is not that Beckett's stage is meaningless, then; it rather offers 'there is no meaning' *as* its meaning; it does not lack signification but *signifies* a playworld devoid of signs. In constructing loci and dramatic action out of no more than theatre's raw materials, Beckett depicts a realm composed solely *of* the material, one without a conceptual dimension. By prompting spectators to seek meaning in a locus which has none, he signals not merely a world which is inscrutable but one in which meaning is absent.

This absence is literalised in Beckett's dramatic craft, for each of his works lacks several of the elements we expect of theatre. With minimal sets or none at all, his plays lack defined 'place', and none have a narrative in the usual sense. Dimensions of movement are often missing from Beckett's stage. Winnie begins *Happy Days* buried to the waist in earth, and *Rockaby*'s lone protagonist, W, is fixed in her rocking chair, while other characters remain entombed in wheelchairs, giant urns and dustbins. A comparable absence is evident in the constraints Beckett imposes upon characters' use of space. May in *Footfalls* trudges the same path repeatedly, the unnamed protagonists of *Quad* (1984) walk the lines of an invisible pattern on the stage floor, while in *Act Without Words II* (1959) Beckett contrives what he terms a 'frieze effect', mounting his characters on a narrow platform which runs the width of the stage so that they can proceed in only one dimension. Dialogue may be similarly lacking, for words may be severed from any tangible speaker by being recorded on tape, denied response in Beckett's actual or *de facto* monologues, or, in his mime plays, absent entirely. Even that most basic component of the live medium, the human figure, appears in partial form, so that, as we have seen, in *That Time* and *Not I* the audience is presented with only a face or a mouth. Indeed, in *Breath* (1970) no character appears at all, the stage remaining empty but for a pulsating light, a recorded birth cry and 'miscellaneous rubbish'.

All these are specifically theatrical absences, 'gaps' in the inventory of theatre's readable components, and therefore augment the stage's signification of non-signification. But equally, with the stage and the other-place built of the same materials, they function as absences in that hypothetical realm that is the locus. Beckett's dramas deal less in plots than in *situations*, for they entail placing characters in markedly restricted circumstances. For our purposes such situations have two key qualities. They first shape all the unfolding action, determine all that his characters can do or be. Buried in earth, locked into chairs and rooms, dustbins, spatial confines and repetitive movements, the fictional 'lives' of Beckett's protagonists are dictated by the circumstances in which they are depicted. At the same time, those circumstances are emphatically physical, composed of concrete checks and barriers, constraints placed upon the life of the body. As we have noted, most forms of conceptual thought view material reality as shaped according to an immaterial design. Our lives have a meaning or purpose, we assume, one transcending mere physical survival, because they are part of a 'higher' order. But the 'lives' of Beckett's characters are determined by the brute material circumstances of their dramatic situations. From the audience's viewpoint characters *are* their lives, and on Beckett's stage their lives are their situations. He thereby depicts existence as a purely creatural affair, one which cannot 'transcend' the material for it *consists* of the material.

Devices such as these, then, operate both at the level of interpretation and of action. They also function imagistically. All elements of Beckett's theatre combine to infer an other-place whose primary quality is its austerity. As we noted, his plays lack narrative, his sets are bleakly bare and often dimly lit or cast in shadow, while each of his loci is characterised by the notable absence of some dimension. Similarly, most of Beckett's protagonists are in some way physically or sensorily impaired, suffering blindness or amputation, paralysis, dementia, speechlessness or decrepit old age. As we have seen, in certain of his plays, particularly later works, disability takes more abstract forms, with characters reduced to faces or mouths, immobilised, or shown manically speaking or pacing the stage. Such images collectively figure an existence shaped by privation, the lack or loss, the absence, of some fundamental faculty or dimension of human experience. By dramatising humankind's encounter with extraordinary physical limits, Beckett illustrates the earth-boundness of human existence, the merely material level at which life, he believes, is lived.

Such images function in an oblique way. Darkness, silence, disability, immobility, scarcity – each of these is negative; each is one pole of an existing dichotomy, the opposite of a positive term, and is defined by that term. Thus it is as part of a dichotomy that we as members of the audience perceive and interpret them. We understand the significance of darkness as the lack of light, read immobility as a loss of free movement, perceive physical impairment in reference to an ideal of the able body, and so on. Our very experience of interpreting Beckett's work therefore entails an implicit comparison in which it is found lacking – simultaneously a comparison with life and with theatre, the cultural situation in which we have placed ourselves, the medium whose expectations we bring to the event. Thus reading his stage itself involves the recognition of an absence; we perceive his loci as worlds of the negative in reference to implied realms of the positive which we must posit as part of our act of reading.

Beckett's critique is not of a particular order of meaning but of meaning-making itself; not a specific symbolic construction of reality but the very act of symbolisation. To effect this critique on the stage, however, he uses symbols. It is true that he communicates his ideas primarily by subverting such signs, prompting spectators to seek conceptual signifieds and then denying them. But this too is an act of signification, for, as we have seen, when a stage component is denied conceptual meaning it functions as a sign of that meaning's absence. Even when subverting given cultural meaning, one can only use cultural means, for to undermine existing signs *on a stage*, an acknowledged space of signification, is to create new ones. Beckett is in the somewhat paradoxical position of mounting his critique using precisely the process he criticises.

This is emblematic of a more fundamental paradox. For Beckett the recognition that reality is ultimately devoid of meaning is a positive act, for it enables us to extract maximum value from our lives, to experience the fertile diversity of existence in a phenomenal world. But human beings are meaning-making animals. The process that is human consciousness consists of projecting structures upon reality; human subjectivity orders the world of objects it perceives, is *comprised* of its structured perception of that world. There is no escape from such subjectivity. Truly to 'experience' a world without meaning would be to lose consciousness, one's ability to be *aware* of reality's meaninglessness; to stop being human. The only alternative is to understand such meaninglessness intellectually, to represent and conceptualise the illusory nature of representation and conceptualisation. This is indeed the alternative Beckett offers, the meaning that there is no meaning. But this is itself a conceptual paradigm, a mechanism for explaining reality, and so an example of that process of human symbolisation he disavows.

HABIT

Faced with the 'perpetuum' of reality, Beckett argues, the usual human response is to impose form and meaning upon it. Humanity, he asserts, is equipped with two faculties to aid it in this, the first being its capacity for 'habit'. He states:

> Habit is a compromise effected between the individual and his environment ... [but] the world being a projection of the individual's consciousness (an objectification of the individual's will, Schopenhauer would say), the pact must be continually renewed, the letter of safe conduct brought up to date. The creation of the world did not take place once and for all time, but takes place every day. Habit then is the generic term for the countless treaties concluded between the countless subjects that constitute the individual and their countless correlative objects.
>
> (Beckett 1965: 19)

A 'pact' is made between the world of objects and the subject who perceives it. Human consciousness projects its own constructions onto the universe, quantifying it and rendering it knowable. Since individuals alter over time, comprising 'countless subjects', reality must continually be remodelled; as we ourselves are remade each day, so the world must be conceptualised afresh to accommodate us. This ongoing process is *habit*, the 'perpetual adjustment and readjustment of our organic sensibility to the conditions of its worlds' (Beckett 1965: 28), a constant reordering of ourselves and the universe to remake them into the person/place we know. Habit thus returns us to an existence which is familiar, links the unknowable present to the known, already-formulated past, reaffirming our conception of reality and hence our place within it.

Beckett renders 'habit' on his stage in the form of activity which is gratuitously structured. The tramp-like Vladimir and

Estragon spend all of *Waiting for Godot* anticipating their rendezvous with the mysterious figure of the title, and pass the time philosophising, bickering and comforting each other. Much of their behaviour is overtly artificial. Their dialogue is theatrical, comprising tightly timed question-and-answer exchanges, poetic speeches and *stychomythia*, a mode of dramatic duologue composed of short lines uttered by alternate speakers. Their physical activities are similarly contrived, often consisting of clown routines: falling over and struggling to get up, gazing at the sky in comic unison, exchanging three bowler hats in a complicated slapstick that leaves each wearing the wrong one.

It is once again via an 'absence' that Beckett makes habit out of such theatrical material. In most forms of theatre, actions – words, activities – comprise the building blocks of narrative. Activities produce results, words effect change, and by such means the story develops meaningfully over time. Thus it is by reading actions, divining the logic governing their occurrence, that we as spectators interpret the play's events. But Vladimir and Estragon's activities evidence no such logic, and no such movement forward in time. Denied an explanation for action as it occurs, the audience can only wait for the play's conclusion to account for it retrospectively. But *Waiting for Godot* does not conclude, it simply ends; Godot fails to arrive and we never discover why they wait for him. The usual cause-and-effect narrative is absent, there is no developmental logic to grant actions a purpose within the playworld. But beyond the playworld, in the auditorium, this lack of meaning is itself meaningful, for without purpose activity functions as a sign of purposelessness; failing to move forward in time, actions are revealed as a way of *filling* time, of waiting. As Vladimir and Estragon perform their contrived dialogues and routines, it becomes apparent that they are *acting*, manufacturing the appearance of a life imbued with form and meaning. Their actions are in a Beckettian sense habitual, a way of ordering their world and their lives using the only resources which, as tramps, are available to them: their own behaviour.

Thus *Waiting for Godot* presents it audience with the spectacle of ordered activity. By denying that activity a meaning within the playworld, Beckett presents it to the audience as a *sign* of meaninglessness. In *Endgame* such activity, such habit, is inscribed into the social order, for the play's central characters, Hamm and Clov, act out the roles of master and servant. Hamm is disabled, unable to leave his wheeled chair, and orders Clov to bring him various objects, to monitor the world outside, and to wheel him to precise positions about their dilapidated room. The audience is thus confronted with a series of structured movements through the bounded space of the stage/room. Clov enters and leaves on command, positions and climbs his ladder to peer through the window in a comically ritualised sequence of steps, and in angular, chess-like moves wheels Hamm across the stage.

But as in *Waiting for Godot*, all such activities are revealed to be pointless. Hamm's moves about the room are always contained within that room; his movements 'write' his confinement in stage space, demonstrating their own futility. Blind as well as paralysed, he cannot know where Clov has positioned him, and the post-Holocaust world outside is dead and unchanging – it does not need to be monitored. Hamm enforces his commands by threatening to withhold the key to the larder. The larder, however, is in another room where Hamm cannot go; we realise he must give the key to Clov each day. Just as Clov's tasks are revealed to be pointless, we realise Hamm's commands are without force, and that their master–servant relationship is a kind of game whose rules require both parties' consent. Hamm and Clov's rituals, 'moves' and hierarchical relationship are their own end result. Like the chess game suggested by the title, they are a way of ordering the characters' lives and the confined world of their room.

As director of his own plays Beckett worked with extraordinary precision, demonstrating the exact movements, stage positions, duration of pauses and so on that he required. Similar precision is evident in his writing, certain of his plays describing in detail the characters' gestures and movements, facial expressions and even behavioural minutiae. This enabled him to construct habit out of the performances' own components. *Happy Days* opens on a bare landscape to show Winnie, its central character, buried to the waist in a mound of earth. Upon being woken by a bell, she commences a stream of tasks: praying, brushing her teeth, rummaging through her handbag and applying make-up. Winnie's every action – the opening and closing of her eyes, the turning of her head – is scripted, and all these micro-activities are coordinated with her relentlessly optimistic speech. The result is a continuous and highly orchestrated verbal/visual text, so that, as in *Endgame* and *Waiting for Godot,* the audience is provided with an image of structured activity. Once again, however, such activity is stripped of purpose. Winnie ostensibly speaks and interacts with her husband, Willie, who lies out of sight behind her mound of earth. But Willie replies only occasionally with a word or a grunt. Winnie is speaking to herself; her words and gestures are revealed as a way of masking the void of her life, imposing meaning on an existence which has none.

As we noted, in later plays such habitual activities tend to take more basic forms. The lone character of *Rockaby,* W, spends the play in a rocking chair, her taped monologue coordinated with the chair's regular (mechanically controlled) back-and-forth motion, while May, the protagonist of *Footfalls,* walks the breadth of the stage and back again along a fixed path of nine steps. It is with simple movement – through space, in time – that W and May structure their fictional lives and worlds, literally ordering the time/space 'perpetuum' of the locus. In other works language performs a comparable function, the characters of *Play* (1963), *That Time, Ohio Impromptu* (1981) and *Not I* seeking to organise themselves and their pasts via the act of speaking. Although in plays such as these the shaping of the time/space of the locus is quite literal, the resulting image is more abstract. As spectators we may bring our experience of theatre to bear on Vladimir and Estragon's routines or Winnie's words/gestures, and so initially seek to read them for more conventional meaning. But comprised of activities in their pure, physical form, W's rocking and the words of *That Time's* old man suggest no such possibility, effectively signalling that they must be translated directly into abstractions: 'movement', 'speech'.

Perhaps the purest example of this abstraction is in the television play *Quad,* where action again takes the form of temporally structured movement. The 'set' of this piece consists of a square pool of light, six paces by six, projected onto the stage floor. Four cowled and anonymous performers enter one by one, each walking to the rhythm of his or her own distinctive percussion, to march along lines running parallel to the square's sides. They also walk the diagonals that join its corners, deviating only to circumnavigate the 'danger zone', a smaller square area in the centre which they are instructed to avoid.

In performance the total effect is ritual-like as, resembling monks or religious celebrants, the walkers describe a coordinated pattern in sound and, particularly, movement. For the spectator, however, there is no pattern, for on the floor there is only a solid square of light. The pattern, the purpose ordering their actions, is absent, it does not exist – or rather, it exists only in so far as the walkers' steps trace its lines upon the stage; it 'exists' in the minds and actions of the characters. Their dramatic lives are shaped by the figure, but the figure is itself created by those lives. The walkers' activities are habit; the structure is an illusion, projected onto a void, with those human subjects fabricating what they believe they perceive.

In this sense *Quad*'s pattern is reminiscent of some conceptual paradigm. Just as the human 'annexation' of reality entails imputing to it a design and reproducing that design in one's actions, so *Quad*'s walkers trace a shape upon the stage floor, their *dramatic* world, as if it represented that realm's inherent order. But the visible, 'known' world of *Quad* is limited. The stage outside the pattern's boundaries is beyond the performers' tread, and so remains unquantified, in darkness and unknowable, while the danger zone at its centre is forbidden them. The danger zone is thus like the Logos that we discussed in relation to Brecht. In Derrida's usage, the Logos is that assertion which lies at the heart of all discourses, and to which all other assertions must refer in their claim to truth. But it must remain unexamined; only when the existence of God goes unquestioned does the intellectual edifice of Christianity hold together. Similarly, *Quad*'s danger zone, the centre which anchors its shape in space, must remain unexplored, for if it were shown to be hollow – or the pattern's reach shown to have physical limits – it would be revealed as a mere construct, a figure drawn by human action upon the 'perpetuum' of the stage floor.

With no possibility of purpose, a future goal, human action cannot move forward in time. Habit therefore lacks development, merely repeats: *Quad*'s walkers retrace their path, W continues her rocking. This is central to Beckett's dramatic proposition, for in a world without purpose time becomes a dimension of pure decline, a principle expressed in Beckett's dramatic action and imagery. Winnie begins *Happy Days* buried to the waist but by the second act she is buried to the neck, while Pozzo becomes blind during the interval of *Waiting for Godot*. Perhaps the supreme example is *Breath*, where a birth cry and a death rattle follow each other in quick succession, life being imaged as the moment of dim light that falls between. The decaying or disabled body illustrates the action of what Beckett terms the 'time cancer', that inevitable descent into deterioration and death that begins as soon as we are born. Indeed, Beckett's work is filled with testaments to time as a corrosive force: characters are invariably aged, infirm or unkempt, environments are dilapidated, clothes threadbare and / or anachronistic, and the basic stuffs that make life bearable in Beckett's universe – food in *Waiting for Godot*, painkillers, bicycle wheels, coffins and sugar plums in *Endgame*, toothpaste, Vaseline and 'universal pick-me-up' in *Happy Days* – run out.

This conception of time itself negates the kinds of paradigms customarily used to structure reality. Rationalism addresses time as a dimension of meaning, locates prior causes to explain effects. It is inherently optimistic; the world, it asserts, can be understood and therefore altered, reshaped to make a better future. Sacred paradigms similarly peer ahead, to the realisation of a perfect, non-material state of being. But devoid of such designs, the Beckettian universe can offer no such future. With death and deterioration, disability and scarcity, Beckett represents the end of rationalist and theological time, the demise of those world views which seek to bind the present to the past and future to form a meaningful continuity.

This view of time is most importantly a formal feature of Beckett's work. Habit merely reiterates the same visual and verbal forms for the spectator; words circle and meander, walking and rocking redraw the same shapes in space. Equally, his plays do not develop, for, lacking a narrative in the conventional sense, they do not move forward in time, nor conclude; Godot does not arrive, W simply stops rocking, and Mouth in *Not I* begins and ends the play in the midst of her relentless, disordered speech. With no possibility of meaningful development, time in Beckett's theatre describes a path of circularity, a continual present without the potential for change.

For Beckett, then, the sense we make of our world, the order we project upon it, is illusory, all supposed meanings being no more than constructs fostered by habit. In this sense Beckett's view is supported by much modern theory. Structuralism and that collection of diverse perspectives termed Post-structuralism both focus upon the human act of sense-*making*, starting from the assumption that all meaning is of human manufacture. This is perhaps not incidental, for the *émigré* Irishman Beckett spent many of his formative years as part of that milieu of French intellectualism which gave birth to such as Claude Lévi-Strauss, Jacques Lacan, Julia Kristeva, Jacques Derrida and Jean-François Lyotard, figures central to critical theory as it has developed.

But while this view of meaning and subjectivity is well supported and theoretically sound, nevertheless the account offered by Beckett's drama is incomplete, for it does not acknowledge what is perhaps the most important factor in humankind's fabrication of sense. In Beckett's plays habit is represented as an essentially individual act; characters behave in a vacuum, rock, walk and talk in order to build an ordered universe out of nothing but their own activities. In social reality, however, we never have the opportunity to order the 'perpetuum', the blank sheet of reality, for ourselves, for the paradigms our culture provides dictate the terms out of which sense can be made. In behaving in a 'habitual' way – acting, thinking and speaking as if the world possessed order and meaning – we actually reproduce the conceptual structures circulating in a social reality not of our own making.

This socio-cultural dimension is missing from Beckett's model. As we noted, even when subverting given orders of signification Beckett employs signs, tokens which function on a cultural level. Although such signs – objects without a conceptual dimension, actions without purpose – offer meanings different from those we expect, they employ the same mechanism of signification, the combination of material object and immaterial concept. There is no meaning in Beckett's loci, but for the audience that fact is meaningful. As we noted, 'there is no meaning' is itself a meaning, a conceptual paradigm which explains reality, but one which fails to explain how the *effect* of meaning is created, and what ends – cultural and, most importantly, political – are served by the meanings to which we are heir.

VOLUNTARY MEMORY

Beckett's critique of the human manufacture of meaning complements his view of human subjectivity. Within the sacred paradigm of premodern society the self was conceived as a part of God's design, as a soul. But in the modern period this view was superseded, and the inaugural theorist of the new model of the subject, the humanist individual, was René Descartes (1596–1650). With his formulation *cogito ergo sum*, 'I think therefore I am', Descartes asserted that the mind's existence is proven by its awareness *of* itself. Our knowledge of the world may be in doubt, he argued, for it is perceived via fallible human senses, but we perceive our own mind directly. The 'I' of Descartes's dictum is therefore a stable entity, one which is both autonomous – possessing a power to *know* which is independent of the body and the world – and enduring, its identity consistent over time. It thus provided the reliable and objective vantage point required by reason and science; by subjecting the world to the mind's scrutiny in order to determine its underlying laws, finding causes for the effects perceived, the stable humanist individual rendered reality knowable to reason.

Both models, the soul and the Cartesian individual, conceptualise the self as an unchanging immaterial essence separate from the material body. But as we have seen, for Beckett the self is not stable but continually shifting. He states:

> Yesterday is ... irremediably part of us, within us, heavy and dangerous. We are not merely more weary because of yesterday, we are other, no longer what we were before. ... Such as it was, [yesterday] has been assimilated to the only world that has reality and significance, the world of our own latent consciousness. ... The individual is the seat of a constant process of decantation, decantation from the vessel containing the fluid of future time, sluggish, pale and monochrome, to the vessel containing the fluid of past time, agitated and multicoloured by the phenomena of its hours.
>
> (Beckett 1965: 15)

In Beckett's view, then, the subject constantly alters as it moves through time. The self exists in a permanent 'now', for as the future becomes the present we are changed by it, become a different self, an 'other'. Stable identity is therefore an illusion, one conjured by what is for Beckett the second of humankind's sense-making faculties, what he terms 'voluntary memory'. Voluntary memory involves recalling the past into the present, remodelling it so as to reflect our current identity, and thus fostering the appearance of continuity; by reviewing yesterday, conceptualising it afresh from the perspective of the self of today, we nurture the illusion that our former self was the same, and that consequently we are essentially unchanging. The stable 'I' of Descartes's dictum is therefore for Beckett a chimera. It is no more than the 'plagiarism of oneself', the automatic redrawing of yesterday's self by today's to create the impression that they are one.

This shifting self is figured in one of Beckett's earlier plays, *Krapp's Last Tape*. Krapp spends his seventieth birthday replaying tape recordings of his own voice, made on previous birthdays as part of a long-standing ritual. The tapes recount past experiences and insights; as an aspiring poet, the young Krapp once sought to deny himself physical pleasures in pursuit of his art. But time has changed him. On reaching a point on one tape where his younger self is about to describe a great revelation, the ill-humoured Krapp impatiently winds forward; at another he consults a dictionary to find the meaning of a word, 'viduity', that he once used freely. The aesthetic concerns of the young man are of no interest to his older, altered self, who concentrates instead on the purely bodily delights of drinking, eating bananas and replaying accounts of past sexual exploits.

It is once again by combining the use of theatre's raw materials with a theatrical absence that Beckett illustrates in *Krapp's Last Tape* his conception of the self. As spectators we usually build our view of a dramatic character by synthesising information drawn from different sources, weaving together their words with their actions, the words of others, visual appearance, accounts of past events and so on to form that unity which is the fictional individual. But *Krapp's Last Tape* signals this act of synthesis to be inappropriate. The bulk of the play's words emerge from the tape, so that language is primarily the medium by which the spectator learns of the younger Krapp. The older man is in contrast signified visually, via physical presence, and we see him eating, loading the tape and pausing to stare into space. As the older man disparages the opinions of his younger self, and proves to have forgotten what he once knew, we are made aware that the two cannot be viewed as a single individual, one identity. Whereas words and visual image and so on usually combine, in *Krapp's Last Tape* they signify separate selves. In this play it is the stable self in the form of unitary character which is absent.

As Beckett's later work tended towards greater abstraction, this subversion of the Cartesian self became more thorough-going. As we noted, the stage picture of *That Time* consists of an old man's lighted face on a darkened stage. A taped voice is broadcast from three discernibly different positions about the stage, and although it is the same voice, it recounts separate narratives, describing what appear to be events from three different periods of the man's life. Segments of these stories are played one after the other in altering sequences, and between each tripartite sequence there is a pause during which the old man's breathing is audible. In the last sequence the voices fall into what seems to be chronological order, beginning with the tale of youth, then middle and old age.

The face is the pre-eminent symbol of the self in both ordinary social exchange and the theatre, and so crucial to the audience's interpretative activities. Even if we forget a character's name we usually remember the actor's face and affix to it the character's attributes. Faces thus anchor all the information offered by other means, are the signifiers upon which we unify data to construct coherent dramatic personae. Aside from the old man's face, however, the only information offered in *That Time* derives from the voice, a source fragmented into three and constantly shifting; the voice(s) offer data but their reliability is in doubt. More-over, the pauses with their audible breathing indicate a part of the old man's psyche which is anterior to such data, pre-dating that linguistic alignment of the past into its proper order with which the piece ends. *That Time* concludes with the voices played in their chronological order and the old man smiling. His past, it is implied, has been properly structured, its jumbled fragments rewritten into a meaningful, narrativised sequence, 'voluntarily remembered' to confirm his identity of today. But for the audience the process is undermined because it is shown to *be* a process, the stable self a construction. In atomising the stage's elements, Beckett fragments the components out of which the fictional self is usually synthesised, denying the audience a unified sign of character.

Whereas *Krapp's Last Tape* depicts the dissolution of fixed identity, *That Time* enacts its successful fabrication. But in both plays the self is represented as a product of language. Language is the primary tool with which we conceptualise the world and our place in it, and in Beckett's work the failure of the self is most often figured in language's breakdown. The character of Lucky in *Godot* spends most of the play silent, speaking only when commanded by his master, Pozzo. When he does speak his words issue forth in a stream lacking all grammar and syntax – those *structures* which permit meaning – a parody of rationalistic discourse in which references are made to unlikely, very physical authorities, 'Fartov and Belcher', but which makes no discernible sense. Comparably structureless speech is found in *Not I, Rockaby, Footfalls* and, predictably, *That Time*, plays whose characters lack a stable sense of self.

What is the relationship between the self and language? We can best explain in reference to the Structuralist (or, arguably, Post-structuralist) psychoanalyst Jacques Lacan. For Lacan human subjectivity is formed over two stages of an infant's development, termed the Imaginary and the Symbolic. The first, the Imaginary, is the pre-cultural stage. The child enters the Imaginary with no sense of itself as a separate entity. It experiences the flow of impulses and sensations about its body but does not distinguish between itself and the world at large, for it has no conceptual tools with which to do so. The distinction only becomes possible once the child has undergone the 'Mirror Stage' (see Lacan 1977: ch. 1), where it sees itself reflected in a real and/or metaphorical mirror; reflected, for example, in others' responses to it. For the first time the child (mis)perceives itself as a unity, a whole separated from the rest of the world by the perimeter of its body wall forming a border or threshold. This is the inaugural experience upon which, Lacan argues, a sense of selfhood will later develop, for it permits the infant to conceive of reality and its own position within it as a series of oppositional pairs, of inside (the body) and outside, self and other, the subject and the objects it perceives.

However, the infant does not yet have a true sense of identity, of selfhood. This is formed when it enters the next stage, the Symbolic. The Symbolic is the stage of culture during which the child learns and adopts the extant signifying systems of the society into which it is born, the most important of which is language. It is in language that the child finds a sign with which it can represent itself, the word 'I'. With the adoption of 'I' selfhood is completed, for the 'I' permits not merely awareness but self-awareness; with the 'I' the infant represents itself *to* itself, fosters the illusion of a stable, continuous identity 'proven' by its ability to perceive itself.

More than any other signifying medium, then, for Lacan it is language which permits the illusion of Cartesian selfhood. We might reformulate 'I think therefore I am' from a Lacanian perspective to read 'I know that I exist because I can perceive myself', for the key quality of Descartes's model is not its powers of pensive reflection but of self-reflection. With 'I' the subject has a mechanism for its self-representation, a means of creating with a material sound the phantom, the immaterial concept, which it then identifies as its own being.

More than a means of self-expression, then, language is the physical medium – concrete sounds, ink on paper – in which selfhood is manufactured. *That Time* shows identity constructed in the act of ordering material words – not the past but *verbal accounts* of the past – whereas in *Waiting for Godot, Footfalls* and others the loss of self is accompanied by a breakdown of speech. Equally, in other of Beckett's plays we see characters urgently speaking as a means of affirming their existence. Winnie talks for two acts, although by the second her words have become disjointed. As we noted, she ostensibly speaks to her husband Willie, but he answers rarely. Winnie's 'conversation' with Willie is a useful fiction, enabling her to continue talking while fending off the knowledge that she speaks to herself. Words are her Symbolic mirror; with language a means of representing oneself *to* oneself, the act of speaking is analogous to selfhood *per se*, a process of continual reaffirmation which fosters the belief that there is indeed a self to affirm.

The fabrication of a stable self via 'voluntary memory' and habit's ordering of reality are for Beckett two sides of the same process, for the 'pact' between the world of objects and the subject who perceives it in fact gives form and meaning to both. By projecting a design upon the world I render it knowable to me: in doing so, however, I adopt the persona of the individual who 'sees' and 'knows' in that manner, represent myself *to* myself as the 'I' who holds that knowledge and perspective. The interdependency of these two processes is implicit in most of Beckett's works. By enacting the roles of master and servant, Hamm and Clov sculpt both their world and their identities, while in walking *Quad*'s characters pattern their lives as well as the stage. But it is in one of Beckett's late plays, *Ohio*

Impromptu, that we see these two processes operating most clearly in unison.

In *Ohio Impromptu* two identical old men sit about a table, Listener listening while Reader reads to him from a book. The story Reader tells seems to record the sad events of Listener's immediate past, the loss of a friend or loved one and his subsequent retreat to the isolated spot near 'the Isle of Swans' where the audience finds him. The purpose of the reading, we are told, is to provide 'comfort'. As Reader reads, Listener periodically raps the table, a call for the last sentence to be read again. As the reading progresses the story moves forward in time to describe the very situation now being enacted on the stage: a man appeared, Reader says, to offer the protagonist of his story some comfort by reading to him from a book. The piece ends with Reader closing his book and the two men moving in perfect synchronisation; lowering their hands to the table, raising their heads, and finally staring at each other unblinkingly.

According to the story we hear read, then, Listener has suffered some loss which has caused him to retreat from the world, and left him speechless, bereft of any means of manufacturing an 'I'. Reader mirrors him, both in appearance and, at the play's end, in movement. He thus offers Listener an image of himself *for* himself. Reader reinforces this by telling his companion a story, a cause-and-effect narrative in which the events of Listener's past are ordered into a meaningful sequence. In doing so Reader not only imposes a design upon Listener's past, he also offers him a stable identity as the hero of the story, a linguistic persona with which he can identify. Thus the fabrication of a self in this play simultaneously involves reordering reality; Listener is constructed *as* the person who lived the rewritten events described.

This principle is reproduced in the spectator's interpretative experience. Listener and Reader are mirror images. In effect, they appear to be facets of the same individual, the former in need of affirmative self-reflection, the latter *being* that reflection. The loss Listener experienced, it is inferred, was of Reader, his own 'I'; the self, this play implies, is a story we tell to ourselves in order to convince ourselves that our *self* exists. But as members of the audience we too seek to interpret the story as an account of Listener's past, in order to make of him a rounded character. In recognising Reader as Listener's *alter ego*, however, we must necessarily acknowledge that the resulting fictional self *is* fictional. Thus the stage is without a self, and the audience is denied that concept underlying our view of character, the construct we use to interpret what takes place. The very means offered spectators for making the onstage figure of Listener into a character, Reader and his story, ultimately undermine that process. If the self is a story we tell ourselves, then character is also a fiction, one the audience itself manufactures.

But Reader and his story do not explain all of Listener. Listener periodically raps on the table, calling for passages to be reread, thereby signifying a part of himself which is beyond the story, outside language and the 'I' it offers. Indeed, it is that part which, by rapping, prompts the manufacture of the 'I'. This pre-self is signified in some form in most of Beckett's plays. Winnie's activity in *Happy Days* is not entirely continuous, for it is punctured by pauses in which she stares silently into space, her face inexpressive, her body frozen. As spectators we read such hiatus as Winnie's dawning awareness of her real condition; her optimistic persona slips as she recognises the meaninglessness of her existence, buried in the earth, alone and declining. These pauses therefore act as signs of a part of Winnie not contained by the 'I' she constructs *for* herself in her habitual words and actions – or, equally, a part of her which escapes the audience's usual conception of 'character'. Krapp's similar pauses, the old man's breathing in *That Time*, the sudden halts in W's rocking in *Rockaby* or in May's pacing in *Footfalls* – all these signal a region of the subject beyond those personae viewed as the self, both by the fictional subjects onstage and the real ones in the auditorium. If the 'I' is a sign, a concept attached to a material signifier, the self that is expressed in those interruptions is beyond signification and the ordering of the self/world it effects. It is the human being as material thing, the creature that lies beneath our illusion of selfhood.

The ultimate dramatic depiction of this pre-self is in *Not I*. The play begins before anything is visible, for the hubbub of a woman's voice is heard as the houselights go down. When the curtains part they reveal a spotlit mouth hanging in darkness 8 ft above the stage floor (another figure, the robed Auditor, is described in the playtext, but in directing his own play Beckett omitted this character). As she is seen, Mouth's voice rises in volume to become audible. Her speech is repetitive and peppered with pauses as, in urgent and disjointed snippets, she tells the story of a woman who cannot speak. She describes the moment when, walking in a field, the woman passed out, coming to consciousness again to find herself talking frantically and uncontrollably. While recounting the tale Mouth refers to the woman as 'she'. Five times she arrives at the brink of using another pronoun, only to veer back to the third person. Gradually it becomes evident that Mouth may be telling her own story, and that the word she is repeatedly drawn to, but avoids using, is 'I'.

When we first see her, Mouth is talking, for she is revealed in the midst of speaking her self into existence, a process which will culminate when she successfully represents herself *to* herself. But Mouth circles and never says 'I'. To say 'I' would be to demonstrate that the self is manufactured of merely material speech, subverting precisely that illusion of non-material selfhood she seeks to conjure. Mouth therefore finds herself in the same dilemma as other of Beckett's characters; like W in *Rockaby* or *Quad*'s walkers, she too must attempt to create with merely material resources a meaning which transcends materiality. But lacking a fully developed identity, Mouth is trapped in a Lacanian quandary. Selfhood consists of representing oneself to oneself with 'I', but for a non-self, a mere body, to do so would prove the resulting construct to *be* a construct, and so undermine the whole project.

The audience finds itself in a similar quandary. Most forms of theatre require that we impute to characters a non-material subjectivity, an 'I'. It is in reference to this hypothetical self that we endow dialogue with meaning, interpreting words as the expression of their speaker's will, thoughts and desires. But the audience of *Not I* is denied a whole individual, or even a face. The image we are presented with is an emphatically visceral, corporeal one; tongue, lips, teeth, all moist with saliva and engaged in physical motion. Consisting of no more than a bodily organ, Mouth resists all efforts to make of her a 'character'. Her words are disjointed, and, without an adequate visual image of a fictional individual to invest them with meaning – to make of them self-expression – they threaten to revert to mere sounds, material 'signifiers' without a signified, speech with no speaker. The spectator is, like Mouth, caught in a paradox that cannot be resolved; the one's attempt to construct a dramatic character is thwarted by the mere materiality of the visual/verbal image, while the other endlessly circles in language but always speaks as *she*, not *I*.

In plays such as these, then, Beckett dramatises the human subject's manufacture of its own illusory self. Voluntary memory entails narrativising, making-sense of one's past, and in so doing adopting the subject position offered by that narrative, that sense, as the site of a fictional 'I'.

This conception of the self, like Beckett's notion of habit, lacks a cultural component. In his dramatisations, selfhood is manufactured by the individual alone: the old man of *That Time* recounts and reorganises his own past life, Mouth and Winnie speak, and Reader is inferred to be a part of Listener's psyche. But just as we are never afforded the opportunity to order our world for ourselves, so in reality we are not the sole agents of our own selfhood. As we noted in the Introduction, subjectivity is culturally derived, built of those positions offered in discourse; in Lacan's terms, we define ourselves within a pre-existing Symbolic. The 'I' we adopt, then, is manufactured elsewhere.

This cultural dimension is most important for its political consequences. Language is not a neutral mechanism, it is the primary medium of ideology, the means by which those ideas which serve the interests of society's elites are fostered as truth. Thus the self's construction within language is inevitably political, and subjectivity is always implicated in operations of power.

Moreover, that power is geared to real, material ends. Subjectivity consists of ways of viewing the world, and by shaping our view of the world, ideology governs our ability to act upon it. It is this which Beckett marginalises. Hamm and Clov's hierarchical relations are depicted as a construct built of mutual assent. But in social reality the master–servant relationship which theirs infers is one of class, founded upon real inequalities over which servants such as Clov have no control. We never see the construction of 'a self' for it is always a *particular* self, one built of the positions made available by culture, either reproducing or challenging existing ideologies.

THE MATERIAL STAGE

The feature of Beckett's theatre which determines its dialogic relations with the audience is its indication that it is to be read

in two contradictory ways. Beckett's stage first offers signification of a symbolic order, both by establishing a locus for the
action and, with testaments to absence, by nurturing an imagistic reading of its elements. The spectator is thus invited to
interpret the stage in the Abstract register, to transpose its parts
into both components of an other-place and symbols of nega-
tivity.

Beckett reinforces this Abstract reading by encouraging intense
interpretative focus. As we noted, in his roles as playwright and
as director, Beckett worked with great precision, regulating the
stage picture, the actor's gestures and behavioural minutiae,
blocking and even the duration of pauses with extraordinary
exactitude. One effect of this is to rid performances of 'noise',
random signification that might obscure the practitioner's intentions. But the resulting clarity and sharpness of line itself
functions as a sign, signalling to spectators that every detail is
significant and therefore warrants superlative scrutiny. A similar
effect is created by his theatre's minimalism. When we encounter
stages bare of sets, events and narrative, and action which
consists of no more than clowning or talking, walking or rocking,
we subject those elements to close interrogation. When the stage
offers so little, we assume a corresponding importance to what
there is, and so are encouraged to look beyond the material object
for 'higher' meaning.

These features signal to spectators that the stage must be interrogated to render Abstract meaning. Others signify this meaning
to be of a certain order. Although Beckett's stage proffers a locus,
his dramatic situations resist translation into any *specific* other-
place. Presented with Winnie buried in earth, it is apparent that
we are to view the locus as a realm of ideas, albeit that the
central idea is of the failure of ideas. Moreover, these ideas are
signalled to be of a general kind. Winnie's state can be taken as
a metaphor of ageing, futility or of existential incapacity: her
situation implies all these and more, indicating that its true
meaning is figured in each, and is therefore more profound than
any one. This is true of all Beckett's works, for when confronted
with the characters of *Play* entombed in urns, Mouth talking in
the darkness, or W rocking to the rhythm of her own clipped
speech, we interpret their predicaments in terms of philosophical generalities. The details of Beckett's stage pictures
are similarly non-specific. Costume is always anachronistic

135

and/or idiosyncratic and 'place' is drawn in broad strokes: shafts of light in the darkness, bare stages, simple, emblematic props. It is therefore impossible to site characters and action in particular socio-historical circumstances. This is of course appropriate to the kinds of ideas with which Beckett deals. His concern is with what we may call the 'human condition', not the situation of particular human beings at specific times and places, but that of humanity *per se*. It is *universal*, and its universality is conveyed by the generalised quality of what we are shown; these are not particular places but no place, and therefore all places.

These techniques prime the audience to interpret the stage's components symbolically. For stage signs to function successfully in this way, in the Abstract register, they require a logic of interpretation, a Law of the Text. The audience must find that area of potential meaning shared by all or most of the performance's elements, and use it to decode those elements *en masse*. In most forms of theatre this presents no difficulty, for spectators are usually well schooled in the kinds of simple interpretative strategies required to turn the stage into a locus. We know that the playing space must be viewed as an other-place, and all that falls within it as objects of that world: we know that actors are to be taken as characters, hypothetical subjects, and words and actions as their expressions. Once the locus is established in the audience's gaze, the Law of the Text governing that locus can be sought. The sequence of events, the narrative, can be read to divine the 'causes' of that world's 'effects', the forces which power its occurrences. Characters' words and actions can be interrogated to yield an underlying logic of human behaviour; a Stanislavskian text will render a psychological causality, a Brechtian text a socio-political one.

These are very simple processes, and they underpin our understanding of most forms of theatre. But it is precisely interpretative assumptions such as these that Beckett denies his audience. The physical components of the other-place remain ambiguous, for, composed of theatre's own materials, they fail to distinguish fully the fictional place from the real site of performance. Nor are the occupants of that other-place unproblematic. Confronted with the manically speaking Mouth, perhaps our first response is to try to view her as a hypothetical subject, a 'character' in the usual sense. We thus attempt to see her words

136

as self-expression, and assume that the events they describe constitute her past. But Mouth cannot be ready successfully in this way, for *Not I* refutes the very notion of the self on which our idea of 'character' rests; there is no coherent self in the play-world and so we cannot use that concept to interpret what we see and hear. Similarly, we are denied narrative. Action in Beckett's plays lacks purpose, events do not conclude, and we are offered no means of ascribing to the playworld a causal 'physics'.

This is not to say Beckett's stage permits no symbolic reading. Rather, the symbolic meaning we derive is that there is *no* symbolic meaning. But we can only ascertain this *by* reading the stage symbolically: it is in addressing its materials as signifiers that we discern their lack of conceptual signifieds; the purpose-lessness of Vladimir and Estragon's actions are revealed when we seek their purpose; only our assumption that Mouth should be viewed as a character leads us to discover the absence of self. The experience of interpreting Beckett's theatre is therefore an ambiguous one. We project fragile structures of interpretation – link words to images to create fictional selves, ascribe a purpose to actions – only to have our activities demonstrate their own misassumptions; an Abstract reading is signalled as appropriate, but the fruits of that reading paradoxically indicate its inappro-priateness. As the concepts we use to read the stage symbolically are shown to be futile, so we are denied the mechanisms neces-sary to interpret its elements as parts of an other-place. Objects taken for signs revert to objects, characters become actors; the Abstract locus signals that it is a Concrete platea, and that the only meanings on offer are those we impose in our inter-pretative gaze.

By this means Beckett reproduces his vision of a reality devoid of conceptual meaning not merely in the playworld but also in the audience's experience of attempting to interpret it. Seated in the auditorium, we too try to elicit conceptual meaning from merely material phenomena, address physical sounds, objects and actions as signifiers in order to divine their signifieds; and like Beckett's characters, we too are brought to the recognition that they are merely material things. In fact, the spectator's activ-ities parallel those of Beckett's characters point for point. Like Mouth we try to construct from words a self, or, in *That Time*, a past; like Vladimir and Estragon we await the arrival of Godot;

just as *Quad*'s walkers inscribe a pattern on the empty floor with their pacing, so we, in seeking the purpose of their organised activity, draw that same pattern in our mind's eye. And just as these attempts in the playworld are revealed to be constructs, so they break down in the auditorium; the 'symbolic' objects are of the platea – not an other-place but a stage – and we are made aware of our own meaning-making activities. Thus Beckett reiterates the theme of his drama in its form, and so in the dialogic relations it demands of its audience. In tandem with his critique of meaning in the world, he subverts the meaning-making mechanisms of the theatrical medium itself.

We may therefore describe Beckett's work as a form of 'metatheatre'. Literally the prefix *meta* means 'beyond' or 'above', but in contemporary critical usage it is usually taken to describe work which is self-reflexive; metatheatre is theatre which is in some sense *about* theatre, concerned with its signifying processes, revealing them to an audience. Because of its subversion of theatre's sense-making mechanisms, it might be assumed that Beckett's stage achieves an effect comparable to Brecht's. In fact the opposite is true. Brechtian Epic theatre poses the platea against the locus, the Concrete register against the Abstract, to render all meanings provisional as in ordinary social space. But Beckett effectively banishes the platea altogether. The audience's activities, and the social space in which they are enacted, are made to bear the same meaning – that there is *no* meaning – as the stage. If realism is concerned to make theatre resemble reality, Beckett asserts that reality is like theatre, a realm where meaning is manufactured. There is no provisionality to this proposition, it is not presented as Brechtian 'opinion', for it is verified by the audience's own experience. In this sense Beckett extends the locus to absorb the auditorium itself. Social space is rendered symbolic, symbolising the emptiness of symbols. The world is itself a locus, albeit one without a conceptual dimension, and this, paradoxically, is the only meaning which Beckett's stage admits.

Beckett's theatre is not difficult to place culturally and historically. Towards the middle of the twentieth century there emerged a body of philosophical writing concerned with humankind's conceptual ordering of its world. Building upon the work of Søren Kierkegaard and Edmund Husserl, philosophers such as

Jean-Paul Sartre and Martin Heidegger, and writer Albert Camus, developed the doctrine of Existentialism. The viewing subject and the objects it views, Sartre asserted, are defined in a process which is *relational*, human beings perceptually shaping their world and, in doing so, defining themselves. To live 'authentically' is, for Sartre, to live with the recognition that all such meanings, and the self they reflect, are indeed constructs. These principles were realised in the novels and plays of Sartre and Camus themselves. But whereas the ideas their dramas dealt with were radically new, both dramatists communicated them via quite traditional theatrical means. It was with another new dramatic mode, which Martin Esslin dubbed the 'Theatre of the Absurd', that such principles found formal expression (see Esslin 1968). In the plays of Beckett, Eugène Ionesco, Jean Genet, Arthur Adamov and Harold Pinter, the vision of a meaningless reality was complemented by theatrical forms which problematised customary meaning-making strategies, comprising a tradition whose influence is visible in the work of dramatists ranging from Edward Albee and Tom Stoppard to David Mamet.

But Beckett is, more importantly, part of a longer and more diffuse tradition within modernism. In the late nineteenth and particularly the early twentieth century there emerged a number of movements, groups and individual artists whose work in various ways ruptured extant modes of sense-making. In the view of the Surrealists, for example, orthodox art inherently supported bourgeois culture, the prevailing aesthetic and ideological order. They therefore sought to explode customary modes of seeing by creating artworks which refuted existing logics of interpretation. By offering as works of art cups and saucers lined with fur, or flat irons with nails welded to their smoothing surface, Surrealists presented their audiences with the inexplicable. Cups are supposed to hold liquid, a function denied them when fur-lined, just as an iron is stripped of its given purpose, its cultural identity, when adorned with nails. The principle behind such works is one of juxtaposition; by combining components with no culturally given connection, artists created artefacts which could not be explained by extant logics. They thus prompted viewers to seek a link – between fur and cup, iron and nails – which lay beyond those modes of meaning contemporary society made available.

Such objects do not remain inexplicable forever, of course, for today's art historians have little difficulty in interpreting them. Rather, by demanding that viewers seek an interpretative logic outside culture's given formulations, they force a change in that culture. They thus precede the developments which they themselves prompt, and this is one of the reasons why such artists and movements are generally referred to as the modernist avant-garde. Radical artistic experiment, the challenging of existing ideas of what art should be and do, provokes the generation of those new logics necessary to understand such experiment, and this was of course a key feature of modernism. Writers from Mallarmé to James Joyce, painters such as Picasso and Cézanne, whole movements like the Surrealists, Dadaists and Futurists – these and many others produced works which, in their own time, forced an alteration of culturally constructed aesthetics.

Aesthetic challenges of this kind have a broader, socio-political significance, the modernist avant-garde performing what is, for cultural theorist Jean-François Lyotard, a key historical function (see Lyotard 1984: 71–82). As we noted in the previous chapter, many areas of modernist thought were rationalistic in colouring, the period as a whole constituting something of a renaissance for the reasoning mind. But such thought, Lyotard argues, has an inherent capacity for totalitarianism. Reason presumes that it is able to explain all of the universe, that its formulations are 'commensurate' with the real world; that everything is encompassed, 'presented', within its theories. Claiming a monopoly of truth, it thus marginalises all other views and representations, establishing a hegemony of ideas. By 'presenting the unpresentable', creating works which signify a missing meaning, Lyotard asserts, the modernist avant-garde demonstrated the limits of accepted reason. In so doing it revealed reason's conceptual constructs to be constructs, not 'commensurate' with the world but imposed upon it.

Lyotard's notion of 'presenting the unpresentable' applies directly to work such as Beckett's. Perhaps the most important response avant-garde pieces elicit when first shown is incomprehension. Surrealist works were presented as 'art' yet were impregnable to those conceptual tools used for art. Offered as meaningful yet invulnerable to interpretation, the observer is left with his or her perception of the piece as intellectually impenetrable, a mute 'thing'. Thus the avant-garde work effects a momentary signification of its own materiality. This is perhaps the key quality linking Beckett to this tradition, for with its absences of meaning, his drama refutes those interpretative strategies basic to theatre, forcing us to recognise that the stage is a material place. The Surrealist René Magritte painted a picture of a pipe bearing the legend 'This is Not a Pipe'. The paradox is not difficult to resolve once we recognise the materiality of the thing itself; it is not a pipe, it is a *painting* of a pipe. It is a similar principle we find in Beckett's theatre, for he offers his audience not a world but the theatrical representation of a world, and is careful to ensure that we remain aware of the distinction.

But although in Lyotard's view the avant-garde performs a radically subversive role, the political status of Beckett's theatre is, as we have seen, ambiguous. Beckett's project clearly has the potential to counter ideology. Ideology propagates conceptions of reality which covertly favour elites over other social groups, and by asserting that truth and meaning *per se* are illusory, Beckett undermines the very ground on which it stands, providing an epistemological weapon for those who seek to oppose it. This perhaps takes on greater significance in the context of twentieth-century history. A series of impending disasters brought about by reason and science – the nuclear arms race, environmental disasters – and the perversion of rationalist and supposedly 'liberating' discourses such as Marxism, have illustrated that discourse is never politically neutral, never merely 'true' or 'false', but can always be co-opted, mobilised in support of a position of power. All discourses are therefore potential instruments of power, and so the subversion of meaning-making *per se* may be regarded as a radical act; by showing his own theatrical events to be material things, constructions of meaning, Beckett contributes to a cultural awareness that all meanings are constructed.

At the same time, however, there are negative consequences to Beckett's philosophical position. In an absolute sense, all meaning is indeed manufactured, and discourse's claim to truth is therefore illusory. But the history of humankind is the history of words *taken for* meaning. Discourse and representation do not exist in a space of pure concepts, they are always a part of existing political contests, deployed by one group or another in struggles involving real material power. Consequently, words

141

and meanings always carry specific political freight, always mean something for someone to some end.

It is this side of meaning-making, discourse/representation as a practice of *power*, that is marginalised by philosophical positions such as Beckett's. As we have seen, his vision is of a universal order, concerned not with the situation of particular human subjects in specific periods and cultures, but with that of humankind *per se*. His depictions of *particular* circumstances are therefore metaphors of generalities. He uses ageing and disability to figure the essential materiality, the corporeality, of the human condition, employs images of women buried in earth and suffering from mental illness to depict a universal existential state, and shows class structures as merely a means of endowing reality with form and meaning. But disabled people are not metaphors. Like women, they live their lives in circumstances of real disadvantage, circumstances which are not the result of a universal human condition but specific and socially derived; they are born not of a need to give life structure but of relations of power, created by human beings and perpetuated in human society. In positing an existential situation common to all, Beckett implicitly disregards the things which distinguish us, and most importantly those systematic political inequalities that determine our lives. Life may in reality be a meaningless void for each of us, but the void is less comfortable for those who find themselves without the real social, political and economic power to cushion its blows.

This is an unavoidable quandary. Beckett's position is unquestionably a progressive one, tending towards the subversion of ideological mechanisms. But dealing with meaning as an absolute rather than as a discursive *effect*, he can make no distinctions. Thus his assertion that meaning is illusory inevitably undermines not only discursive formations of an ideological kind, but those which are radical and empowering as well. The real social and political results of such a position, however, are not equal. In negating progressive discourses – for theories of class, race, gender and disability are also attempts to quantify and 'annex' social reality – as well as reactionary ones, Beckett implicitly subverts attempts at change. He thus inadvertently favours the *status quo*, the social order which already exists, in which inequalities of power are already constituted.

5

PETER BROOK
AND RITUAL THEATRE

RITUAL THEATRE

From his directorial début at the age of seventeen, Peter Brook (b. 1925) quickly rose to become a leading figure of the British theatre establishment. Although noted for daring *coups de théâtre*, his early work deviated little from conventional theatrical aesthetics. In the 1960s, however, he embarked upon a course of experiment which was to lead him away from orthodox stage practices, resulting in a series of pioneering productions which were to establish his work internationally. In the international theatrical scene Brook found other practitioners whose work echoed certain of his own ideas and aims, in particular his desire to create what he has termed a 'theatre of ritual'. It is this project, particularly evident in Brook's productions of 1970 and after, which we shall focus upon here.

The theatre of ritual was in part Brook's response to what he sees as the major problem facing the modern world, its descent into a state of spiritual decay. Modern western culture, he argues, is dominated by rationalism, a mode of thought able to grasp only the concrete, material world. As a consequence, all other, immaterial dimensions of life have been neglected. In previous epochs special events, *rituals*, were enacted to affirm the life of the spirit. By collectively celebrating the sacred and divine, the magical and mythical – what Brook calls the 'Invisible' – communities maintained their systems of belief. Indeed, in the so-called Developing World, where the process of modernisation and rationalisation has yet to be completed, rituals still perform this role, and the Invisible remains a vital part of life. But in the West, Brook argues, we have 'lost all sense of ritual and ceremony' and so have been brought to the brink of spiritual and social collapse. His *The Ik* (a 1975 dramatisation of Colin Turnbull's anthropological study *The Mountain People*) ostensibly charted the destruction of a Ugandan tribe, the breakdown of its entire social and familial order after being forcibly resettled far from its ancestral homeland. Brook, however, makes the comparison with the West explicit:

> In the same way, in our world . . . We try to believe that family bonds are natural and close our eyes to the fact that they have to be nourished and sustained by spiritual energies. With the disappearance of living ceremony, with rituals empty or dead, no current flows from individual to individual and the sick social body cannot be healed. In this way, the story of a tiny, remote, unknown African tribe in what seems to be very special circumstances is actually about the cities of the West in decline.
>
> (Brook 1987: 136)

With no living rituals to maintain the life of the spirit, the West faces social disintegration.

What is meant here by 'ritual'? In recent years a great deal has been written on the subject, with particular focus on ritual's relationship with theatre. Here, however, we shall begin by examining the term in its basic, most material sense.

We most often use 'ritual' in reference to a particular species of performed event, activities especially (although not exclusively) characteristic of premodern societies. In the general sense, the purpose of these activities is not functional but symbolic, for the primary goal of religious celebrations, shamanistic ceremonies, totemic and initiation rites and so on is to image the divine, to create in the profane world a moment in space/time that is sacred. Brook clearly employs 'ritual' in this sense; his aim is to create what he has called a 'Holy Theatre', a 'theatre of the Invisible-made-Visible'. But at the same time, his use of the term is also informed by his readings in anthropology, especially the work of the French anthropologist and founder of modern Structuralism, Claude Lévi-Strauss. From a Lévi-Straussian perspective, one of ritual's most important functions is to perpetuate the community's sense of group identity. The ostensible purpose of a ritual may be to celebrate spiritual beliefs but its actual effect is to assert the communal nature of such beliefs, writing them into the collective cultural consciousness so that they become a part of our individual sense of identity. Ritual, then, provides a means of reaffirming the social whole. In participating in the ritual, we demonstrate our allegiance not only to a common creed but also to the community which espouses it.

Thus the modern world's neglect of rituals, and the loss of that spirituality they affirmed, has caused what Brook perceives to be a *social* collapse. It is in this sense that he seeks a ritual theatre, one which, in celebrating the Invisible, offers its audience an experience of *communitas*. He is concerned, then, not only with theatre as a means of representation but also with its *performative* powers, its ability to establish a sense of communality and so heal the 'sick social body' of the West. The primary question for Brook is therefore how to restore to theatre this ancient ritual function of maintaining the communal whole, how to create what he calls a 'necessary theatre':

> How to make theatre absolutely and fundamentally *necessary* to people, as necessary as eating and sex? I mean a theatre which isn't a watered-down appendage or cultural decoration to life. I mean something that's a simple organic necessity – as theatre used to be and still is in certain societies. Make-believe is *necessity*. It's this quality, lost to Western industrialized societies, I'm searching for.
>
> (Heilpern 1989: 22)

THE UNIVERSAL LANGUAGE OF THE THEATRE

For Brook human existence is at root multi-dimensional, comprising many different planes of experience, the social, spiritual, political and so on. Although no culture, and no theatre, is able to encompass all these, most figure a rich diversity. But the orthodox theatre of the West, Brook maintains, is unable to express any such multi-dimensionality, for its stage is dominated by 'styles'. 'Styles' in Brook's sense are established dramatic formulae which represent only one of reality's planes. The style of theatrical realism, for example, may deal in a variety of different characters and events, but depicts each only in its 'Visible', concrete dimension, so that 'the so-called real dialogue and the so-called real acting do not actually capture that totality of information, visible and invisible, that corresponds to . . .

reality' (Brook 1987: 84). Nor is this confined to realism. Although Brook admires and is influenced by such as Artaud, Meyerhold, Brecht and Beckett, each is what he terms a 'subjective' artist, describing his own narrow, partial vision: Brecht the political, Beckett the existential and so on. While the safe, commercial theatre of the West – what Brook calls the 'Deadly Theatre' – employs many styles, each depicts only one facet of life, and none is able to incorporate the Invisible.

Brook therefore seeks to escape such cultural tunnel vision by creating a theatre able to depict any and all planes of human reality. His work has been described as a search for a 'universal language of the theatre' and for the 'wellsprings of drama'. Either phrase will serve, for both express Brook's desire to return to a theatre which is deeper, more essential than the differences of class and nationhood which divide contemporary humanity, one able to reach beneath the Babel of cultures to both speak to all people equally, regardless of their diverse origins, and to communicate those Invisible dimensions of experience that have been lost to the West.

Brook's first step in attempting to create this universal language is the elimination of all that is culture-bound, and his key concept in this respect is the 'empty space'. He states:

A *real* silence contains potentially everything. And it's not for nothing that, for instance, the whole of Japanese thought, the whole of Zen thinking, continually comes back to emptiness as the root out of which anything can come. And that's why, for me, the theatre starts and ends within a bowl of emptiness, which is an empty space and a great silence.

(Peter Brook interviewed on *The South Bank Show*, London Weekend Television, 1989)

The 'bowl of emptiness' that Brook seeks, then, is a kind of theatrical *tabula rasa*, a space where nothing is set and all is therefore possible. His first step towards this is in using a literally 'empty space' to play in. Shakespeare, he argues, was the most complete dramatist because his vision was 'global', encompassing almost all facets of existence. But he was only able to achieve this breadth because his plays were enacted on a bare stage and so could move freely between different kinds of reality; in *A Midsummer Night's Dream*, for example, passing from civilised Athens to forest wilderness, but also from wakefulness to dreams, from the material world to a magical, spiritual realm, offering an 'objective' vision of reality which spans the 'subjective' theatres of Brecht and Beckett combined.

With the empty space we see figured one of the most consistent principles of Brook's later work, what he calls 'pruning-away'. Like Grotowski's 'via negativa', it consists of reducing theatre to its essentials, stripping off the baggage of culture and custom to begin again from zero. Bare stages have been a feature of Brook's theatre since his 1962 production of *King Lear*, taking a variety of forms: the minimalist, laboratory-like white set of *A Midsummer Night's Dream* (1970), the carpet that was unrolled in the village square as a playing area during his 1972 tour of Africa, or the various open and sand-strewn spaces in which his most monumental work, *The Mahabharata* (1985), was staged. All metaphysical claims aside, it is perhaps *The Mahabharata*, Brook's dramatisation of the ancient Hindu legend of humankind's creation, which best illustrates the empty space's *practical* utility. The nine-hour epic journeys from battle-fields to palaces, forests, mountaintops and humble peasant huts, moving from the ordinary domestic world of human beings to the mythic realm of legendary heroes, and the divine, Invisible domain of gods and spirits. These would demand very different kinds of set; a realistic domestic backdrop would hamper any attempt to depict mythic or divine events. Only by eschewing sets entirely was Brook able to depict the range of loci, and thus the range of reality's planes, that this magical tale described.

More important for Brook than its literal emptiness, however, the space must be empty of 'style'. The Elizabethan stage, he maintains, was unfettered by generic proscriptions and mixed realistic theatre with other 'poetical' devices – verse, soliloquy, 'far-fetched plots' – to build a multi-dimensional world. Similarly, the list of Brook's later productions reads like a record of experiments with existing forms. His *King Lear* bore the hall-marks of Beckett's absurdism, while the work-in-progress perfor-mances of his 'Theatre of Cruelty Season' in 1964 sought to give Antonin Artaud's theories a concrete form. But more significant from our viewpoint are those of Brook's productions that blend different practices. In *US* (1966), a 'group-happening-collaborative spectacle' dealing with the Vietnam war, natural-istic scenes jarred against darkly humorous comic-book sketches, evocative, symbolic images, monologue, giant stage mannequins, and direct audience-address of the aggressive 'confrontational' mode pioneered by American companies such as Julian Beck and Judith Malina's Living Theatre. Brook's 1964 production of Peter Weiss's *Marat/Sade* juxtaposed the techniques of Brecht and Artaud, creating a 'jangle of styles' comprising Epic oration and songs, and grotesque Artaudian shrieks and bodily contortions. By mixing techniques from different styles in this way, Brook sought to blend their different constructions of reality, to create a multi-dimensionality – what he terms a 'cubism of the theatre' – comparable to Shakespeare's.

The most distinctive feature of Brook's later work, however, is its *interculturalism*, its incorporation of techniques, images and texts drawn from the theatres of the non-western world. In 1970 Brook founded the International Centre for Theatre Research (CIRT) in Paris, assembling a multi-national group of actors – each bringing their own cultural 'colour' – to explore theatre practices from around the globe. Thus CIRT actors' performances have often been shaped by formal Asian disciplines such as Japanese martial arts katas, Yoga, T'ai Chi and Indian narrative dance, while the devices of *Nôh*, Balinese mask and puppet drama, and the traditional Chinese circus have all featured in Brook's productions. Costume in his work is often based on Asian clothing, whereas music has drawn upon the traditions and/or instruments of Japan, Africa, Bali, Sri Lanka, Australia, Turkey, Iran and India.

Brook's intention is not to reproduce these other theatres, he asserts, but to take from them that which he believes transcends their source culture, to find the universal in the particular. Indeed, we can see all of his borrowings, eastern and western, as part of this search for the universal, an attempt to escape the confines of style by collapsing many styles. But the practices he takes from the Developing World must be seen as especially significant because, originating in societies that have yet to undergo the West's rationalisation, they are more suited to depicting those Invisible realms of experience lost to western theatre.

Brook's borrowings are not limited to the stage, however, for his work also incorporates skills from beyond theatre proper. Forms of 'action painting' have featured in several productions, with red paint poured into buckets or over actors' heads to represent blood (*Marat/Sade* and *The Mahabharata*), and acts of violence scrawled onto screens instead of enacted (*The Screens* [1964]), whereas in *US* a performer was painted in two colours to depict symbolically the war's splitting of Vietnam. Brook is also an experienced film director and, as David Williams notes, in *The Mahabharata* he used the stage equivalent of cinematography (see Williams 1991: 117–92). The play takes the form of a story told by Vyasa, the tale's author, to a boy who represents humankind. When the boy is puzzled by the appearance of a new character, the demigod Karna, Vyasa effects the equivalent of a filmic 'freeze-frame' with the words 'I stop all motion', immediately halting the action. He then initiates a dramatised, film-like 'flash-back' which explains that Karna is the issue of a union between a mortal woman and the Sun, and is actually the half-brother of his present enemies. In a similar vein, 'close-ups' and 'panora-mic' shots, slow motion, reverse shots, changes in 'depth of field' and 'split screen' effects are all used to tell this epic tale whose threads are numerous and complex.

Perhaps the most ingenious of Brook's innovations is his use of *objets trouvés*, 'found objects' employed to depict elements of the playworld. In *The Mahabharata* bows and arrows were repre-sented by simple bamboo sticks, and a chariot by two warehouse pallets laid end to end. Forest undergrowth was figured with coils of wire in *A Midsummer Night's Dream* and in Brook's amalgam of Alfred Jarry's 'Ubu' plays, *Ubu aux Bouffes* (1977), an industrial cable spool became a war machine on which Ubu rode, crushing his enemies as it rolled forward. This too is emble-matic of Brook's 'pruning away'; just as the empty space is a kind of return-to-zero, with nothing fixed and all possible, so the objects brought into it are addressed as semically empty raw materials, to be transformed into elements which are meaningful in new ways.

We can separate Brook's use of *objets trouvés* into two general categories. In the first they are employed synecdochally, as parts representative of greater wholes. In *Ubu* three bricks arranged in a hearth-shape successfully implied an entire dwelling, while in *The Mahabharata* a (second) chariot was suggested with a single wheel held upright by an actor. This kind of synecdochal signification is fundamental to Brook's practice at all levels. Locations may be indicated very succinctly, a carpet and some cushions representing the luxury of a king's court, and some mats, crockery and everyday utensils connoting the simplicity of peasant life in *The Mahabharata*. In *The Conference of the Birds* (1973) the birds themselves were characterised using synecdochal signs, with the hawk evoked by two bent fingers forming a beak-like hook, the parrot with head movements and a wicker grid held before the actor's face as a cage, and the peacock with a fan held over the head like a crest and one knee raised to imitate that bird's 'proud' stance.

In the second category are found objects used in a metaphoric fashion, representing something else on the basis of a shared quality, which renders them similar. Thus the cable spool represents a war machine because it is ridden and, rolling forward, crushes what lies in its path. In *A Midsummer Night's Dream* the objects of a spinning plate on a stick, 'found' in the Chinese circus, depicted a flower because of their general similarity to a bloom on a stem.

Such objects do not innately resemble the things they represent but become metaphors in the way they are used. As we have noted, a signifier (material sound or image) only becomes attached to a specific signified (concept), only forms a *sign*, by relating to the other signs that comprise the performance. But on Brook's bare stage the audience is in large part denied such helpful context. Practically the only other meaningful, *semic* elements are those provided by the actors; their words and costumes, certainly, but especially their actions. It is the performers' magician-like manipulation that makes Brook's metaphoric *objets trouvés* 'similar' to the things they represent, for only when the actor adopts a stance reminiscent of archers on Mogul reliefs do the sticks become bows and arrows, just as the cable spool is recognisable as a war machine only when it is ridden.

As the raw materials of signification, found objects on Brook's stage are manipulated, *transmuted*, to form signs. We can view such transmutation as part of his quest for a universal, transcultural language, for it entails stripping the objects of their given cultural significance. A chariot, say, placed on a stage, would call to mind not only a corresponding object in the play-world, it would also say much about the locus in general. If the chariot were Roman in design, or merely recognisably 'ancient', it would infer a particular time and place, and also the mode in which the story is to be presented, the production's 'style'. A mimetic prop, then, automatically plugs into a network of existing cultural associations, and hence established and limited cultural meanings. But Brook's metaphoric *objets trouvés* deny such associations; a 'war machine' represented by a cable spool infers no specific place/time. Indeed, such objects explicitly offer meanings other than those usually ascribed them. A cable spool seen on a roadside would evoke a number of associations for the competent western observer, of industry and high technology, and hard physical labour perhaps. But placed on an empty stage, manipulated by performers, it is divested of its everyday connotations and denotations. As raw material for fresh signs, such *objets trouvés* refute their usual cultural codification.

The cumulative result of the devices we have examined, Brook's diverse borrowings and transmutations, is a theatre of massive eclecticism. In his production of *A Midsummer Night's Dream*, the vocal and characterisation skills of Britain's Royal Shakespeare Company were used alongside stilt-walking, bubble-blowing, juggling and trapeze. Indian finger bells and side drums accompanied Titania's entrance, and the fairies signified their other-worldliness with the hand and neck movements of Thai dance and by carrying Perspex versions of Polynesian 'spirit batons'. The forest undergrowth, represented by emphatically 'modern' coils of silver wire, was lowered from fishing rods operated by mischievous fairies, while, as we have seen, the magic flower 'love-in-idleness' was a spinning plate balanced on a stick. We noted that this device was taken from the Chinese State Circus, the source of many of the production's images, from the design of its costumes (flowing silk robes in bright, primary colours) to the unfurling of a black cross-hung flag or *gonfalon* in response to Oberon's command that Puck 'overcast the night ... with drooping fog'.

But we must question whether such devices genuinely enable Brook's work to communicate on a universal, transcultural level. As we noted, Brook's work is informed by his reading of the structural anthropology of Claude Lévi-Strauss. It is therefore appropriate that we examine his theatre through the lens of Lévi-Strauss's theory.

Building upon Saussure's semiotics and the work of Russian Formalist Roman Jakobson, Lévi-Strauss argued that not only language, but culture in its entirety, is a system, consisting of elements arranged in structural relationships. Far from emerging out of pure creativity or inspiration, cultural artefacts such as myths and stories – indeed, all meaningful objects – are created via a process he terms *bricolage* (see Lévi-Strauss 1966). Literally, the *bricoleur* is the jack of all trades, the handyman whose distinction is that he builds things out of the remains of other things. For Lévi-Strauss all cultural objects are born of a similar process. The cultural *bricoleur* constructs his or her works out of the fragments of older works, assembling new artefacts from existing cultural materials. However, these re-used materials bring with them their former meaningful relations with other elements of the system, retain in the interpreter's gaze those structural connections that originally determined their significance. Thus the *bricoleur* effectively builds not just with old materials but also old elements of meaning, uses not just signifiers but signifiers/ signifieds – signs. As a consequence, new artefacts do not create entirely fresh meanings but redeploy existing semic fragments. New artworks are actually reconfigurations of old components, so that even novel artefacts operate within the boundaries of the same semiotic system, the same cultural 'set'.

One might assume that Brook's borrowing from a range of styles, cultures and media, and his semic recharging of objects via transmutation, have the potential to escape the limits of any culture, to speak to people of all societies equally. But that would be to misinterpret Lévi-Strauss's model. In his conception, stories, artworks, signs and so on possess no inherent meaning, only the meaning ascribed within, *by*, the system. It is in our agreed, cultural understanding of objects, our encoding/ decoding, that meaning is generated. It is this very specificity of meaning that is Lévi-Strauss's primary focus, for his interpretation of anthropological artefacts involves situating them in their source cultures. Viewed from that perspective, if Brook's theatrical 'artefacts' are meaningful for their primarily western audiences – and they are – it is not because they communicate on a universal level but because they successfully function within that 'set' which is western culture.

RITUAL AND THE INVISIBLE

As well as being an example of 'pruning-away', a means of divesting objects of their immediate associations, 'transmutation' also images a kind of theatrical alchemy, a transformative 'magic', which echoes the magical metamorphoses of real rituals: the Christian transubstantiation of wafer and wine into the body and blood of Christ; divination ceremonies where material objects physicalise a celestial plan: rites for the evocation of spirits, ritual possession, shamanistic medicine – all of which give physical form to the paraphysical, like Brook's transmutation using objects of the Visible world to figure the Invisible.

What does Brook mean by the Invisible? He gives no precise definition but, as we noted, he deems it to consist of those 'sacred' realms of experience which lie beyond the concrete world and our rational grasp of it; magic, myth, the spiritual and so on. Once these would have been communally expressed in religious beliefs and practices, but modern society lacks a shared belief system. Yet, Brook argues, such metaphysical dimensions can still be found in art. He explains:

> We are all aware that most of our life escapes our senses; a most powerful explanation of the various arts is that they talk of patterns which we can only begin to recognize when they manifest themselves as rhythms or shapes ... we recognize that a magical thing called music can come from men in white ties and tails ... [but] Despite the absurd means that produce it, through the concrete in music we recognize the abstract.
> (Brook 1972: 47)

While the abstract Invisible cannot actually appear in the concrete world, for Brook it *can* manifest itself in its *effect* on that world. By definition the intangible cannot take a tangible form but is discernible in art via the 'shapes', 'rhythms' and 'patterns' that it causes, its aestheticisation of physical reality. Brook's Invisible, then, is to appear to the spectator as beauty, an extraordinary ordering of the material that figures the immaterial divine.

It is this kind of extra-ordinary aesthetic ordering that we see in Brook's transmutation of found objects. At first sight the use of a spinning plate to represent a flower seems a vast over-investment of effort, for it would be easier, cheaper and more plausible to use a real or synthetic flower. But *A Midsummer Night's Dream*'s love-in-idleness is not merely a flower, it is a *magical* flower, and it is this magical quality which Brook conveys by the magician-like skill of plate spinning. Music expresses the

Invisible not in the concreteness of its sounds, he argues, but in the way they are organised to form an ineffable beauty. The sounds do not *become* the Invisible, they 'manifest' it, provide for their listeners an experience of what lies beyond them. Similarly, a plate and stick are everyday material objects, but they display a formal harmony which for Brook transcends that earthliness once one is set spinning atop the other. They thus act as an interface between the Visible and Invisible, the mechanism by which one shapes the other.

This is one of the senses in which we may term Brook's a 'ritual theatre'. Rituals take a variety of forms, of course, but we have described ritual *per se* as a fixed sequence of actions whose purpose is not functional but symbolic. Its symbolic status is crucial, for the aim of ritual is to figure a transcendent cosmic order, imprint upon the physical world the shape of that which is by definition *meta*-physical, literally *beyond* physicality. This order may be of many kinds, from the pantheon of gods or spirits evoked in a religious ceremony to the 'natural' social order celebrated by rites of initiation into adulthood, or the more abstract celestial harmony of Shinto figured by the Japanese Tea Ceremony. But it is always transcendent, for this is ritual's defining property. In popular usage a 'ritual' may be any sequence of repeated actions, as in 'the ritual of making the morning coffee'. This is not ritual in our sense since it is merely habitual and defers to nothing beyond itself. With ritual proper the structure of actions/words always mirrors an order that lies beyond the tangible world, and so beyond the materiality of its own activities, providing for that order a tangible correlative.

The key quality of ritual as described, then, is its ordering of the profane material plane, for in this ordering is imprinted the pattern of the sacred. Patterning is a characteristic of rituals around the world. Many involve the deployment of bodies in space to form horizontal and/or vertical patterns: the priest in a Christian Mass proceeds along a symbolic path through the laity and ascends to the heights of a lectern; spiritualists form a circle of hands. Movement may be comparably patterned, coordinated in dance and procession, or simultaneous bowing, kneeling and so on, while voices are often orchestrated in song, chant and ritualised response. Indeed, such coordination is one mechanism for creating that experience of group identity, of *communitas*, we described earlier, for with orchestrated song and dance, choreographed gesture, procession and so on, ritual provides the community with a physical correlative of its conceptual unity. Our unity is 'written' in our behaviour; by acting in unison we demonstrate our one-ness, both to our fellows and, equally importantly, to ourselves.

This ritualistic ordering of the concrete world finds its theatrical equivalent in Brook's ordering of the material stage, complementing that aesthetic patterning featured in the transmutation of *objets trouvés*. Regular CIRT practice included group exercises with bamboo sticks to build rhythms, shapes and coordinated movements, and such arrangements feature periodically in Brook's productions. Blocking, the arrangement of figures about the stage area, is often highly stylised: the Pandavas, the five heroic brothers of *The Mahabharata*, first appeared in a symbolic arrowhead formation, one of the piece's many emblematic configurations, while *The Conference of the Birds* employed *Nôh* drama's own schematic blocking conventions to comparable effect. Brook also exploits vertical space, so that in *A Midsummer Night's Dream*, trapezes, stilts and raised catwalks actually elevated the fairies above the mortal characters, inferring their otherworldliness, their place on a different, more ethereal plane. Although such use of space/movement features in many theatres around the world, it is less common on the orthodox western stage, and Brook's consistent and emphatic use of it lends his theatre a ceremonial colouring. Indeed, he sometimes augments these practices with real and/or simulated formal or ritual actions. In *The Mahabharata* characters greeted one another in the traditional Indian manner (a shallow bow with hands held palm-to-palm before the face), while warriors ritually baptised their weapons before a battle, kneeled and bowed to their enemies prior to combat, and performed simple victory dances when triumphant.

Aesthetic ordering is nowhere more effective, however, than in the use Brook makes of the actors body. As we saw, preparatory training for Brook's actors at the CIRT included work on such Asian disciplines as T'ai Chi, martial arts katas and Indian Kathakali, and these were augmented by modern, western techniques such as Moshe Feldenkrais's system of movement. Although different in style, all these nurture onstage movement which is highly formalised and linearly paced. The stress that each places on balance, dynamic unity and rigorous bodily awareness/control creates an overall regime of movement –

what we might call a 'kinescape' – which has an observably considered and *deliberate* quality. The emphatic actions of a karate kata, Kathakali's traditional language of movements and gestures, and the slow, graceful and flowing body sculptures that T'ai Chi describes in space – all these work to shape subtly even simple actions on stage, giving them a hieratic, symbolic colouring. The ultimate effect is to denude movement and gesture of all that is erratic, rendering it disciplined and ceremonial.

Although Brook offers more esoteric explanations, from our materialist perspective his theatre's distinctive features are nevertheless physical. Transmutation, the sculpting of space / movement and of the body – these effect what we might term the 'ritualisation' of the stage, granting it a recognisably ceremonial *appearance*. Such devices are familiar from, for example, television documentaries, and to a lesser degree from our own social experience. They are therefore able to signify. Their 'specialness', their extra-ordinary aestheticisation of the physical stage, indicates to the viewer that their meanings are of a metaphysical kind; when we see movement crafted in so purposeful a fashion we must assume that there is indeed a purpose, an ordering principle which lies beyond, transcends, that movement's own materiality. Ritualisation, whether on the stage or in a space of ritual proper, effectively signifies that its activities have been shaped in accordance with some other design, the profane, material plane made to figure the immaterial and divine.

Brook's most focused attempt to create both a ritual theatre and a universal theatrical language was *Orghast* (1971), the CIRT's first production (for a detailed account, see Smith 1972). Like Jerzy Grotowski, Eugenio Barba, Beck & Malina and others, Brook's founding of this company represents an investment in the idea of a *community* of actors and the possibilities for collective creativity and research that arise from it. Speaking of *Orghast*, Brook described the purpose of this research:

the basic theme of the work is the examining of forms of communication to see whether there are elements in the theatrical vocabulary that pass directly, without going through the stage once removed of cultural or other references. And the reason for exploring this is to break down

156

the almost obligatory compartmenting and narrowing
of the theatre form into the sort of theatre that suits one
particular streak of society.

(Smith 1972: 248)

In *Orghast* Brook sought to operate outside what he has termed
the 'normal channels' of culture and, particularly, rational
language. By bypassing these – indeed, by developing methods
which eluded rational quantification entirely – he hoped to
communicate with his audience on a universal, precultural level.

Performed only twice in Persepolis as part of Iran's Shiraz
Arts Festival, *Orghast* was written by the poet Ted Hughes, and
was his and Brook's attempt to create an ur-myth meaningful
for all spectators regardless of their origins. The story told how
the marriage union of Moa (material fire; fertile, mutable,
feminine) to Sun (spiritual fire; ordered, unchanging, masculine)
resulted in the birth of King Krogon, who, possessing the qualities of both parents, sought to resolve them, to impose order
upon the natural universe, and in so doing became a dictator.
His rule was challenged by Pramanath (Prometheus), who
appeared to battle Krogon, their struggle shifting across the
piece's divine and secular realms. This story, clearly able to bear
psychological or political interpretations, is most importantly an
allegory of socialisation, the tale of humankind's acquisition of
culture and language. Its conception of humanity as schisma-
tised, torn between the cultural and the natural, parallels Brook's
own view of western society as polarised between the Visible
and Invisible, the rational/material and spiritual/imaginary, and
reflects the CIRT's search for a means of transcending cultural
differences.

Orghast featured most of the practices we have described,
and had a markedly ritualistic colouring. Brook made use of
available resources, staging the play's two segments at sunset
and sunrise, and at the ancient tombs of two Persian kings. The
tombs provided a 'found' set which enabled him to work
spatially, positioning performers on and about the structures,
and at different heights on the surrounding rock faces.
Movement tended to be of two kinds, either deliberate and
ceremonial or else explosive and emotionally charged. Vocal
work similarly consisted of both 'primitive', 'primordial' sounds
and harmonious, choral drones which had been improvised by

the company. Materials with great but generalised symbolic weight were used, particularly fire, with a fireball lowered down the face of the first tomb, burning spectacularly against the black backdrop of the night. Together the symbolically loaded time and place, arresting images, and formalised soundscape and kinescape evoked a potent sense of ritual, a combination of the ceremonially disciplined and the ecstatic and 'primitive' that pervaded the entire event.

Orghast's most intriguing feature, however, was linguistic. Along with small sections in classical Greek, Latin and Avesta (an ancient Persian tongue used in Zoroastrian religious ritual), the dialogue was in 'Orghast', a 'language' Hughes invented for the play. In this respect *Orghast* bore the stamp of perhaps the most enduring influence upon Brook, that of the French surrealist Antonin Artaud.

Artaud staged few productions and our knowledge of his ideas derives largely from his polemical writings. In these he railed against a world in which, he believed, the natural self had been repressed in the interests of civilisation. In the theatre this repression took the form of a preoccupation with realism, character psychology and, most importantly, language. Dealing only with such superficial levels of human existence, for Artaud the orthodox stage could engage only with the socialised, surface personae of its audience. In reply he sought to pierce through such superficialities to provoke responses of a primal kind. To this end he stressed theatre's physical and sensual dimension; in his productions actors were made to strike statuesque, *in extremis* postures and perform emotionally heightened gestures, and were blocked and moved in space in highly choreographed arrangements, while sets were deliberately stylised and anti-realist. More important for our purposes, Artaud emphasised language's phonetic qualities. Since words were, he believed, the primary vehicles of repressive reason, his 'Theatre of Cruelty' strove to denude them of sense, obscuring rational meaning with stylised diction, rendering pronunciation staccato or musical, turning words into sounds as a means of reaching the spectator's natural, prelapsarian self.

Brook and Hughes's reasons for creating a new language for *Orghast* reveal a purpose similar to Artaud's. Modern languages, they assert, function intellectually and so are confined to the communication of cultural references. This is doubly true of

Western tongues, which, due to the West's preoccupation with rationalism, lack all 'vitality'. 'Orghast', in contrast, was to work 'viscerally', appeal directly to the body and the emotions, those human faculties often believed to be natural, untainted by culture and intellect. With its 'musicality' and 'percussive' qualities, 'Orghast' was to bypass linguistic sense and elicit direct, instinctual responses from the audience, functioning, according to Brook and Hughes, in the same way as ritual incantation. Thus although 'Orghast's' 2,000 words could be deciphered by Hughes and some of the company, its most important characteristics were onomatopoeic: rough-sounding words were to convey violent concepts, the syllable 'ull', reminiscent of the sound of swallowing, indeed meant to swallow or absorb, while 'Orghast's' general phonetic coarseness expressed its primitive character. By exploiting this linguistic sensuality, Brook and Hughes sought to circumvent cultural divisions and communicate with all members of the audience 'directly'.

In this respect *Orghast* was not an unqualified success. While many spectators were moved, particularly by the company's vocal work, the story proved largely incomprehensible. This was particularly serious for Brook's theatrical project. He had attempted to create an event that was equally accessible to spectators of any cultural origin, but had succeeded instead in bewildering and even alienating some.

The limited success, or partial failure, of *Orghast* is symptomatic of a more general problem in Brook's conception of culture, one which impacts upon his desire for a theatre of ritual. As we noted, ritual acts as a kind of social cement, bonding disparate individuals into a communal whole, and it is partly for this purpose that Brook seeks a ritual theatre. He does not proffer his audience authentic rituals, however, but the trappings of ritual: sculpted movement and space, hieratic gesture, 'magically' transmuted objects. Indeed, he cannot offer his diverse but predominantly western audiences genuine ritual because, like all acts/objects which presume to proffer meaning, rituals are always culture-specific. While it is true that rituals the world over have common elements, in particular cultures those elements mean particular things. The speaking of nonsensical words, for example, features in the ceremonial acts of many societies. But whereas for certain fundamentalist Christian sects this signifies 'speaking in tongues', in a Jamaican Voodoo *hounfor* it indicates something quite different – the speaker's possession by a spirit of the Voodoo pantheon. Equally, although in a general sense the patterned dispersal of bodies in space featured in many rituals is symbolic of the material world's subordination to the immaterial, in different cultures it would infer a *different*, immaterial key into models of the transcendent which are specific to the societies in which those rituals are enacted.

Components of ritual therefore possess no inherent meaning, only that meaning derived from our cultural interpretation of them. They function as signs; the physical acts/objects are signifiers, inferring concepts, signifieds, which are not isolated but a part of a conceptual system, each deriving their significance from systematic relationships with other signs – deriving, that is, from the system(s) that comprise a particular culture. A communal interpretation of any ritualistic component therefore requires that all members of the audience possess the same cultural knowledge. It is true that some performance signs can communicate similar, very general ideas to people of different cultural origins, but they always remain at the level of the general – not the 'universal' but the unspecified, the vague; ritualistic patterning signifies 'the Invisible' but not any particular belief system; fire signals the 'primitive'.

Brook's practice ultimately indicates rituals to be interchangeable, all indicating essentially the same Invisible. This is a western cultural perspective, a view of ritual from *outside* any society where it remains a meaningful activity. He thus offers spectators the appearance of ritual, but an appearance hollowed of ritual meaning, presenting signifiers whose signifieds derive primarily from western culture's conceptions of *other* cultures.

THE TWO WORLDS

Although the experience of *Orghast* crystallised the issue, the question of stage–auditorium communication, the relationship between actor and spectator, had always been crucial for Brook, for he views that relation as the basis of theatrical *communion*. Reality, he maintains, is always experienced on two different levels as 'two worlds'. He states:

> There are two worlds, the world of the everyday and the world of the imagination. When children play they pass

'speaking in tongues', in a Jamaican Voodoo *hounfor* it indicates something quite different – the speaker's possession by a spirit of the Voodoo pantheon. Equally, although in a general sense the patterned dispersal of bodies in space featured in many rituals is symbolic of the material world's subordination to the immaterial, in different cultures it would infer a *different*, immaterial key into models of the transcendent which are specific to the societies in which those rituals are enacted.

Components of ritual therefore possess no inherent meaning, only that meaning derived from our cultural interpretation of them. They function as signs; the physical acts/objects are signifiers, inferring concepts, signifieds, which are not isolated but a part of a conceptual system, each deriving their significance from systematic relationships with other signs – deriving, that is, from the system(s) that comprise a particular culture. A communal interpretation of any ritualistic component therefore requires that all members of the audience possess the same cultural knowledge. It is true that some performance signs can communicate similar, very general ideas to people of different cultural origins, but they always remain at the level of the general – not the 'universal' but the unspecified, the vague; ritualistic patterning signifies 'the Invisible' but not any particular belief system; fire signals the 'primitive'.

Brook's practice ultimately indicates rituals to be interchangeable, all indicating essentially the same Invisible. This is a western cultural perspective, a view of ritual from *outside* any society where it remains a meaningful activity. He thus offers spectators the appearance of ritual, but an appearance hollowed of ritual meaning, presenting signifiers whose signifieds derive primarily from western culture's conceptions of *other* cultures.

THE TWO WORLDS

Although the experience of *Orghast* crystallised the issue, the question of stage–auditorium communication, the relationship between actor and spectator, had always been crucial for Brook, for he views that relation as the basis of theatrical *communion*. Reality, he maintains, is always experienced on two different levels as 'two worlds'. He states:

> There are two worlds, the world of the everyday and the world of the imagination. When children play they pass

Schechner's Performance Group. As we noted, in *US* Brook used the kind of 'confrontational' theatre techniques pioneered by Beck & Malina's Living Theatre. Performers addressed spectators directly, at times aggressively, challenging their customary, passive relationship to the stage and so the status of the locus as separate from ordinary social space. But while such strategies do indeed challenge traditional distinctions between the real and fictional worlds, they offer no way of integrating them, no mechanism for establishing imaginative 'communion'. It was in *A Midsummer Night's Dream* that Brook addressed this communion directly.

Shakespeare's play lends itself to a metatheatrical reading. Characters take on other personae, knowingly or unknowingly mount entertainments, and are beset by delusions, all of which mirror theatre's own conventions and devices. The play depicts concentric layers of illusion: the 'rude mechanicals' stage a drama for their Athenian masters, who, blundering through the forest, inadvertently provide similar amusement for the fairies, while they are themselves watched by the real spectators. Brook's production extended this logic to acknowledge the audience's own role. The stark, white box set, drenched in bright Brechtian light, rendered all action up to the audience's critical eye, making its artifice evident. The rear flat was surmounted by a catwalk on which the fairies would stand, looking down at the action and reminding spectators that they too occupied a special vantage point from which to enjoy the spectacle. The play ended with actors walking into the auditorium to greet members of the audience, interpreting the line 'Give me your hands, if we be friends' literally.

This interpretation, however, was accompanied by equally metatheatrical devices. We have seen that many of these were taken from the Chinese State Circus; the ethereal fairies descended to earth on trapezes, a magical flower was imaged by the 'magical' skill of plate spinning, and Puck's 'invisibility' consisted of his walking on stilts while the frantic Athenian lovers, Demetrius and Lysander, dashed about the stage, around and between Puck's wooden legs, unable to 'find' he whose voice tormented them. These techniques were to provide a secular equivalent for the play's magic. In no sense, however, are they magical. They are skills and obviously so, and such skills are the domain of actors, not fairies; of the platea, not the locus. The very means used to conjure the play's imaginary place/time, then, served to remind the audience that these events were actually occurring in the real world of the everyday.

We can explain this deliberate puncturing of the imaginary world by referring once again to ritual proper. As we noted, the ritual event acts as the interface of the physical and metaphysical realms, the mechanism by which each meets and shapes/ gives shape to the other. This determines the interpretative logic proffered its participants. Those taking part in ritual are not required to believe that their own, real world has *become* the divine; there is no 'illusion'. Observers of a ritual evocation of spirits, for example, are not asked to accept that a dancer has become transformed into a celestial being, but that spirit and dancer, and their respective realms, have momentarily merged. Even in cases of ritual 'possession', Brook points out, performers remain themselves at the very moment that they embody something else (see Heilpern 1989). In fact it is crucial that it be so, because the event presents a transmutation of the profane into the sacred, the ritual act being the bridge by which those two conceptually exclusive planes touch. Thus, to use our own terminology, ritual requires that its participants view the Abstract and Concrete, locus and platea, as coexisting – view the ritual event as the point in space/time where these permeate each other.

It is in this light that we can view the techniques of *A Midsummer Night's Dream* and their subversion of illusion. As symbolic of a flower, the spinning plate that was love-in-idleness was part of the (Abstract) locus. In revealing the artifice involved in creating that symbol, however, it placed itself in the (Concrete) platea (this was emphatic, for as the plate slowed and began to wobble the audience was reminded of the skill required to manufacture that symbol, the real-time hours of practice that made it possible). The audience was therefore required to reconcile the two registers within the device, find some way to interpret plate/platea and flower/locus concurrently, and an appropriate interpretative logic was offered by the device itself. Manufactured by a special stage skill, the flower signalled that it was *dependent* upon the platea, and dependent at the most basic, mechanical level, for the objects were similar only when the plate (bloom) was balanced on the stick (stem). The dependence was mutual, for just as the locus was built of the skills of the platea, so the platea was given its shape by the locus. As in ritual proper, the act of performance placed itself conceptually 'between' the two worlds as the interface or bridge by which they met.

The spectator must therefore acknowledge Concrete object and performer, and cooperate with him or her to build of the performance an other-place – not to see the spinning plate as the illusion of a flower but as 'manifesting' a flower. Brook's imaginative and spiritual 'communion' between actor and audience is in reality an interpretative relationship, a semiotic collaboration wherein both contrive to translate material signs into elements of a hypothetical world. By this means Brook offers not the image but the *experience* of an everyday realm suffused by the imaginary, an experience which is founded upon the act of encoding/decoding.

Whereas Brecht proffered the platea and locus in contradiction, then, Brook shows them as interdependent, and this is implicit in many of the practices we have examined. His bare stages and customary bright lighting thwart attempts to conjure theatrical 'illusion', revealing the stage's artifice. The techniques of ritualisation – transmutation, the patterning of space and the performance's 'kinescape' – all indicate the presence of Abstract meaning not despite but *through* their overt, Concrete contrivance, 'manifesting' the locus in the devices of the platea. Many of Brook's intercultural borrowings similarly advertise their own artifice. In *The Mahabharata* clandestine acts were performed behind a *tira sila*, a semi-transparent cloth used in Kathakali, which actually called attention to the concealment being effected. As well as being worn, the Balinese masks used in *The Conference of the Birds* were held at various distances from the actors' faces, just as the actors remained in plain view while manipulating the bird puppets through the air in a simulation of flight. Indeed, Brook's performers stared concentratedly at the puppets as they worked, drawing the audience's gaze to that very contrivance by which those elegant patterns described in space nurtured the image of divine beauty. With these and other devices Brook shows a fictional world dependent upon the real stage – less a 'Visible' suffused by an 'Invisible' than a platea and locus which both feature in our interpretation.

One thread that runs through much of Brook's work, including his 'two worlds' theorum, is Zen Buddhism. Zen teaches that self-reflexive thought causes one to quantify reality, to under-stand life instead of simply living it. Self-awareness, abstract knowledge, memory, consideration of future consequences – these interpose between the individual and the immediacy of experience so that the individual lives at one remove from the world about him or her. The result is a schism between thinking and doing, so that the this-ness of things is lost in the cacophony of thoughts that crowd about them, and the now-ness of the moment is denied by a consciousness that stands outside the flow of experience. In response Zen seeks the fusion of thinking and doing into Being. By concentrating on the moment of per-ception and the uniqueness of the object perceived, it strives to cultivate an inner harmony, to unify the fractured, alienated self by immersing it in unmediated experience.

Zen permeated western thought in the 1950s and influenced many areas of artistic production in Europe and, particularly, the United States for the next two decades. It underlies Brook's notion of the 'empty space', as he acknowledges, and informs his disavowal of the intellect and even his work with performers; like Grotowski, Brook encouraged his actors to overcome the divide between thought and deed, to respond on stage in the now-time of the event 'like a cat' (see Heilpern 1989: 146). Similarly, Zen parallels his desire for a theatre where the other-place/time of the locus coexists with the real place and time of the audience. It was in pursuit of this goal that Brook led the CIRT on its tour of Africa, for accounts of which I am indebted to John Heilpern's excellent and entertaining chronicle (1989).

For Brook, Africa offered unique opportunities. There, he asserts, the imaginary world of myths and spirits is still an accepted part of the everyday, for 'What western analytical minds call the superstitious attitude of the Africans is nothing but a natural, free passage of one sort of reality to another' (Cohen 1991: 150). African audiences were also unfamiliar with the West's equivalent theatrical division, the stage/auditorium divide. As Heilpern observed, Africa was to provide a 'natural audience ... one in which both sides – actors and audience – relax to the point where judgement and defense melt into shared experience' (1989: 87), thus offering the CIRT a laboratory situation in which the fruits of their research could be tested in a truly 'empty space'.

The company took to Africa only some poetry, a few simple props – some large boxes, their usual bamboo sticks – and the skills they had developed. With these they toured villages and small towns giving 'carpet shows', so named because they were performed on the large carpet that the company would unroll as a 'stage' in any convenient public space. The shows consisted largely of miming, clowning, movement and music, those means which are often thought capable of communicating in the absence of a shared language, and took their names from the objects/actions around which they were built: *The Box Show, The Walking Show, The Shoe Show*. All were based on simple scenarios. *The Shoe Show*, for example, began with a large pair of army boots being placed on the carpet. Performers would enter, put on the boots and mime a magical transformation: a beggar became a king, an old woman became beautiful and young. But these scenarios provided only a framework, for the minutiae of each show were improvised during the performance. Brook's key words for the shows were 'simplicity', 'energy' and 'danger', and he encouraged his performers to be spontaneous and highly responsive to the audience, to sense when those watching were losing interest and adapt their performances accordingly.

The carpet shows represented the most thoroughgoing, practical application of Brook's ideas; theatre at its most pruned-away, in its emptiest space, at its most transcultural and universal, and featuring perhaps the most radical of transmutations. Most of all, they sought to eradicate the divide between the spectators' everyday world and the imaginary world of the performance directly. Built out of improvisation, and responding to the audience on a minute-to-minute basis, the shows were emphatically of the now-time and this-place, spectators and performers occupying the same conceptual space. In this sense they epitomised that 'communion' Brook believes to be the essence of necessary theatre.

However, responses to the shows varied in ways that were not always predictable. In the Algerian town of In Salah *The Shoe Show* provoked an enormously positive response from those who gathered to watch, whereas in a small Nigerian village it was greeted with silence. It ultimately became clear that the show's basic premise was actually very culture-specific. To the performers it had seemed based on an obvious and universal idea – magical objects transform people – but this was only because this trope was familiar from fairy tales. With no such tales in their own culture, the Nigerian village audience had no way of understanding what was being represented. A similar revelation followed performances of *The Box Show*. Heilpern notes:

> in Paris [Brook] thought *The Box Show* a direct and simple piece of theatre. Perhaps an audience schooled in Beckett or the Theatre of the Absurd might have found the boxes a powerful image. Yet . . . the boxes seemed highly complex in Africa. They seemed presumptuous. They were shown to be no more than what they were – a theatre convention that could have no meaning to people who couldn't recognize the convention.
>
> (Heilpern 1989: 89)

Even so simple an object as a box proved far from culturally neutral and, invited to interpret it, the audience was puzzled.

It finally emerged that shows had proved problematic at some sites for an even more fundamental reason. Not only were some of the audiences unfamiliar with fairy tales, they lacked experience of theatre of any kind. In the culture of that village where *The Shoe Show* failed, 'performance' consisted of dance and song – indeed, spectators referred to the CIRT actors as 'dancers'. The audience was therefore unaware of the theatrical conventions necessary to make-sense of the piece. When one actress entered the playing area stooped over to depict an old woman, spectators were nonplussed. Was she ill? Was she shamming old age? If so, why? The audience was not privy to western theatre's basic convention, that actor A is to be read as character X. Indeed, when one performer bowed even this was greeted with consternation; even simple movements could prove culture-specific. This is not to say that the villagers or performers were naïve. Rather, the agreed cultural codes which would have made theatrical communication between audience and actors possible were absent.

The Nigerian village audience's interpretative difficulties illustrate the most fundamental flaw in Brook's project, for his search for a universal theatrical language is based on a misunderstanding of what language actually is. As we have seen, Brook attempted in many of his productions to operte at least partially outside language and culture, to reach beneath all social over-lays and grasp those means and meanings common to all humankind. He conceives of language as the medium through which meaning is communicated. But language, and culture generally, is in reality the medium in which meanings are *created*. Meaning does not occur in the non-human world; it is made, and made with those conceptual tools human society provides. There is no meaning outside culture because culture is the very mechanism which allows meaning to exist.

This reflects upon all Brook's attempts to reach his audiences on a universal or acultural level, and all the means he has employed to that end. Despite his reorganisation of theatrical space and relationships, all his works were performed on what are ultimately stages, acknowledged spaces of representation, and remain performances, acts of signification; and signification and representation involve shared cultural codes. Physicality, non-rational sounds, music, rhythms and so on may seem to operate in an acultural way but on a stage they are still signs, culturally derived tokens offered and received in the knowledge that they are fabricated; screams emanating from the stage of *Orghast sig-nified* the 'primordial' and 'primitive'. If shared cultural codes are not available the audience will either be unable to read the event, like the Nigerian audience of *The Shoe Show*, or else interpret it using its own codes; the company was baffled when, giving an impromptu performance of *Orghast* near Kano, Nigeria, the audi-ence collapsed into laughter, until it was explained that an 'Orghast' phrase they had used, 'bullorga torga', was similar to the local *Hausa* slang for 'vagina'. Culture is inescapable, and it is from a cultural perspective that we must view Brook's theatre.

SIGNIFYING THE INVISIBLE

The stage is a material place and its expressions are concrete things. When it communicates with the audience, offering mean-ings and provoking responses, it does so by tangible means; it produces signs, cultural constructs which are read using equally cultural interpretative strategies. It is with such constructs that we must account for Brook's theatre.

All actions, words and images in Brook's later work appear upon bare or nearly bare stages. For Brook these are a means of eliminating cultural accretions to start again from zero. But such empty spaces are not without their own significance. As we noted with Brecht and Beckett, the bare stage constitutes a non-signifying field – it *signifies* that it is non-signifying – and so focuses the audience's gaze upon what falls within it. Like the painting mounted within a white border, any object, action or character placed on a bare stage becomes subject to intense inter-pretative scrutiny. We are aware that it alone has been chosen and seek in it a significance commensurate with its isolation.

To this already highly charged space Brook introduces an even greater intensity. We have noted that 'ritualisation' – trans-mutation, the sculpting of movement and blocking – expresses the tangible world's subjugation to the 'patterns', 'rhythms' and 'shapes' of the Invisible. That is not to suggest that ritualisation signals the presence of a genuinely spiritual realm; rather, it acts as a *sign* of the Invisible, indicating that something momentous is being expressed. Beyond any specific meaning a spinning plate or sculpted kinescape may infer, ritualisation *per se* tells us that what is taking place is of great significance.

It is in this semically fertile arena that Brook's performers effect their acts of transmutation, and transmutation itself is also readable. Being transformed, the stridently modern cable spool signals that its meaning transcends its modernity – indeed, trans-cends its social, functional identity. Manipulated by performers, it becomes a 'war machine'; not a chariot or tank, say, but an abstract category of which chariots and tanks are merely the specific examples. That is, it is signified as having the status of *universality*, and this is true of all Brook's borrowings from other theatres, cultures and media. When a simulated karate kata is used to express militarism, the fact that the story is *not* set in Japan tells us that its significance is too profound, too 'global', to be limited to one culture. The very contrast between the culture-specific signifier (cable spool/kata) and supposedly super-cultural signified (war machine/militarism) indicates that the sign, the union of the two, invests the particular with the universal. This is augmented by the extra-ordinary quality of Brook's devices; we understand that, to require a spinning plate for its depiction, love-in-idleness must be viewed as a very special flower. Thus the alchemical transformation of objects and techniques that pervades Brook's stage operates as a sign, signifying that its meanings must be read as universal.

Brook's theatre not only primes its audience to scrutinise the stage intensely, then, but also to seek meaning of a universal order. The Brookian event signifies its own status as an interface or bridge between real social space and what lies beyond. To determine the nature and meaning of that 'beyond', to weave the stage's signs into a single other-place, a locus, the audience must seek a Law of the Text, that potential for interpretation shared by all or most signs, and so the logic available for their reading *en masse*.

This logic is provided less by the literal, denotative meanings of the Brookian stage's devices and images than by their connotations; and, ironically, their connotations when viewed from a western cultural perspective. Brook's 'pruning-away', the supreme *simplicity* that is a feature of all levels of his work, is not symbolically neutral. His bare stages and Grotowski-like 'poverty' of means – his use of sticks and bricks and cable spools instead of expensive props, and the actor's body and skills in place of high technology – actually key into an extant and very current cultural iconography in the West, for with such 'primitivism' Brook signals his stage's *asceticism*, its rejection of western materialism to embrace the life of the spirit.

'Spirituality' as an interpretative logic is inferred in a range of Brook's practices. By evoking comparison with genuine rituals, his stage's ritualisation calls forth imagistic associations of the metaphysical, while its 'magical' transformations imply shamanistic qualities. But the most important elements are Brook's borrowings from the Developing World, and particularly from Asia. As we have seen, costume is often based on Asian clothing, the musical instruments and traditions of the Developing World are used, and elements from the theatres of India, Iran, China and Japan periodically appear. One of the most evocative features of Brook's work is the appearance of the performers themselves. When characters clad in simple, hanging robes in black, white or earth colours appear, moving and speaking in a ceremonial manner, asceticism is inevitably suggested. Recollections are summoned of the self-imposed poverty of hermits, mystics and gurus, images of Christ and Buddha and Indian *sadhus* or holy men. Images like these evoke associations of mysticism for the modern western observer, and most of Brook's work from *A Midsummer Night's Dream* on is pervaded by this aura of eastern-ness.

The mystical associations traditionally ascribed to the East are highly suspect. At the very least, they reduce the complexity of many cultures to a single figure of *western* iconography. Of course, in the West various connotations gather about such images, and, on its own, Brook's 'orientalist' symbology probably could not establish an interpretative logic for the text as a whole. But the Law of the Text is that potential for interpretation shared by most or all of the stage's signs, and is derived from those signs *en masse*. When images of Asia are placed alongside 'magic', hieratic gestures, and ceremonial movement and blocking, and matched with a monk-like austerity of means – all these situated on an unadorned playing space – the connotations they all share are of the religious and spiritual. Brook's theatre offers not ritual but the trappings of ritual; does not deal in the sacred but images it, and does so most emphatically by employing icons of the East as seen through western eyes.

As we noted, Brook's theatre implies no specific belief system but a supremely general notion of 'spirituality'. This generality is significant. He seeks to depict a metaphysical realm which by definition cannot be realised on the physical plane. By signifying that his theatre has a spiritual dimension, but refusing to offer a definite spiritual meaning, Brook subjects the spectator to a simulation of the Invisible's ineffability. By pointing to the realm beyond the stage but never elucidating, providing the 'bridge' but no detail of what lies on its other side, Brook provides the interpretative *experience* of a dimension the spectator can never fully know.

This is not to suggest that Brook's productions are in some sense unsatisfying. Indeed, they do provide a 'communal' experience, but as we have seen, the community in question is an interpretative one. For Brook, only the audience's imaginative input makes the theatrical event 'complete'. This is one of the motives behind his ubiquitous principle of 'pruning-away', because, he argues, 'theatre is the art of suggestion, not statement':

> Nothing is richer than the images that the imagination can produce. ... And this is the principle of staging that goes through everything; that given a choice, we've tried to prune-away and eliminate, with the help of the actors, with the actors' body language, with their gestures, with their

voices, so that it's one colour, one movement, one element like a ladder or a stick, that suggests something – that is a suggestion and not a statement.

(Peter Brook interviewed on The South Bank Show,
London Weekend Television, 1989)

Minimal, partial and metaphoric images, then, engage the spectator's imaginative faculties, producing a richer *conceptual* text than could be realised literally onstage. This is a perceptive observation from Brook, and clearly his work nurtures such engagement. So many of its images demand to be read: spinning plates ask of spectators that they make the imaginative connection with a flower, and the same is true of action painting, karate katas, coils of wire that represent forest undergrowth and carpets and cushions which suggest a king's palace. At the same time, the connection is easily made, even when the images are quite abstract; one need not intellectualise the link to appreciate that elevating fairies on trapezes indicates their ethereality. Our pleasure derives not from the complexity of such images but from their ingenuity, from the jolt of recognition when the meaning becomes apparent.

Thus the spectator is presented with a stage which elicits intense interpretative scrutiny matched by images which demand their own decoding – but images so easily decoded, and so self-conscious of their ingenuity, that at the moment of experiencing delight we are aware that other spectators are also decoding and experiencing similar pleasure. Our own pleasure, our own reading, is mixed with the awareness that this is being experienced by the audience collectively. Our collaboration with the performer is thus extended into an appreciative collaboration with the other spectators, with the result that interpretative communion is broadened into an experience of *communitas* – based not upon any contact with the divine, of course, but upon an awareness that we operate in unison with our fellows.

It is in this last sense that we may term Brook's a ritual theatre. Lévi-Strauss explains:

Ritual ... *conjoins*, for it brings about a union (one might even say communion in this context) or in any case an organic relation between two initially separate groups, one ideally emerging with the person of the officiant and the other with the collectivity of the faithful. ... There is an asymmetry which is postulated in advance between profane and sacred, faithful and officiating, dead and living, initiated and uninitiated etc., and the 'game' consists of making all the participants pass to the winning side by means of events.

(Lévi-Strauss 1966: 32)

Union with the 'officiants', the performers, may be established in interpretation, but, as we have seen, Brook seeks to go further; to counter the western individual's general experience of alienation, that loss of a sense of communality which has, he argues, resulted from the West's spiritual decline. Although he does not genuinely achieve this, with his 'incomplete' imagery Brook does fabricate its simulacrum, for although the audience remains physically passive, as in orthodox theatre, his images provide a means of *interpretatively* coordinating disparate spectators. Such images and their decoding thus provide an equivalent of the unifying mechanisms of dance, procession, chant and so on found in ritual proper; in self-consciously reading the Brookian theatrical event together, communally, we demonstrate our one-ness to each other and to ourselves.

Far from being universal, Brook's theatre is very much of its time and place, for it stands at the intersection of several western traditions. In the latter part of the nineteenth century there began to emerge critiques of western society's rationalism and materialism which used premodern cultures as their point of comparison. Friedrich Nietzsche's *The Birth of Tragedy* (1872) was perhaps the first such text to turn an analytical eye upon theatre. Nietzsche argued that drama was born out of the ritual celebrations of ancient Greece, where it negotiated two opposing aesthetics, the Apollonian and Dionysian. Whereas Apollonian art such as poetry is intellectual and coolly considered, the Dionysian is sensual and communal, as in the massed rhythms of dance. While he maintained that both represent necessary facets of human experience, Nietzsche implicitly favoured the Dionysian for its power to disrupt the rational, offering it in critical comparison to the contemporary world.

Nietzsche is important in two respects. With its suspicion of modern reason and its pairing of drama with ritual, this early work expressed ideas that were to prove formative in the development of certain trends in modernism. The so-called 'Cambridge School' of academics – Francis Cornford, Gilbert Murray, Jane Ellen Harrison and, most importantly, J. G. Frazer of *The Golden Bough* – similarly traced modern culture to its 'roots' in previous ages, linking drama to its supposed ur-form in the ritual dance or *sacer ludus* of the Festival of Dionysus of classical Greece. Nietzsche can thus be seen as having initiated a tendency towards nostalgia within modernism, a sublimated critique of the present married to a yearning for a fictionalised Golden Age of the past. Later Artaud was to rearticulate ideas of ritual, sensuality and the pre-civilised self reminiscent of Nietzsche's in his own, rather unique brand of surrealism.

But for our purposes *The Birth of Tragedy* is equally significant for the image it offers of the human subject as polarised between the rational and intellectual on the one hand, and on the other, the sensual and instinctual. This dichotomy, later so evident in Brook's work, was to prove crucial to modernist conceptions of the self, reiterated in some of the key discourses of the early twentieth century. In Freudian psychoanalysis, the self is in its initial stages of development driven by the 'Pleasure Principle', the basic urge to satisfy its desires. But soon this must be accommodated alongside the 'Reality Principle', formed when one encounters a pre-existing reality – notably, a *social* reality – which checks, modifies and rechannels desire's path to gratification. Although by no means the same as the Nietzschean dichotomy, Freud's Reality and Pleasure Principles nevertheless proffer an opposition between nature and culture as fundamental to humanity: a modernist vision of the self existing in a primal state and a social self which represses it, shaping its drives to meet social norms.

But in order to appreciate Brook's historico-cultural significance fully we must also locate his work within a more specifically artistic tradition. As noted in the previous chapter, the first effect of those discourses central to modernist thought was the undermining of existing world views. The work of Freud, Marx, Nietzsche, Einstein and others challenged the certainties of the old dispensation, and responses to this were by no means universally positive. Disturbed by the empiricist and rationalist leanings of Impressionism, for example, Gauguin sought to rediscover an art which retained an element of mystery, finally retreating to the 'primitive' cultures of the Pacific in search of it. Painters such as Van Gogh, the Fauvists and even

Picasso displayed a comparable, if less pronounced, desire for the primitive and simple. This suspicion of the new is even more evident in literature. The novels of D. H. Lawrence image a modern self riven between the intellect and the spirit, and hark back to a lost time in which the individual was whole and the community intact, embodied in peasant-like figures who exist in intimate contact with the natural world. The early poems of T. S Eliot represented modern existence as arid and sterile, and in *The Waste Land* (1922) he argued for the recreation of a stable, unified culture able to offer the individual a sense of stability and continuity with the past. Indeed, in so much of the writing of the early twentieth century we see a nostalgia for a lost Arcadia, the use of myth as a means of obliquely suggesting the new age's continuity with the old, a rediscovery of 'spirituality' in an epoch whose key discourses rejected it – all this at least partly the result of a disenchantment with the modern world, resulting in attempts to rediscover what, it was felt, had been 'lost'.

Such ideas carried less weight as the century progressed – perhaps because they were in part a response to the newness of the new world – but after the Second World War were mobilised afresh, stepping to the centre of the cultural stage. Out of what we might call the neo-romanticism of the 1960s youth movement, the period in which Brook's more radical experiments in theatre began, a militantly 'alternative' culture developed, one critical of western materialism and calling for a return to nature and to spiritual values. This took its most vocal form with the 'hippies' but actually had a much broader purchase, surfacing as a new interest in natural lifestyles, communal living, health foods, vegetarianism and holistic medicine, and as a rejection of the industrial West's urbanism and established patterns of work and leisure. It became partially interwoven with 1960s and 1970s drug culture and its claim to offer new states of consciousness, represented in Timothy Leary's call to 'Turn on, tune in, drop out'. Many of these ideas have recently reappeared, finding a new home in the 'New Age' and 'Green' movements of the 1980s and 1990s.

Most of this finds resonance in Brook's ideas and practices. It is therefore not incidental that an important feature of the period was its fascination with non-western, especially Asian, cultures. In the neo-romantic view, Asia had largely escaped the modern

West's afflictions, retaining both a contact with nature and a spiritual dimension to existence. Youth culture in the West blossomed in the late 1960s and 1970s with a diversity of Asian cultural artefacts, not only kaftans, incense sticks, ginseng and sitar music, but also more obviously spiritual imports such as Yoga, Taoism, Buddhism, I Ching, gurus and Transcendental Meditation – as well as, ironically, Chinese and Japanese martial arts. James Roose-Evans made the point succinctly:

> Brook, like Grotowski, and countless numbers of ordinary people, is turning towards a re-examination of spiritual values ... in the West especially, many more people spend large sums of money attending day and weekend courses in Tibetan chanting, meditation, Tai Chi and other alternative and holistic practices. Much of this activity reaches loopy proportions, spawning religions of ego, but underneath this movement there lies, indisputably, a hunger for and need of rituals that will enshrine the fears, yearnings and conflicts of people today.
>
> (Roose-Evans 1989: 196)

In the theatre, this neo-romantic outlook is not exclusive to Brook. Director Eugenio Barba has written of what he calls the 'Third Theatre' (see Roose-Evans 1989: ch. 17). If the first is Brook's commercial 'Deadly Theatre', and the second comprises the orthodox, director-controlled avant-garde, the Third Theatre consists of companies that function cooperatively and experimentally, seeking to create not merely a new theatre but a new, ritual-like theatre *experience*. Into this category we can place Barba's own work with the Odin Teatro, as well as the theatres of Grotowski, Beck and Malina, Schechner, Augusto Baol, Tadashi Suzuki (of the Waseda Little Theatre, Tokyo) and Luis Valdez (of El Teatro Campesino), all of whom share some or all of Brook's practices, aims or principles, and have developed their own form of what we have called ritual theatre.

Moreover, these ideas have impacted upon the study of theatre. Barba and Grotowski have both been involved in 'Theatre Anthropology', researching the performance practices of non-western cultures, while under the auspices of such as Schechner and the late Victor Turner, a new discipline, 'Performance Studies', has sought to place theatre proper within a wider context of rituals, sports, games, and even 'social dramas' such as trials and social crises. Turner in particular argued that all such activities carried out the same *performative* function, as mechanisms for dealing with social schisms, reintegrating the communal whole (see Turner 1987).

But the political implications of Brook's work are ambiguous. Like neo-romanticism in general, Brook's theatre represents a genuine disaffection with and response to a perceived deterioration in the conditions of life under mechanistic western capitalism. The radicalism of the 1960s and 1970s, with its pacifism, libertarianism and lauding of communality, provided a rallying point for those seeking change. Similarly, by offering in microcosm a vision and experience of another mode of existence, theatre such as Brook's reiterates a comparable critique, offering a point of potential resistance to the conditions of contemporary life.

It should be remembered, however, that the image of existence offered by Brook's stage is a mythical one. Far from being free of 'styles', for example, Shakespeare's theatre was far less tolerant of experiment than our own. Brook's work implicitly looks back to a prelapsarian past, a Golden Age when human beings were whole, at one with themselves and the community. But beyond the impulse to nostalgia, there is no reason to suppose that human subjects in past or other societies experienced any less alienation than in the modern West. It is ironic that Brook and others look to the Developing World, to societies deeply impoverished and oppressed precisely by western materialism; such poverty only appears attractive to those who are not forced to experience it.

Nor are such images neutral. If modern life is degraded, it is because of the material circumstances in which most people live, not the absence of an Invisible. But the effect of certain of the theatrical tendencies and theories mentioned is to obscure this. Performance Studies effectively strips human activities of what is most particular and meaningful, rendering real political relations – relations of power – the expression of some supposed 'universal' impulse. Similarly, work such as Brook's dehistoricises and depoliticises precisely what is historically and politically specific. When modern life and theatre is related exclusively to a mythologised past, or to equally fictionalised cultures of the Developing World, what is effaced is an understanding of current conditions in the West, the kind of 'rationalistic' knowledge necessary if one is to change things. Historically, religion and systems of spiritual belief have most often functioned in the service of those with material power, at the very least reconciling the oppressed to their lot. By focusing on the immaterial, one effaces the concrete; by positing a mythological past as a model for the future, and metaphysics as the means of reaching it, theatre such as Brook's effectively obscures the real forces which determine life today, the very conditions which are the ultimate source of that theatre's own disaffection.

6

ROBERT WILSON AND THE THEATRE OF VISIONS

THE THEATRE OF DREAMS

Emerging out of the innovatory ferment of 1960s New York 'loft culture', the early work of Robert Wilson (b. 1941) was eclectic, comprising film, set design, an installation entitled *Poles* consisting of 600 telephone poles erected in a field in Ohio, and a number of performance pieces. In all media he was experimental, his early performance works evidencing that rejection of existing aesthetics characteristic of the forms of 'live art' developing in the United States at the time. In 1969, however, Wilson's work took a new direction with a piece that set the tone for most of his later productions, the kind of theatre for which he is now most widely known, and which Stefan Brecht has termed the 'Theatre of Visions' (Brecht 1978). This piece was entitled *The King of Spain*.

The King of Spain was a spectacular, large-scale production performed within an orthodox proscenium arch stage. Much of the action took place in a Victorian drawing room, the location conjured with traditional *trompe-l'oeil* effects, flats painted to create realistic illusion. But the illusion was interrupted. A section of the room's rear wall was missing and through the gap a second part of the set was visible, representing an area of sunlit countryside. The figures who entered the room seemed undisturbed by this anomaly, behaving for the most part in the kind of dispassionate and genteel manner appropriate to their environment. Yet their activities were incomprehensible; characters piled straw on the stage, lit a shelf of candles, played indecipherable games at a table and slid brass rings along a wire. Periodically an athlete in shorts and singlet appeared in the meadow 'outside', running across the room's missing slice. The piece drew to a close as a set of giant mechanical cat's legs walked across the stage, its body 'out of sight' in the flies. No explanation was offered for any of these occurrences, for like all Wilson's 'plays', *The King of Spain* had neither plot nor dialogue, and followed no discernible logic. Spectators were left to make of the piece what they could.

This lack of any apparent sense is a consistent feature of Wilson's work, for it is central to his theatrical project. Human beings, he maintains, always register the world in two ways, on two separate 'screens'. The 'exterior screen' is the place of conscious, public meanings, where we ascribe to objects and events the same significance as our fellows. But at the same time we each register those same images on our 'interior screen', where they are perceived subjectively, our imaginations granting them meanings personal to ourselves. Both screens operate throughout our waking lives, so that we continually perceive reality in both a cultural and an individual, acultural way. But in the modern world, Wilson argues, people are beginning to turn from the outer towards the inner. He explains:

> More and more people are turning into themselves. . . . You can see it in the subways, where everyone is bunched together, and nobody is looking at anybody. What they are doing is signing off. They have to because there's so much overload. . . . It's actually a means of survival.
>
> (Innes 1993: 202)

In a society where life is lived at a frenetic pace, where we are bombarded with media 'messages' and forced to share our personal, expressive space with others in congested public areas, this retreat into a private, contemplative world is for Wilson a necessity, a means of individual 'survival'. It is this view of contemporary existence and its problems which informs his work. Most forms of theatre coerce the audience into accepting their proffered meanings, reproducing the wider social situation in which the personal is overwhelmed by the public. Wilson in contrast seeks to cultivate each spectator's individual response. By creating works which elude fixed, given meanings and public logics, he in effect aims to merge the two screens, to access the imagination of each member of the audience via the emphatically 'exterior' instrument of the stage.

This aim of accessing the personal and imaginative is evident in Wilson's work with performers. For his early New York productions Wilson formed and became artistic director of a company, naming it the Byrd Hoffman School of Byrds after the dance teacher who had helped him overcome a childhood speech problem. All but one of the Byrds were untrained; indeed, Wilson plucked several from the street. Their work was consequently free of pre-formed 'styles', the performance signatures – regimes of movement, kinds of diction and so on – indicative of particular schools. Similarly, in the experimental workshops conducted in his loft Wilson encouraged Byrds to approach performance without aesthetic preconceptions. Rather than attempt to reproduce something resembling conventional dance, for example, they were to explore their own distinctive ways of moving, or else develop new, idiosyncratic kinesics. Time was spent freeing Byrds from such impositions, effectively teaching them *not* to 'act' (see Shyer 1989: 9–10).

By such means Wilson permitted performers an opportunity for free expression, certainly, but those same practices offered a comparable *interpretative* freedom to spectators. Movement is rarely entirely functional or natural; one need only compare everyday western movement to the way people walk, sit and gesture in African or Asian societies to recognise that our use of our bodies is culturally shaped. The competent social subject 'writes' his/her culture's kinesic codes in moving, and also uses those same codes to 'read' the movements of others. This is equally true of the stage, for our reception of stage movement entails consciously or unconsciously comparing it with extant performance aesthetics. But in nurturing movement unrelated to existing forms, Wilson encouraged kinesics unreadable by available means. It is not merely that Byrds moved in ways that were 'original'; rather, in doing so their movements signalled their difference from given kinesics, indicating that they could not be interpreted using those codes. The 'dance' that was a feature of Wilson's productions with the Byrds – tightly choreographed arrangements of unconventional steps, sequences of inexplicable gestures – eluded not only the codification of dance proper, but also established notions of grace, beauty and so on. A comparable 'kinescape' characterised Wilson's later productions, for the choreographers with whom he worked after breaking with the Byrds – particularly Lucinda Childs – similarly deal in movement which resists easy categorisation. With no cultural logic available to interpret it, the spectator must respond subjectively.

Perhaps the most successful means Wilson employed to generate such idiosyncratic expression/interpretation were his collaborations with artists who were sensorily or intellectually impaired, and who moreover conceptualised the world in unique ways. The first of these to contribute to his theatre proper was the painter Raymond Andrews. Andrews is deaf and without speech, and, when he and Wilson first met, had never attended school. He had thus been excluded from the world of the exterior screen, the aesthetic ideas and norms of the society in which he lived. In response, Andrews had developed his own thoroughgoing interior life. He was not only an accomplished visual artist, possessing an extraordinary sense of colour and spatial composition, his paintings also provided Wilson with an entirely original iconography, a network of images that was unique to his imagination.

Perhaps the most fruitful of Andrews and Wilson's collabora-tions was *Deafman Glance* (1970). The curtain rose on the striking third section of this piece to show a forest spanning the width of the stage. Half-visible figures – silver-painted nudes, dwarfs, a man swathed in bandages and walking on crutches, a magician in top hat and tails – wove slowly through the forest, while behind it the outline and tip of a pyramid could be seen. In the foreground stood a fairy-tale hut adorned with horns, antlers and animal bones, and a dining table presided over by a Byrd costumed as a green frog. In this downstage area enigmatic, ritual-like actions were enacted: a papier-mâché ox was cere-monially beheaded; wooden pens were built on the backs of four tortoises; a figure in ecclesiastical robes was placed in a glass coffin and carried offstage. During the piece a white rabbit, three women carrying babies, performers bearing sheets of shim-mering glass, and a host of other figures, appeared to dance or conduct activities. The entire segment was watched over by a boy, played by Andrews himself. At several points the chair on which he sat moved as if under its own power, finally flying into the air so that Andrews hovered over the scene, surveying his imagistic domain.

As a young man Wilson trained both as an architect/interior designer and as a painter. It is perhaps for this reason that his is a spatially and visually oriented theatre, dealing in such fantastical, carefully constructed stage 'pictures', mobile *tableaux vivants*. But *Deafman Glance* was extraordinary not merely for its images but for their diversity, their apparent lack of any guiding rationale. If a connection existed between those images it was inaccessible to audiences, for it derived not from a shared culture but from Wilson's and Raymond Andrews' interior screens.

Stage tableaux of this kind are characteristic of a relatively recent trend in performance in the United States, for Suzanne Lacy, Alwin Nikolais, Claude Van Itallie, Peter Schumann (the Bread and Puppet Theatre), Michael Kirby (the Structuralist Workshop) and Richard Foreman (the Ontological-Hysteric Theatre) have all dealt in similarly extraordinary yet elusive imagery. But such iconographic *diversity* is most pronounced in Wilson's theatre. Animals are legion in his work, with performers costumed as apes, lions, walruses, owls and black, brown and white bears – and, in *The Life and Times of Joseph Stalin* (1973), fifty dancing ostriches – sometimes sharing the stage with real dogs, snakes, camels and goats, as well as mechanical tortoises and stuffed ravens. These may appear alongside giants, dwarfs, winged women and other characters reminiscent of myths and fairy tales, as well as cowboys and Indians, and elements drawn from the symbology of science fiction: astronauts, space ships, futuristic cars and so on. Some of his characters are eminently recognisable. Certain of his works are ostensibly based on the lives of famous historical personalities, so that Freud, Stalin, Edison, Einstein, Abraham Lincoln and a host of others have trodden his stage. All such images may appear in several productions, for Wilson recycles his work, repeating elements or even incorporating whole acts from previous plays into new ones. Thus *Stalin* re-used part or all of five previous productions, while dinosaurs and various 'monsters', trains, pyramids, fish, volcanoes, geometric shapes sculpted in light – these and other motifs recur throughout his *opus*, deployed alongside new elements to create new wholes.

For our purposes imagery such as this achieves two important effects. First, it results in theatrical texts with quite literally a dream-like quality. In Freud's view, our dreams deal in materials and concerns which are ordinarily repressed, banished from consciousness. To elude our mental censor these concerns are translated, the 'latent dreamwork' of our unconscious recoded to form the 'manifest dreamwork' that we actually dream. This translation is effected via two processes, which Freud terms *condensation* and *displacement*: condensation involves representing a number of anxieties using only one symbol, while displacement entails severing them from their original source and affixing them to some new, innocuous object. Both processes result in images which bear an inexplicable sense of importance. Our dreams are thus laden with elements which, the dreamer feels, are of great significance, but which remain beyond his or her understanding.

Wilson's works offer audiences a comparable interpretative experience. Dinosaurs, cowboys, space ships, Abraham Lincoln and Albert Einstein – these are not merely images, they are *icons*, the kinds of symbols that continually circulate through our culture's visual media. They are therefore highly resonant, inevitably bringing with them a wealth of ideas and associations. A similar symbolic density is suggested by the 'rituals' that abound on Wilson's stage. We have noted that, regardless of whether such acts are explicable or not, 'ritualisation' *per se* infers its own symbolic status, for when we see performance space/time shaped in so purposeful a fashion, we assume that there is indeed an underlying purpose, and so seek that purpose in our reading. In fact this sense of purposefulness pervades all levels of his theatre. Wilson plans and directs his productions in minute detail, carefully organising his painterly stage pictures, choreographing movement and sometimes synchronising it with music, and so on. The result is a discernible craftedness, an observable precision about the work as a whole, which indicates its own significance.

Elements such as these invite interpretation, advertising that they can be read. But the striking diversity of Wilson's imagery ensures that all such attempts at reading are frustrated. As we noted, the events and objects that appear on his stage obey no discernible logic. A single action or object – a half-hidden pyramid, the beheading of an ox – might suggest any number of possible readings. But this plurality is never contained, meaning is never fixed, because the images together conform to no consistent rationale. Thus Wilson's stage offers the spectator no Law of the Text, no shared, culturally derived order of meaning by which the stage's elements may be decoded *en masse*. By filling the stage with objects/actions which seem to declare their own decodability, but which deny attempts to subsume them within a single

184

interpretative discourse, Wilson both encourages interpretation and ultimately denies it. The result is a stage filled with iconographic components which, like genuine dream-images laden with a sense of portent, suggest their own symbolic status while refuting all attempts to discover what they are symbolic of.

Writing of *Deafman Glance*, the surrealist poet and novelist Louis Aragon declared Wilson to be the modern inheritor of surrealism. Although anachronistic, the comparison is illustrative. Rejecting the world of consciousness and its socially derived meanings, surrealism sought to express what it saw as the 'higher reality' of the unconscious, often drawing upon the metaphor of the dream. Surrealist artworks were, it was claimed, borne out of the raw stuff of the inner self, unshaped by public structures of meaning; that such works were an expression of that self was, for surrealists, sufficient to make them art. Wilson's productions are similarly the detailed and painstaking realisation of his and his co-workers' initial vision, but a vision which is not necessarily accessible to an audience. By both encouraging expression free of cultural norms and seeking the non-orthodox view, he apparently liberates his theatre from the need to make discernible, public sense, and his audience from the meanings of the exterior screen.

But this claim to aculturality, this liberation of the audience from given meanings, warrants scrutiny. As we noted, Wilson deals less in images than icons, visual tokens drawn from existing cultural networks. Indeed, the potency of his stage pictures derives in no small part from the familiarity of their components. Dinosaurs, space ships and so on bring with them dense cultural freight and it is inevitably this with which the spectator engages. Nor are the original elements of his productions disengaged culturally. We have seen that idiosyncratic movement, for example, *signifies* its invulnerability to customary codes. In declaring itself beyond the sense of readable culture, such movement claims for itself an identity in *relation* to culture; paradoxically, the identity 'acultural' is itself a cultural one, a significance which derives from a given, public perspective.

THE INEXPLICABLE OTHER-PLACE

If the first effect of Wilson's imagery is to render his stage dream-like, the second is to establish a locus. This too is a consequence of its lack of discernible sense. When we see huge mechanical cat's legs prowl *The King of Spain*'s drawing room, a giant Abraham Lincoln strolling beneath an airborne flying saucer in *the CIVIL warS: a tree is best measured when it is down* (1981), or the eponymous, genteelly dressed hero of *The Life and Times of Sigmund Freud* (1969) in a rough-hewn cave surrounded by wild animals, it is apparent that events on the stage are governed by logics alien to our usual experience. Inaccessible to everyday modes of sense, such juxtapositions of disparate elements effectively signal that the playing space is to be viewed in a way different from ordinary social space. They grant it a quality of emphatic other-ness, their very strangeness separating it from the world of the onlooker, encouraging audiences to view the stage as the site of an other-place.

This effect is achieved even in those of Wilson's productions which seem least to demand a locus. *I Was Sitting on My Patio This Guy Appeared I Thought I Was Hallucinating* (1977) was a smaller-scale piece, a partial return to Wilson's pre-*The King of Spain* aesthetic. In its two separate acts Wilson and dancer/ choreographer Lucinda Childs recited the same senseless monologue, speaking directly to the audience as if from the platea. But *Patio*'s refusal to proffer definitive meaning – its indecipherable words/word-like sounds accompanied by equally unreadable movement – effectively signified the action's conceptual distance from the reality of those who watched and listened. In Wilson's 1986 production of Heiner Müller's play *Hamletmachine*, the performers were arranged as the sides of a square in a bare playing area. As each in turn spoke a part of Müller's fragmented dialogue, he or she would perform a simple movement; take a half step, swivel a quarter turn on a chair, and so on. Over the span of the piece each performer spoke and moved four times, but was otherwise silent and still, effectively demanding that spectators assume an other-place as the site of such impenetrable occurrences.

Wilson signals this other-ness perhaps most clearly using theatrical special effects. The *King of Spain*'s giant cat's legs and the levitating chair of *Deafman Glance* are more than matched by the moving life-sized train that crossed the stage in *Einstein on the Beach* (1976), and the elephant's trunk which emerged from the wings in *Death, Destruction and Detroit* (1979) to scoop a child from his chair and whisk him into another world. Most spectacular perhaps was the finale of *Stalin*, in which an elderly couple, an exploding star, a pegasus and the image of the city of Moscow in flames seemed to float in the sky. People and objects fly, giants walk the stage and space ships traverse the heavens in Wilson's theatre, like his fantastical imagery inferring a world which operates according to a different 'physics'.

The most distinctively 'special' device of this order is slow motion. *Deafman Glance* opened on a tableau of a mother and her two children, and for the first half-hour nothing moved. The mother then rose from her chair and, after pouring glasses of milk for her offspring, stabbed them to death, the whole procedure taking a further thirty minutes. Slowed action of this kind has also been used by Richard Foreman, but is typical of Wilson's work, for in many of his productions events proceed as if under water. Even in pieces like *Einstein on the Beach* where performers moved at something approximating normal speed, other elements such as the trains inched across the stage.

Slow motion is a potently defamiliarising device. Like a bare stage, such 'bare time' provokes great interpretative focus from the audience; when actions are substantially slowed, spectators are encouraged to scrutinise them intensely, to seek in them a greater than usual concentration of meaning. It is thus in the audience's *interpretative gaze* that events are 'made strange'; actions themselves may be prosaic but slow motion prompts us to view them as extraordinary. This defamiliarising effect is augmented by the extreme length of many of Wilson's plays: *Deafman Glance* lasted eight hours, *Stalin* twelve, while the mammoth *KA MOUNTAIN AND GUARDenia TERRACE: a story about a family and some people changing* (1972) ran for seven days and nights. With performances of such duration, and with slow motion, the audience's perception is of time stretched, the ordinary laws governing phenomena warped or suspended. The stage world is thus presented as a realm where events proceed according to principles different from those of the auditorium, and its status as other-place is reinforced.

Wilson's use of traditional stage technology – as in special effects: performers suspended from wires, a mechanical elephant's trunk – is central to his practice, for his signification of a distinct locus is often reliant on the kinds of techniques and skills long used to effect theatrical 'illusion'. Perhaps the most obvious of these is scenic design and construction. *The King of*

Spain's juxtaposition of interior and exterior settings was disorientating precisely because both sets were conjured so realistically. Wilson usually works in large spaces and his sets often proffer spectacular vistas: open landscapes with wide horizons and broad, star-studded skies, monumental architectural constructions, grand interiors. The seven acts of *Stalin* moved from a beach to (another) drawing room, a cave, a forest, a temple's interior, a bedroom, and finally the barren and volcano-strewn surface of a planet in space. Each location was conjured with remarkable plausibility, largely due to such venerable stage mechanisms as *trompe-l'oeil* scene-painting, sophisticated lighting, and so on. *KA MOUNTAIN* was staged on a real mountain in Iran and utilised the terrain's natural features. But Wilson augmented these with, among other things, a giant whale, a biblical ark, several dinosaurs, a graveyard, some cardboard waves and silver rockets, a simulated New York housing project composed of fifty identical pasteboard houses, and several hundred papier-mâché flamingos.

Sets and scenic arrangements of this kind provide more than spectacle. As we have seen, Wilson's imagery is markedly non-consistent. Conforming to no *one* interpretative logic, the objects/actions that appear on his stage do not of themselves demand to be read as components of a *single* text, appearing instead as a collage, elements yoked together rather than integrated into a whole. But in signifying one defined 'place', Wilson's sets establish a space of symbolisation able to encompass them all. They may not be consistent but they are all symbols, to be read in the Abstract register, and so to be viewed as occupying a space that is unified *conceptually*.

This conceptual unity of space works to redefine the fantastical diversity of Wilson's iconography, for, as a feature of a defined other-place, the non-consistency of his imagery becomes a characteristic not of the stage but of the locus. The event is thereby proffered not as an illogical performance but as the presentation of a world whose 'logic' is itself illogical. Paradoxically, the images' very non-coherence thus becomes the basis of their coherence, the quality they share and which signals to audiences that they are to be addressed as parts of a single whole. Like the realism of the paintings of Magritte or Dali, the fantastical plausibility of Wilson's stage pictures rework their non-consistency into a feature of another realm.

In later productions Wilson moved away from mimetic sets, often working instead with lighting, simpler designs and a limited palette. But with such means he achieved a similar visual splendour. In *Death, Destruction and Detroit*, eighty recessed spotlights shone directly upward, creating a wall of light as backdrop, while on the set of his most recent work, *Doctor Faustus Lights the Lights* (1994), stood large, Gordon Craig-like flats, shafts of light streaming between them to fall onto a darkened stage. Although these do not depict another world in the same way as earlier sets, they do have a comparable semiotic effect, their spectacle making of the stage a distinctly special space.

Central to this kind of scenic 'illusion' is Wilson's use of perspective. Traditionally the key device in establishing theatrical perspective is the proscenium arch stage, and in particular the arch itself, the 'frame' which stands between the main stage and the auditorium. For our purposes the arch performs two significant functions. First, it signals to the spectator that all that falls within it must be viewed in a special way. Like the frame in which a painting is mounted, the arch marks a symbolic boundary, separates the figures, objects and actions of the performance from surrounding social space. It can therefore prove instrumental in establishing a locus, for it physicalises the *conceptual* difference in the way spectators are to view the production, signalling that the stage is to be addressed as an other-place and that its parts are to be interpreted in the Abstract register.

But this symbolic inclusion of the production's elements in a special space effects a complementary exclusion. The second function of the proscenium arch is to mask the offstage area. The edges of the set, props hanging in the flies until they are to be lowered, stage machinery, the dry ice machine, the actors watching from the wings, waiting for his/her cue to come on – all these are obscured, the literal devices by which theatre effects its constructions hidden from view. It is not that the arch permits perfect 'illusion', of course, for audiences always remain aware that the event has been manufactured. Rather, in removing theatre's meaning-making mechanisms from the spectator's gaze, the arch excludes artifice, signs of 'authorship', from the space of the readable theatrical text, indicating that it is not to feature in our interpretation.

These two functions performed by the arch are complementary. Separating-off the stage, nominating it as a special space,

189

enables the audience more easily to view it in the Abstract register; in tandem, obscuring artifice effectively banishes our recognition of the Concrete platea. With seating arranged to limit and control the audience's sight lines, the proscenium arch is therefore a key tool for establishing a locus. It is for these reasons that the use of this design of stage (and to a lesser degree, its ancestor, the 'picture frame' stage) historically coincides with the modern period's development of more illusionistic forms of theatre, culminating in the nineteenth century with the emergence of realism and naturalism – forms which strove for a peerless simulation of reality – and with the mythical worlds of fabulous creatures and events figured in the operas of Richard Wagner.

Wilson is unusual among modern, avant-garde theatre practitioners in that he employs the proscenium arch for its full illusionistic potential. This is due in part, perhaps, to his training as a painter; the arch 'frames' his stage pictures, is a means of controlling spectators' sight lines. But the perspective that the frame provides has a more than merely practical function on Wilson's stage. By obscuring artifice and forcefully separating the playing area from ordinary social space, the arch enables him to establish a radically *other*-place, reinforcing the loci depicted in his sets. Indeed, Wilson frequently augments this with additional perspectival effects. His painted backdrops are sometimes contrived so that landscapes appear to dwindle into the distance. They thus grant the relatively shallow stage a greater depth, conjuring the visual impression of a reality which continues beyond the confines of the real playing area – creating 'illusion', certainly, but also marginalising the real space of the platea and its artifice. He achieves similar results with stage objects. The train that crossed the set in scene one of *Einstein on the Beach* reappeared in scene four, this time much smaller and at an angle, thus seeming to recede towards the horizon of a fictional world whose dimensions transcended those of the stage.

Those practitioners who do employ perspective, however, often use it subversively. In Foreman's *Pandering to the Masses: A Misrepresentation* (1975), the rear walls of the initially shallow playing space opened up to reveal a deeper, raked stage behind. The performers on the forestage were telescoped, and the audience was forced to adjust its view to account for the resulting dislocation of sight lines. Wilson uses perspective in an equally ironic fashion. In *the CIVIL warS* a performer of restricted growth stood in the foregound, a giant on stilts behind him, and to the rear, on the set's painted 'horizon', a soldier of ordinary size, contriving an impossible 'perspectival' view. In a similar vein, one section of *KA MOUNTAIN* was performed behind a proscenium frame erected on open ground, the real mountain behind it acting as 'fictional' backdrop; throughout the third segment of *Deafman Glance* an angler sat with his line draped over the edge of the stage, trailing into the auditorium.

But for the modern spectator such visual pranks actually do little to undermine the other-place. Frequently they achieve the opposite, for they evoke the *idea* of perspective, drawing it into the viewer's interpretative consideration. For Wagner and naturalists like Strindberg it was necessary to demarcate a locus unequivocally, for the principle of so marked a separation of real and symbolic spaces was still relatively novel. But for today's audience it seems self-evident, a given; indeed, we might view the history of theatrical experiment in the twentieth century, the work of Brecht, Beckett, Pirandello and others, as an attempt to go beyond that space and its illusion. Thus in bringing the concepts of perspective and a separate space into the modern spectator's interpretative gaze, Wilson is free to manipulate them, to use them to reinforce the locus's other-ness. Just as his inexplicable imagery signals a hypothetical realm which is fantastically distinct from the auditorium, so Wilson's perspectival jokes signify a world where customary logics do not operate; including, paradoxically, the laws of perspective.

STRUCTURATION AND DISCONTINUITY

The second disabled artist with whom Wilson collaborated was Christopher Knowles. Brain-damaged at birth, Knowles had difficulty functioning in the social world but possessed an extraordinary ability to conceptualise *systems*, elements placed in complex interrelationships. This expressed itself in his approach to language. In his poetry Knowles used words primarily as material phenomena – sounds or shapes on paper – arranging them to form audial and/or visual patterns. Moreover, he could do this almost instantly. In *Spaceman* (1976), his third piece with Wilson, Knowles typed during the performance, his structured word-collages appearing on one of the stage's twenty television monitors. Thus, although he performed with Wilson in a series of pieces, for our purposes Knowles's most significant contribution was to texts.

Wilson has worked most often with writers like Knowles or German dramatist Heiner Müller, whose use of language defies existing cultural formations. Speech in Wilson's early works was either inaudible or simply absent, and it was not until *KA MOUNTAIN* in 1972 that words played a significant role. Indeed, none of his works has used dialogue in the conventional sense. Wilson's own playtexts are either compiled out of linguistic fragments – snatches of television programmes and commercials, films, other plays, the 'scream songs' of Byrd Cindy Lubar and even phrases overheard in rehearsal – or else consist of sequences of mutating words and word-like sounds structured according to rhyme and rhythm, their physical, phonetic qualities, rather than sense. Although he did use broadly realistic dialogue in *A Letter for Queen Victoria* (1974), his first collaboration with Knowles, Wilson distributed the lines among performers in a seemingly arbitrary fashion. In *Einstein on the Beach* he dismissed meaningful language altogether, the melodies of Philip Glass's score being sung to the words of the diatonic scale, *doh-ray-me* and so on, and the numbers one to eight.

Language is of course the most important and pervasive medium of human communication, and as such is the primary vehicle of culture. It is a system in the Saussurean sense, an organised structure of signs for the construction and exchange of shared concepts. In using language in anti-sensical ways – breaking the usual ties between a sound/image and its meaning, or between one word and those which follow it grammatically – Knowles and Wilson elude the formulations of the exterior screen. In doing so, however, they reduce words to raw phonetic or visual material which can then be used to create patterns of a different kind. Knowles and Wilson do not structure their words to generate new meanings; rather, they strip words of their usual meaning in order to build new *structures*.

These practices produce not sign systems, structures of sense, but structures *per se*, and such structuration is evident at all levels of Wilson's theatre. As we noted, he plans and executes his plays with an eye for detail, arranging individual components within the greater whole to create painterly tableaux. As a result the time/space of his work bears the stamp of organisation, with entrances, exits and processions across the stage synchronised, and characters blocked to effect visual harmonies. Images and activities may be positioned to imply comparisons, so that in *A Letter for Queen Victoria* a slender black actress, dressed in black and elevated on a ladder, was posed against a more statuesque white actress, dressed in white and standing solidly on the stage floor. Simultaneously each shed her outer garments to reveal costumes of the opposite colour beneath, maintaining the contrast even while inviting comparison. Similarly, 'rituals', activities enacted with scripted precision, feature in almost all his productions, while even idiosyncratic movements are tightly choreographed: arranged into dance-like sequences, repeated as *leitmotivs*, and orchestrated into mass 'ballets'; in *Freud* and *Deafman Glance* thirty performers dressed as black 'mammies' danced in unison, the spectacle transformed into waltzing ostriches in *Stalin*. The overall effect is of a discernible patterning, that 'craftedness' which infers an underlying scheme.

Emphases of this kind are not uncommon in recent American performance. In his theatre-like pieces choreographer Alwin Nikolais typically presented his audience with startling images – dancers swathed in silk or gauze, hidden in great machine-like costumes, or dancing in darkness so that only their luminous masks were visible – using movement to create constantly evolving shapes in time/space. In her *Whispers, the Waves, the Wind* (1984) Suzanne Lacy arranged 150 women in white clothes about white tables on a real beach at La Jolla, California, to construct a complex, repetitive picture; in *The Crystal Quilt* (1987), her meditation on the condition of old age, she used 430 older women dressed in black and seated around tables covered in red and yellow cloths, to create a quilt-like motif. Although different in aim and content, these works display a concern most of all with visual structure *as* structure, individual components being deployed within greater wholes to create patterns which are abstract but emphatically systematic.

Those practices of Wilson's which order the concurrent presentation of objects/events are paralleled by others which pattern the play's development through time. Each of the sets of *Stalin's* seven acts was designed to reflect visually its opposite in the act structure, so that the barrenness of act one's beach scene imagistically recurred in act seven's planet surface, act three's dim and enclosed cave was echoed in act five's temple, and so on. Appropriately, *Einstein on the Beach* was built upon mathematical principles. The piece was composed of nine scenes and incorporated three dominant image-complexes, a train/building, a courtroom/bed and a field/spacecraft. Each image recurred every third scene, so that a train or building, for example, featured in scenes one, four and seven. The spectator was thus offered a continuous scenic picture, each set evoking an earlier one and itself being echoed later.

Such temporal patterning takes its most interesting form in a technique we may call *transformation*, where the image is not merely repeated but evolves. The three cyprus trees that adorned the first act of *Alcestis* (1986) became temple columns in the second, and smoking chimney stacks in the third, while the image-complexes of *Einstein on the Beach* similarly altered with each appearance: scene one's train, reappearing in an altered form in scene four, was echoed in line and graphic style in the image of a building in scene seven. The tree that was the central motif of *the CIVIL warS* was felled near the start, to be refigured in later sections as a series of objects; a log cabin, a boat, a book, finally reappearing as a tree.

For the audience the effect of such devices is more than one of simple aesthetic harmony. Built of semically neutralised materials – meaningless 'words', idiosyncratic movement, repeating designs – the structures Wilson constructs do not offer meaningful connections; the visual echoes between *Stalin*'s sets tell us nothing *about* those locations, any more than patterned word-sounds constitute meaningful utterances. Rather, they present spectators with the fact of structuration, inferring a fictional world whose elements obey some organisational logic, and which are therefore intelligible, decodable.

Thus although there is no rationale to the event – or at least, none accessible to an onlooker – structuration indicates that there is. With its parallels and contrasts, echoings and synchronisations, Wilson's stage invites interpretation, for when we see elements organised and repeated, actions and images compared, contrasted and 'transformed', we assume there is a purpose, a meaning to be read into those relationships. We address such structures as signs; or, more accurately, take them to indicate that the components out of which those structures are built are signs. We therefore scrutinise the literal, visual connections in search of links of a conceptual kind, attempting thereby to elicit the key by which the other-place may be understood.

While such devices encourage spectators to view the stage as a locus, however, others signal the opposite. Not only did the set for *The King of Spain* depict two different locations, the stage was further divided into seven lateral strips, what Wilson calls 'zones'. Most of the play's activities were performed within the confines of one zone, so that, seen from the auditorium, the playing space seemed to be composed of separate tiers, distinct realms between which there was no interaction. Wilson continued to use zones in subsequent productions, most potently perhaps in *Alcestis*, where the upstage area was laid with soil and grass, the middle with tiles reminiscent of an ancient road, while the front of the stage was paved with tarmac, suggesting a locus divided not only spatially but temporally.

Foreman has divided his stage in a similar way, in *Pandering to the Masses* suspending strings across its width to create the effect of a grid or chart. But Wilson's zones are merely the most obvious example of a more general fragmentation of the playing area. Many of his productions have employed raised platforms to isolate some actions from the rest. In *Stalin* the heads of a chorus were thrust up through holes in two small, sand-strewn stages projecting out from the main stage into the auditorium; in *the CIVIL warS* the faces of a similar chorus, eerily lit from below, could be seen under the stage's overhang. The prologue to *KA MOUNTAIN* was staged in a series of rooms about a court-yard, in which apparently unrelated events were enacted, and *KA MOUNTAIN* itself moved gradually up the real mountain on which it was performed, this shifting, mobile space further diffused by the multitude of pasteboard houses, papier-mâché flamingos and so on deployed over the terrain.

This fragmentation of space impacts upon the spectator's reading. Almost all forms of theatre offer us a clearly defined playing area. Most literally, the bounded space tells us what is part of the performance and what is not. It is therefore instrumental in establishing a locus; like the proscenium arch, the borders of the performance space mark an interpretative boundary, signifying that all that falls within their compass is to be read as part of an other-place. In dividing his stage, signifying a multiplicity of spaces, Wilson undermines the locus – not simply by fragmenting space, but by signifying a separation of those fragments, thus effecting a breakup of the other-place in the audience's gaze.

Representing a single fictional world, space is the largest interpretative unity posited by the Abstract register, but its breakup is paralleled on Wilson's stage by a fragmentation of that smaller but equally important unity, the human subject. Like Foreman, Wilson sometimes attached microphones to his actors, relaying their voices through speakers positioned about the auditorium. He has even miked inanimate objects, so that when one character poured a glass of water in *The King of Spain* the sound emerged from places far removed from the action. Similarly, Wilson's choreography frequently requires actors to move only a hand or limb while keeping their bodies still, often emphasising the split by focusing a spotlight upon the moving part. In separating the human action/speaker from its sound/speech, or limb from body, Wilson effects a division of the fictional subject comparable to his fragmentation of space. If his techniques of structuration encourage spectators to address objects/events as parts of a unified text, these devices demonstrate their *discontinuity*.

Signs of discontinuity also disrupt attempts to read the development of Wilson's plays through time. Even when we are offered no story as such, as spectators we still assume that stage events comprise some kind of purposeful sequence. We thus try to link one image with the next, and ascribe significance to changes and continuities, seeking to make of the unfolding action a temporal chain whose links are meaningful; that is, we seek to narrativise it by other means, find a conceptual rationale in the absence of any obvious plot. But Wilson's stagecraft frustrates all such attempts. Objects and actions appear indistinctly in his theatre – figures move half-visibly through forests, the activities of one zone obscure those of another – and several events may occur simultaneously, diffusing action, offering no point of focus. Such strategies deny audiences the means of determining what is or will be significant, which of the event's many fragments can be deployed to form a meaningful chain.

Such narrative discontinuity is evident in Wilson's treatment of iconic figures. As we noted, many of his plays deal with historical personalities: *Freud, Stalin, A Letter for Queen Victoria, Einstein on the Beach* and *Edison* (1979) all feature their eponymous heroes; *Death, Destruction and Detroit* is built around the life of Rudolf Hess, and a host of others, from Ivan the Terrible to Lincoln, Robert E. Lee and Garibaldi, have trodden his stage. We have seen that characters such as these can never be culturally neutral. Audiences inevitably bring to the theatre a host of shared associations, ideas about their lives and personalities, their place in history and so on. In this sense they are already narrativised, informed and explained by existing 'stories'.

But Wilson's treatment refutes all explanations of this kind. In approaching such figures he works subjectively, compiling visual images, isolated historical facts, his personal responses; combining fragments of all kinds to build impressionistic collages. *Einstein on the Beach* incorporated a wealth of images unearthed by Wilson and his collaborators. Some evoked obvious associations with Einstein: a space ship, pages of mathematical computations, a figure who wrote formulae on an invisible blackboard, and a number of clocks, even one which became 'eclipsed', evoking the stellar event on which the physicist's theory of relativity was founded. But other elements remained obscure. Laurence Shyer has described how, after finding a photograph in which Einstein made a curious gesture with his finger and thumb, Wilson made this a motif of the piece's choreography (see Shyer 1989: 226); an experiment he had conducted, which involved shooting light through giant water barrels, was rendered onstage with two performers lying on their backs on glass tables. A bed, a trial, the trains themselves – these and other images were central to the work, yet their connection to its central character was apparent only to Wilson and his circle. Einstein was effectively denarrativised, placed in imagistic networks very different from the cultural texts in which he is ordinarily enmeshed.

Wilson's most potent device for frustrating *temporal* narrativisation, however, is to be found in acting itself. The murder with which *Deafman Glance* opened was carried out not only in silence but also without any visible sign of feeling. The mother's face remained composed and inexpressive throughout, her movements observably controlled even when stabbing her children. The act was thus rendered curiously flat, stripped of any emotional, psychological dimension. This is characteristic of Wilson's work, for whether dancing, speaking, conducting rituals or enacting more everyday activities, performances are most often devoid of the kinds of details – tones of voice, facial expressions, pauses, falterings and small gestures – which customarily indicate 'depth', signify a self lying beneath the character's physical manifestation, the wilful origin of its behaviour.

We customarily interpret action on the stage by seeking the logic which powered it, using what we have learned of the locus, and of the character's personality, situation and so on. That is, we view the action as the effect, looking beyond it in search of its cause. Spectators are usually aided in this by signs that indicate which species of cause should be sought; Strasbergian and Stanislavskian acting provide signs of psychology, while Brechtian theatre signifies social and ideological factors. But Wilson's stage offers no such signs. Just as its events proceed without any discernible logic, so its acting is dispassionate, lacking not only psychology but causes *per se*. Audiences are therefore denied the usual means of interpreting events in terms of their motivating forces. Behaving without discernible reason, characters present the audience with a fictional reality which is *acausal*.

But if dispassionate acting denies spectators an interpretative logic, it is with his stretching of time that Wilson problematises the very process of reading. He has argued that time in his plays is not slowed but natural, corresponding, one might assume, to the pace of the Earth's rotation, the changing of the seasons, and so on. Nevertheless a mechanical tortoise may take forty minutes to cross his stage, and a murder last an hour, and action in his theatre proceeds at a much slower pace than that encountered elsewhere.

Time is of course the dimension of cause and effect, on the stage as in everyday life. We seek to understand stage events as the result of what went before, view the past as the cause of the fictional present. As a consequence, much of our understanding is achieved retrospectively. When an object/event first appears we do not necessarily know what its full significance will be. We therefore hold it in abeyance, developing and adapting our interpretation as connections between it and other objects/events become apparent. The connections thus made plot the 'physics' that governs the unfolding of events, and which we may use to understand them. It is through time, then, that we make full sense of what we see; by tracing connections between objects and actions in sequence, we discern the rationale – social, psychological or, in the case of Brookian ritual theatre, spiritual – with which they may be read.

This tracing of connections is resisted by Wilson's manipulation of time. As we have seen, many of his works are extraordinarily long, and lack all consistency and coherence, narrative (causal) or imagistic (associative). With no means of settling the significance of what we are shown, the material we must hold in abeyance mounts up, gradually overwhelming our capacity. At the same time, slow motion prompts us to greater scrutiny of that material. We usually encounter slow motion in situations where, as in a televised sports 'action replay', slowness enables us to discern details invisible at normal speed; to trace the process, say, by which a footballer scores a goal. We are accustomed to scrutinising the slowed action for greater explanatory information, and therefore take slow motion as a sign of concentrated meaning. But Wilson's theatre refuses to satisfy that expectation, making no such information available. The effect is to render the performance perceptually discontinuous through time. As we examine each action for greater meaning that it can yield, we break it up perceptually, isolate each part within our intense interpretative gaze. Extended over long periods in slow motion, even simple actions are stripped of their sequentiality; walking becomes broken down – one foot lifts, is moved forward, is laid down again – atomised into discrete activities. The very continuity of action in time upon which causal and imagistic connections depend is lost, as we scan each fragment of the sequence for a significance that it cannot render.

THE INTERIOR SCREEN

The key to the dialogic relations proffered by Wilson's stage lies in the contradictory nature of the demands it makes of its audience. His theatre presents spectators with two distinct species of device. First, its evocative yet non-consistent imagery suggests an other-place, a dreamscape whose objects / actions can only be interpreted using logics alien to ordinary social space. Slow motion and special effects reinforce this sense of radical other-ness, while perspective and mimetic or spectacular sets signify a distinct, unified *place*. The latter is augmented by signs of structuration, for by inferring connections between the event's various parts they signal that all must be addressed as components of a single whole. Together these indicate that the event is to be viewed as a symbolic unity, prompting spectators to seek the interpretative key, the Law of the Text, by which it may be read.

Signs of discontinuity, however, signify the opposite. By dividing the playing space, signalling the unrelatedness of the activities of discrete zones and fragmenting the performing subject, Wilson indicates that the event's components should be read separately. Crucially, these work to redefine other devices. Remobilised in a logic of discontinuity, the diversity of Wilson's imagery, expressive of the stage's other-ness, also functions as a sign of its lack of coherence. A similar disunity is effected along the temporal dimension. The diffusing of focus, denarrativisation of culturally resonant figures and dispassionate acting all resist the spectator's attempts to weave images and occurrences into a sequence which is coherent in the Pavisian sense, symbolically unified and therefore meaningful. Slow motion itself, symbol of the stage's other-ness and so of the other-place, similarly deprives the event of continuity, breaking actions into discrete units in the spectator's over-energised interpretative gaze.

This second species of device represents a radical departure from orthodox theatre practice, and, as we noted, effectively signifies the absence of any Law of the Text. But in fact the effect is more profound. We saw in the Introduction that the Law of the Text is ultimately founded in the audience's assumption that the event proffers meaning which is both intentional and organised; spectators address the stage as a source of willed, coherent meaning, as an interlocutor, its partner in dialogic relations, and it is on this basis that we view the event's parts as a readable whole, a text. Thus audiences often 'find' coherent meaning even in accidents, 'signs' which are unintentional. But with signs of discontinuity, indicating that its objects/events are unconnected, Wilson's stage signifies that it cannot be viewed as an interlocutor at all.

Thus Wilson's theatre signals two contradictory interpretative postures. On the one hand it indicates that the stage should be read as a symbolic unity, prompting spectators to seek the law which governs all its occurrences and so is the key to its interpretation; on the other, it presents itself as discontinuous, proffering no unified meaning, readable by no one rationale. These two interpretative logics function concurrently, so that each of the stage's elements is presented as both decodable and impenetrable. Wilson's stage abounds with what appear to be signifiers, material, manufactured phenomena – startling images, patterned word sequences, crafted and synchronised movements and rituals – which advertise their own purposefulness and significance, demand to be scanned for meaning. But such meanings, such conceptual signifieds, are not only absent, their absence itself is, paradoxically, signified.

Audiences are therefore placed in a curious position, for the stage requires of its onlookers massive interpretative activity while reminding them that such activity can yield no real results. The spectator must go about the *process* of reading even as they are informed that there is nothing that can genuinely be read. Frustrated in their attempts to find *intentional* meaning, spectators can only excavate the spectacle of Wilson's stage, fulfil that half of their dialogic role, using their own symbolic resources; making such connections – between material sounds/images and concepts – as their imaginations provide. That is not to say we each develop our own stable interpretation, for without an interlocutor, a unitary 'speaker', we have no basis for assuming that meaning should be stable at all. Rather, interpretation becomes provisional, slips and slides as we affix to the stage's objects/events one concept, then another. The ultimate effect is a dissolving of the fundamental relation of the sign, the tie between the signifier and the signified. By employing two species of device to antithetical ends, Wilson denies the mechanism by which culture *per se* generates its meanings; the 'signs' which his spectators manufacture are personal ones, built upon links born of their own interior screens.

On this basis one might argue that Wilson's theatre accesses imaginative depths unique to each member of the audience; that he succeeds in overturning the cultural, exterior screen in favour of the interior. But this must be questioned. It is true that his theatre does bring our private networks of associations into play. But those networks ultimately derive from our contact with the world, and the world we encounter is predominantly a social one. Thus is true even of infancy, that period conventionally deemed most free of cultural impositions, most 'natural'. In the early stages of childhood we are not fully socialised, certainly, and so have not internalised society's cultural norms. But the world that provides our experiences, and from which we build our earliest conceptual models – our own systems of images – is one already shaped by social structures. The relationships between members of our family (including ourselves) and between our family and others, as well as the rules surrounding such natural, pre-cultural processes as defecating and eating, the kinds of food eaten, the clothes worn – in fact, almost all that we encounter as infants derives from that collection of systems which we call culture. In this sense our imaginations are already colonised by cultural forms; the interior screen is itself built of the exterior.

This leaves little possibility of Wilson's theatre eluding the exterior screen. In reality, its effect is less psychoanalytic than semiotic. We have noted that any sign may be mobilised within various discourses and so may be granted a variety of meanings. Usually the Law of the Text limits that potential over-determinacy of meaning, for by ensuring that all stage signs be interpreted according to one logic, it contains the reading of each. But when the Law of the Text is indicated to be absent, signs retain their potential for multiple interpretation. The spectator is free to play with the different symbolic connections available to each, under the assumption that no one meaning is more intentional than another. Thus it is not that we ascribe the components of Wilson's stage meanings peculiar to ourselves. We grant it unique *collections* of meanings, but meanings nevertheless drawn from an existing cultural pool, reiterating those already circulating in society.

Wilson's project is not entirely unique, for we have seen that other practitioners have experimented with a theatre of structure and of the grand but elusive image. But we can better understand the historical significance of Wilson's work by placing it in the broader context of artistic experiment in America.

It was during the 1940s and 1950s that modern American art first rose to world prominence, and, continuing the tradition of modernism, its ascent involved a wholesale interrogation of existing aesthetic assumptions. Most notable in this respect was the school that came to be known as Abstract Expressionism. For abstract painter Jackson Pollock, even experimental modernist painting had not entirely succeeded in breaking with the traditions of academy or 'easel' art, for it still functioned within the limits of the frame. In Pollock's view, the use of a real or metaphorical frame inevitably rendered painting representational. A picture may be 'framed' in many ways: literally, of course, but also by mimesis, by depicting the world; in composition, by arranging its components implicity to acknowledge the edge of the canvas; or simply by contriving the illusion of a spatial depth distinct from the flatness of the real canvas. The effect of all such frames, however, is to separate the work from the world, indicating that it must be viewed differently. Frames render the painting symbolic, *about* something else. In response Pollock dripped paint onto canvases as they lay on the floor, denying his trained hand the opportunity to work in its customary way, creating works that were two-dimensional – never exceeding the plane of the canvas – unframed, and to a degree unintentional. By such means he sought to ensure that his work remained non-representational, non-symbolic; it was not to be about some other thing but a thing itself.

Although Abstract Expressionism represents a reaction against the perceived shortcomings of modern art, its project was nevertheless high modernist. As we have noted, modernism sought to reach beyond given representations of the world to depict a deeper, truer reality. Taking this to its logical conclusion, Pollock's aim was essentially an escape from representation *per se*, for, unframed, a thing rather than a representation of other things, his painting eschewed 'depiction' entirely to remain genuinely real. But subsequent years saw the emergence of a quite different artistic ethos. In their first exhibition Robert Rauschenberg's 'White Paintings' were lit so that the viewers' shadows fell across the canvases, making their positions a part of the work. The paintings of Roy Lichtenstein reproduced the graphics of comic books, while Jasper Johns painted non-representational signs (numbers, a bull's-eye target, the Stars and Stripes), bringing about a collision between their pure functionality and his painterly representation. Andy Warhol reproduced familiar images – branded soup tins, journalistic photographs, cultural icons such as Marilyn Monroe, Mao Tse-tung and Mick Jagger – reinscribing the visible surface of western mass culture on canvas. Far from seeking to escape representation, these artists dealt in the representation *of* representation, self-consciously framing existing cultural frames.

Such work figured a broader cultural change. The late twentieth century is unique in that, as a partial consequence of new communications technologies, social subjects are bombarded with signification in a way never before possible. Via television, film, advertising hoardings, product packaging, fashion, news-papers and magazines we are the constant target of 'messages'. In Althusser's terminology, we are 'hailed' without pause in both our public and private spaces, proffered commercially and ideo-logically derived subject positions in every sphere of life.

Cultural theorist and Situationist Guy Debord characterised this new era as the 'Society of the Spectacle' (Debord 1977). In previous epochs, he explained, capitalism had taken the useful fruits of human labour and turned them into commodities, replacing real use-value with exchange-value so that *worth* became purely a function of an object's place in the economic system, of what it could be exchanged *for*. But late capitalism, Debord argued, has taken this logic to its conclusion by turning representation itself into a commodity. In the Society of the Spectacle, representations and images are produced and con-sumed *as* images rather than as tokens of meaning. The result is a dissolution of the sign. The primary relation of the sign, between signifier (image) and signified (concept), is over-whelmed by the exchange of signifiers, an economic relation in which each is ascribed value solely in terms of its equivalence to others. Meaning becomes peripheral as signifiers are reduced to mere commodities equivalent to, and exchanged for, other commodities. The effect is to disconnect the subject from reality and from meaning, such that the spectacle of images comes to stand in for reality itself. The Society of the Spectacle thus effects a simulation of a reality that does not exist, with representation abstracted and functioning according to the logic of the market place.

This theory fed into that wider body of writing dealing with what has been termed 'postmodernism'. Postmodernism has been explicated in markedly different ways by different theo-rists, but in the most general sense we can describe it as that moment or epoch which recognises that what we deem 'reality' is itself a representation. Modernism sought to go beyond given representations to reach a deeper, truer reality. This can be seen as a continuation of the Enlightenment project; since the eigh-teenth century, 'modernity' in the broader sense has sought to overcome previous misconstructions of the world to find more accurate truths. But postmodernism entails the recognition that all such truths are themselves constructions, meanings that have been made. Thus postmodern art and theory tends to be

concerned not with depths but with surfaces; representing representation, framing the frame – concerned less with truth and
meaning than with the means by which the *effect* of truth and
meaning are created.

Caught at the surface of representation, the postmodern artist
is left with broadly two options. Recognising that all meaning is
constructed, one can create artworks which expose this, and by
doing so problematise meaning's manufacture; Rauschenberg's
'White Paintings' brought the viewer's own role in meaning-
making into the frame. By this means cultural producers may
provide an empowering understanding of cultural processes,
ultimately undermining ideological constructions of the world
by making apparent the very mechanisms by which ideology is
generated. Postmodern art of this kind continues modernism's
rupturing of representation while disavowing its claim to a
higher truth.

Alternately, one can exploit contemporary culture's celebration
of surface and its resulting relativisation of meaning. If the first
option is radical, seeking to assault mechanisms of power, the
second is reactionary. Whereas Rauschenberg's paintings demonstrated their *actual* relation to the real, work of this kind severs
representation *from* reality, making of art a separate realm which
operates according to the exchange-logic of the market. It is
therefore inherently supportive of the *status quo*. In reproducing
the kinds of images offered by mass culture – Campbell's Tomato
Soup, the face of Monroe – Warhol, for example, ascribes them
value *as* images, signifiers without signifieds, re-enacting the
semiotic logic of late capitalism. Indeed, later artists go further.
Jeff Koons takes objects already recognised as kitsch – a
sentimental toy dog, a model train – and, by reproducing them
in precious metals, renders them 'art'. In granting them value
as the representation of the representation *of* the representation,
all purchase on the real, the represen*ted*, is lost.

It is this cultural logic which is affirmed in the audience's
interpretative experience of Wilson's theatre. Like Warhol and
Koons, Wilson takes culturally resonant images of the kind circu-
lated through the organs of mass culture: kitsch moonlit skies,
cowboys and Indians, Stalin, Einstein and Abraham Lincoln. He
then signals that the meaning to be ascribed them is arbitrary,
a matter of personal choice. His theatre is concerned with the
surface of representation: its depths, its true or false relation to

a tangible, material reality – these are indicated to be irrelevant. Wilson's work does not rupture representation, merely relativises it. He frames the event as symbolic, separate from social space, then denies it symbolic depth, reducing signs to images with no possible purchase on the real. The potential for meaning his theatre offers is, as we noted, always bounded by culture; we play with the associations suggested by his images, but associations drawn from the available cultural pool. The 'freedom' his work offers is therefore the freedom of the consumer, to choose whatever collections of meanings one wishes on the assumption that all are of equivalent value. Representation thus takes on the commercial logic of the market place, with images valued only *as* images, as spectacle.

It is spectacle that Wilson's theatre offers most of all. We can regard spectacle as the literal incarnation of capital, for, prior to any 'message' a work may seek to convey, spectacle first tells us what it cost. It is the guarantee that underwrites the contract between producer and consumer, stage and auditorium, for special effects, large spaces and casts, dazzling and carefully contrived illusion – all these signify value, but a value which is purely economic. Wilson emphasises this by making the event semically gratuitous; for, stripped of given meaning, his theatre consists of the pure expression of its own expense. It becomes the theatrical equivalent of gratuitous consumption, its expenditure of real material resources for the generation of images made more emphatic because those images are hollow.

7

POSTMODERNISM AND PERFORMANCE ART

IT HAPPENS

Central to postmodernism is the recognition that 'reality' is itself a construction, a representation. Human subjectivity makes-sense of its world, imposes upon it a meaningful design using those conceptual tools culture provides. We never encounter the real world, only culturally shaped formulations of it, so that the reality we experience is 'textual' even as we perceive it. But such texts can be disrupted by certain forms of radical cultural artefact, among them what is termed 'live art' or 'performance art'.

For cultural theorist Jean-François Lyotard the postmodern is not an epoch but a moment in which we recognise the limits of representation (see Lyotard 1984: 79–82; and 1989: 196–211). This moment is generated by modernism itself. We have seen that modernism was in large part a reaction against the art and thought of the nineteenth century. The discourses central to its development, the writings of Freud, Marx, Saussure and others, displaced old views of reality and the human subject, seeking to posit deeper, truer laws. This was paralleled by innovations in art. Since in the modernist view perception was mediated by unconscious forces, shaped by ideology and by the systems of signs to which we are heir, reality was by definition other than it appeared. Thus realism, the attempt to simulate that appear-ance, was fundamentally flawed, and the early twentieth century was marked by a series of artistic movements which sought to figure the world in new, non-realistic ways.

But as Lyotard points out, in order to offer new conceptual models of reality, modernist art and thought first had to displace existing ones. The attempts of modernist discourse to reach beyond the surface of the real to its 'depths' subverted previous modes of meaning-making before its own formulations had gained sufficient cultural currency to take their place. It is in this moment – the point at which old views of the world are undermined but new views are not yet secure – that we encounter that which eludes the modes of sense available to us, a necessarily indefinable 'something' that partakes of what Lyotard calls the 'sublime'. He states:

Modern aesthetics is an aesthetics of the sublime, though a nostalgic one. It allows the unpresentable to be put forward only as the missing contents; but the form, because of its recognisable consistency, continues to offer to the reader or viewer matter for solace or pleasure. ... [However] The postmodern would be that which, in the modern, puts forward the unpresentable in representation itself; that which denies itself the solace of good forms, the consensus of a task that would make it possible to share collectively the nostalgia for the unattainable, that which searches for new presentations not in order to enjoy them but in order to impart a stronger sense of the unpresentable.

(Lyotard 1984: 81)

For Lyotard, then, two possibilities for art arise from modernism. The first is what he terms the modernist avant-garde. This 'presents the unpresentable', illustrates that there is something which escapes representation, which eludes available strategies for making meaning. In doing so, however, it proffers that knowledge *as* meaning. By presenting the spectator with the unpresentable in a familiar, accessible form – offering the 'solace of good form' – the artwork renders itself knowable; it signifies that the world cannot be encompassed by available modes of sense, certainly, but that signification is itself a way of making sense of it. Beckett's theatre, for example, declares all meanings to be manufactured, but this paradoxically becomes its meaning, a way of knowing the stage event and the world, albeit as a thing/place defiant of knowing. Thus the modernist avant-garde offers a vision of meaning's absence, of the sublime, but in the process codifies that absence, quantifies the failure of quantification so that our view of the world as a place of meaning is obliquely reaffirmed.

The second possibility, the genuinely postmodern, is more radical, albeit that it also arises from modernism. Avoiding all familiar cultural forms, the postmodern artwork 'puts forward the unpresentable in presentation itself', offers the viewer no way of making sense of it. Instead of declaring meaninglessness as a meaning, it remains meaningless, impenetrable to available strategies of interpretation. But in demonstrating that it lies outside the limits of representation, it illustrates that representation *has* limits. It is not that we can 'know' what is beyond knowledge; rather, we recognise that there *is* something beyond the kinds of knowledge available to us. Thus the postmodern work forces us to recognise that reality is something other than our formulations of it, and that those formulations are therefore constructs; in Lyotard's terms, to recognise 'the incommensurability of thought with the world'.

In practice this entails radical formal experiment. The postmodern artwork is that which is geared towards what Lyotard calls 'novatio'; the relentlessly new, the disorientatingly innovative. Using no aesthetic language accessible to the viewer, it offers no subject position from which it can be viewed. We experience the object as 'pure occurrence', possessing a radical singularity, a uniqueness, in that it is not equivalent or 'commensurate' with any existing thought. We are thus confronted with the fact of the object/event happening before we can know *what* is happening. The ultimate experience of the postmodern work is of 'it happens'.

The degree to which postmodern art in Lyotard's sense can be fully realised is open to question. Human beings are sense-making animals. That is not to say we necessarily understand, or even believe we understand, all that we perceive. Rather, subjectivity, consciousness, is built of the positions we take up in discourse, *consists* of our adoption of ways of making meaning. Since the Lyotardian postmodern artwork is to remain pure phenomenon, a thing which cannot be explained even in terms of its inexplicability, this effectively requires that the viewer lose consciousness – lose not only that mode of sense which would enable us to render the work meaningful, but also those other modes which would enable us to recognise it as senseless.

But if the Lyotardian postmodern work seems unrealisable in an absolute sense, it is nevertheless possible for works to refute existing modes of seeing in ways which are fundamental. As noted in the Introduction, we view objects/events through 'frames', culturally derived categories which, in defining *what* we see, determine *how* we see it. When an object is presented as a painting we approach it in given ways, employing strategies different from those we would use with a sculpture or a dance – or, more significantly perhaps, a teapot or table. All may be aesthetically shaped but we interrogate each differently, and sometimes for different kinds of meaning. Frames, then, constitute the foundations of sense-making, for they determine how we perceive and read works. Thus the exploding of such frames – even in limited, partial and momentary ways – effects the most potent assault against available strategies for making meaning.

One of the genres with the potential to effect such disruption is performance art, for its key characteristic as a cultural form is that it has no given form. 'Theatre' proper as defined today is very diverse, but its diversity has limits which, if exceeded, effectively renders the event no longer theatre; our culture's conception of what theatre is continually alters, but we always *have* a cultural conception of theatre. Performance art, however, has no generic limits, for it uses no single, recognisable aesthetic language. The live art event may consist of anything, and so provokes and satisfies no expectations – its only requirement is that it happens. Consequently it permits no certain framing, denying spectators any secure ways of making sense. In the following sections we shall examine four basic strategies by which performance has courted such explosions of meaning. In previous chapters we have focused upon the work of a single practitioner. But as we shall see, the figure of 'the author' itself constitutes a conceptual frame, a way of directing and organising our interpretative activities along given lines. It is therefore appropriate that this chapter be organised thematically, and address the work of a range of practitioners within the field of performance or live art.

THE FOUND OBJECT

In 1917 French artist Marcel Duchamp exhibited his 'sculpture' *Fountain*, which consisted of an ordinary porcelain urinal. This was one of a series of what he termed 'Ready Mades', common, utilitarian objects – a snow shovel, bicycle wheel, bottle rack –

presented in their unaltered, often factory-fresh state as 'art'. Duchamp's use of such *objets trouvés* or 'found objects' inaugurated a significant trend in twentieth-century artistic experiment. In the next decade Dadaist Kurt Schwitters began his 'Merz paintings', collages of urban junk and debris, while Pablo Picasso built animal sculptures from equally unlikely materials, creating a cow's head out of a bicycle saddle and handle bars, the face of an ape with a toy car, and so on.

Pieces of this kind may offer a variety of meanings. Schwitters' and Picasso's creations provided oblique commentary on society's conception of what is disposable, while Duchamp's Ready Mades, echoing the tone of his bearded and moustached version of the *Mona Lisa*, playfully challenged the seriousness with which artworks were customarily received. But at the same time, all such works highlight a key mechanism in our perception of art. *Fountain's* urinal was not only indecorous, but familiar and emphatically functional, clearly inappropriate as an aesthetic object. It was, moreover, mass-produced and shown in its original form. With nothing added by Duchamp's hand, it offered little possibility of finding in it meanings intentionally encoded by its creator. Yet because it was exhibited not in a lavatory but in a gallery, and was surmounted by its title and the artist's name, *Fountain* signalled that it was to be viewed as a work of art.

The circumstances in which it was shown, then, themselves provoked the generation of the meanings ascribed to *Fountain*, the venue, title and artist's name acting as 'framing signifiers'. As we noted in the Introduction, framing signifiers are the material equivalents of conceptual boundaries, separating the work from the objects of ordinary social space. When a sculpture is placed on a plinth, a painting is framed, or a piece of theatre enacted in a specially demarcated time/space, we understand that the work is to be viewed in a special way. We therefore address it as symbolic, about something else, reading the material object for its conceptual content. Because our reading of framing signifiers is usually unconscious, we consequently regard the meanings we derive as inherent to the works themselves. But by framing objects of such obvious banality, Duchamp foregrounded the viewer's own role in the generation of sense. It is not merely that his Ready Mades lacked symbolic meaning; rather, viewers were invited to find symbolic meaning in objects which were categorically non-symbolic, and, frustrated in their attempt, were thrown back to their recognition of the thing as thing. *Fountain* mockingly asked spectators to find aesthetic value in a urinal, the very experience demonstrating that such values were imposed, and therefore constructed.

This strategy, which we may call 'framing the everyday', was central to modernist experiment. The early modernist movement of Futurism celebrated what it saw as the dynamism of the new technological age of the early twentieth century, the era of aeroplanes, cars and furious factory production. Rejecting the stultifying fixedness of traditional 'bourgeois' artforms – the static representations of orthodox realism, the sculpture standing immobile in the museum – Futurist paintings were filled with images of speed and collision, expressive of the energy deemed intrinsic to the new culture of machines. Most important for our purposes were those innovations by which Italian Futurists sought a comparable liberation from the confines of traditional performance. Futurist cabarets offered audiences a bewildering mixture of non-logical playlets and recitations, and 'music' such as the compositions of Luigi Russolo, who combined traffic sounds with the shouts of crowds to create an 'art of noise'. The leading light of Italian Futurism, Filippo Marinetti, developed a form of poetry termed *parole in libertà* or 'word-freedom', a chaotic stream of words, liberated from the norms of grammar and syntax as well as from the stasis of the written text. Dadaist performance similarly entailed presenting as art events which refuted that categorisation. Tristan Tzara's 'poetry recital' in the first Dadaist review to take place in Paris involved his reading aloud from a newspaper article. The sound of an electric bell rendered his words inaudible so that, true to Tzara's intentions, the sight of his ordinary facial expressions and bodily gestures were all the audience was offered to satisfy their curiosity as to the act's significance.

Today such events are perhaps less inexplicable, for the ideas which inform them are more widely disseminated and understood. At the time of their performance, however, they were imbued with Lyotardian *novatio*, possessing a newness disruptive of given modes of interpretation. Enacted in a recognisable performance venue, and supported by appropriate framing signifiers – including advertisements using such terms as 'cabaret' and 'poetry' – Futurist and Dadaist events signalled their readability to an audience which for the most part lacked the conceptual tools to read them. They therefore remained unquantified, pure acts; they simply 'happened'.

It was in the United States, however, that experiment such as this was carried to its logical conclusion. From its inception in 1933 the Black Mountain College in North Carolina was an important focus for experimental performance, attracting in the late 1940s practitioners such as composer John Cage and dancer Merce Cunningham (see Bigsby 1985: ch. 1). Cunningham eschewed all use of rhythm, narrative and mimesis, the components of traditional dance, instead choreographing ordinary movements such as walking, lifting and jumping. Acknowledging the influence of Duchamp and the Futurists, Cage's compositions used everyday audial materials – radio static and the sound of rain falling, cowbells, beer bottles and flowerpots – challenging audiences to question what defined certain kinds of sound and patterns of sound as 'music'. By performing in obvious art settings sounds so ordinary that they would usually be considered 'noise', Cage illustrated how the musical status of his work rested entirely upon a shared conceptual act, upon his use and the audience's recognition of framing signifiers.

Perhaps the most famous of Cage's works was his piece for piano in three movements entitled 4' 33", first performed in 1952. This 'composition' comprised no intentionally produced sound at all; the audience was informed that everything they heard should be regarded as music, after which the musician sat silently at his piano for the title's stated duration. In performance the piece is surprisingly disorientating. The audience is primed to listen, to find meaningful connections, patterns in sound. But with the instrument silent, the inevitable sounds produced by members of the audience themselves – coughs, whispers, the scraping of chairs – is the only available 'score'. Consequently ordinary background noise becomes subject to an unusual interpretative scrutiny. As the audioscape of the audience, 'found' sound, is framed as symbolic, examined in detail for the aesthetic qualities of musical arrangement, it becomes apparent that 4' 33" is not about silence but the sound of everyday life. Our interpretative focus is shifted, the space of the audience becoming material to be read. Indeed, the audience fragments, separates into distinct individuals as we become sensitive to the sounds we and our fellows produce. With no secure framing boundary, all everyday, environmental sound is potentially a part of the 'text'.

Principles such as these have suffused the practice of live art. In London in 1961 English conceptual artists Gilbert and George declared themselves 'living sculpture'; in their *Underneath the Arches*, announced as 'the most intelligent fascinating serious and beautiful art piece you have ever seen', the besuited artists, their faces painted gold, moved mechanically on a platform for six minutes to the accompaniment of the famous popular tune of the title. In Stephen Taylor Woodrow's *The Living Paintings* (1986) live models, their clothes and bodies encrusted with paint, hung completely still on a gallery wall. It is not that such actions/ objects (walking, the human body) ordinarily lack frames, for everyday life is itself shaped in our perception of it, presumed to express sense of certain given kinds. Rather, as ordinary events they are framed in different ways, credited with 'purpose' instead of overtly symbolic 'meaning', viewed not as signifying but 'natural'. Thus such performances effectively frame other frames. By juxtaposing one mode of sense against another, they demonstrate that different kinds of meaning may be made from the same thing, and that all sense is therefore generated in a process which involves the viewer.

This strategy takes what is perhaps its most fertile form with performances which frame the frames of other modes of performance. The first section of Meredith Monk's *Turtle Diaries* (1986), entitled 'Turtle Cabaret', opened on the image of a female performer, dressed in a sophisticated black skirt suit, stockings and high heels, and a hat whose broad brim hid her face. She held her clasped, spotlit hands before her and, to the accompaniment of fast, electronic music, wove her fingers into various shapes, creating lattices, circles, triangles and so on, all the while keeping her body still. Although the act was mesmerising, it was not at all clear how it was to be viewed until another performer appeared, an elegant middle-aged man smiling and carrying a black box; the box lit up to illuminate the word 'CABARET', and the man winked at the audience, saying 'Have a *really* great time'.

This compère figure thus provided spectators with a frame for understanding what was taking place. His interjection was followed by a series of 'turns': a woman wearing a ballet dancer's tutu tottered awkwardly across the stage; two

performers in white overalls, wigs, masks and gloves bent their
bodies into curious, boneless shapes; two men in large boots
strode back and forth while muttering indecipherable phrases.
In the section's final act six members of the company gathered
on the stage. Monk and another performer played a simple tune
on keyboards which, although repetitive, lacked the predictable
four-bar metre we expect of cabaret music; her companion
adopted the movements and 'suave' expression immediately
recognisable as those of a popular ballad singer. Monk also sang
a melody but in different time, its lyrics consisting of the words
'Sun-Gone-Day' repeated over and over. Her voice was joined
by those of two other performers, who sang harmonic accompaniment to the melody but using other lyrics and, again, a
subtly different metre. While this was taking place three other
members of the company performed a 'dance'; they stood at
ease, intermittently taking steps forwards, backwards and side-
ways, the whole clearly choreographed but according to no
temporal or spatial logic discernible to spectators.

For our purposes the key feature of 'Turtle Cabaret' was its
juxtaposition of contradictory frames. Each kind of performance
of course evokes its own unique interpretative frames, and so
construes its components in distinct ways. A chair placed on the
set of a realistic theatre piece, for example, will be read in
the Abstract register. Its style, size, colour and so on will be
scrutinised on the assumption that these may say something
about the playworld. The same chair on the stage of a comic's
or popular singer's show will be viewed differently, regarded
perhaps as expressing the performer's or stage manager's taste,
no more. Thus while one requires symbolic translation, the other
proffers only visual pleasure, and the latter is indicative of
cabaret in general. The 'variety' show typically consists of acts
which employ some special skill, one not usually possessed by
audience members, and offers pleasures of what seems to be a
sensual, non-symbolic kind: visual and audial spectacle, wonder,
laughter and so on.

It was by posing distinct interpretative regimes against one
another that 'Turtle Cabaret' problematised its own reception. In
indicating that it was to be viewed as cabaret, the compère
offered spectators a way of addressing its parts; they were to be
enjoyed as exhibitions of special skills. But this reading was
disturbed by the acts themselves, for the ballet dancer tottered

clumsily, the dances employed contradictory rhythms and the songs conflicting melodies, while the simplicity of the first performer's hand movements jarred with her sophisticated, vampish clothes. The final turn, reminiscent of the stage 'spectacular', lacked precisely the qualities we expect of such an event. All the acts were clearly the fruit of practice and rehearsal, but employed to contrive an appearance of crudity, naïvety or incompetence; it *was* an exhibition of special skills, a cabaret, but was also in some sense *about* cabaret.

This resulted in a radically uncertain position for the spectator. 'Turtle Cabaret' presented itself as both non-symbolic and symbolic *of* the non-symbolic. In practice, viewing the piece entailed oscillating between different conceptions of what was taking place, an ambiguity which pervaded even the micro-details of the performance. As Monk leaned forward to sing, the movement seemed both purely functional and a sign of a fictional persona; she was a singer yet also a performer playing a singer. This experience of interpretative ambiguity is one conjured by almost all performance art. As we noted, its defining characteristic as a cultural form is that it has no form, and hence permits no unequivocal framing. Typically the spectator seeks to formulate an interpretative posture by cobbling together those proper to other arts, graphic, plastic and performance. In employing the 'found' form of cabaret, Monk proffered frames neither of which were able to encompass the event entirely, thus leaving audiences with a phenomenon which remained to a degree indeterminate.

REFUSING THE FRAME

If 'Turtle Cabaret' framed as symbolic an activity usually considered to be unframed, then other live art adopted the opposite strategy. Gilbert and George's *The Meal* (1969) was an elaborate dinner prepared by Lord Snowdon's butler and a descendant of Mrs Beeton. English artist David Hockney sat as Guest of Honour, and thirty others paid to attend what was both a dinner party and, according to the artists, an important artistic occasion. Having declared themselves 'living sculpture', Gilbert and George had gone still further, denying all separation between their work and their existence as social beings to the extent that a 'private', unwatched event was deemed art. Similarly their

Laws of Sculptors included instructions on dress codes and behavioural decorum, inferring that artists' domestic activities must also be addressed in aesthetic terms, even though no audience witnesses them. If the work of Duchamp, Cage and Monk entailed framing the everyday, Gilbert and George in these later pieces conversely refused the explicit framing of their art altogether.

This principle was taken to its extreme in the performances of New York artist Vito Acconci. For his *Following Piece* (1969) Acconci chose passers by at random and secretly tailed them along the street until they entered a building, whereupon he would choose someone else and begin again. In *Seedbed* (1971) he lay out of sight beneath a ramp in an art gallery, masturbating while visitors walked overhead. These performances were effectively invisible; they had no audience, and so of course went unrecognised, unframed, as art. In contrast, others remained visible but were not discernible as performances. In 1975 artist Claire Watson lived beneath an upturned boat in the English countryside for the duration of several menstrual cycles without changing her underwear. There were no obvious clues to inform local people that she was not simply a homeless person or a hippie traveller; indeed, local people would visit and sometimes bring her food. Whatever feminist concerns may have inspired Watson's work, for our purposes it is most significant in that, although a performance, it went unframed as such. Like Acconci, she provided no framing signifiers, thus encouraging interpretations other than those normally deemed appropriate to art.

The public framing of such works as 'art' can only take place retrospectively, if and when the event features in journals, academic books and so on. The only possible framing signifiers arise from reportage, words and pictures which may appear much later, and may never be seen by those who experienced the events themselves. Describing his involvement with the English performance scene in the 1960s and 1970s, Jeff Nuttall recalled a series of lectures he gave on the college circuit (see Nuttall 1979). The lectures described the fantastically fictionalised lives of obscure Edwardian characters, the details of which were accepted as fact by unsuspecting audiences. These and other of Nuttall's similarly hoax events were not unframed but framed misleadingly, and unless participants happened upon

Nuttall's own account of his career, they would remain unaware of their involvement with avant-garde art; unaware, that is, of how those events might otherwise have been perceived.

Strategies such as these are extreme, perhaps ludicrously so, but they are effective. As we have seen, the categorisation 'art' brings with it a number of expectations. By priming spectators to view the object/event in a certain way, the label itself dictates the kinds of sense that may be deployed in its interpretation, and so the meanings it may generate. By remaining invisible, refusing to frame or framing misleadingly, performers elude this codification of their work. Because of its transience, live performance is an ideal medium for such exercises in refusing the artistic frame. By the time the performance has been recorded – and therefore quantified, fixed in words and photographs, media with their own strategies of sense – it has already irretrievably passed; long before we are made aware of what has happened, it *has* happened.

This eluding and problematisation of frames was developed in its most thoroughgoing form with an American tradition of performance, the 'Happening', a term coined to describe the work of such as Jim Dine, Robert Rauschenberg, Claes Oldenburg and, most importantly, Allan Kaprow. Spectators at Kaprow's *18 Happenings in 6 Parts* (1959) entered the open interior of a New York gallery to find three 'rooms' made of plastic sheeting, in which they were seated to face in different directions. They were then presented with a sequence of events: moving figures, readings, action paintings, slide projections, bells and amplified sound. The performance had no narrative or discernible themic thread, nor did it seem to possess any pre-determined order, different activities taking place concurrently in the three rooms. Moved from one room to another and seated to face in different directions, no two spectators witnessed the same events in the same sequence and from the same angle. No explanations were given for the event, no means to make sense of it, and it was experienced outside of any context save that of 'performance'. The only protocol offered – the sounding of a bell to indicate when to enter certain rooms or when to applaud – followed none of the behavioural conventions of any recognisable artform.

As we have seen, framing signifers may take many forms. Architectural arrangements (raised stages and scaffolds, proscenium arches), confinement within a defined space and/or time, adherence to the characteristics of a known genre – all these may function like the literal frame about a painting, signalling how the object/event is to be read. Even a work's coherence, its status as a unified whole, may serve to render it distinct from ordinary social space. But by eschewing narrative and thematic logic, generic consistency, a unified and recognisable spatial arrangement or even an experience of the same 'text', *18 Happenings in 6 Parts* denied audiences the conceptual markers required to fix its status. Indeed, in later works Kaprow and others moved out of recognisable gallery and performance spaces, for, as illustrated by Duchamp's *Fountain*, venue itself may signify the nature of the event. Kaprow's *Courtyard* (1962) indeed took place in the courtyard of a derelict hotel, while Claes Oldenburg staged performances in a car park, a car wash and a swimming pool. His *Store* (1961) was staged in a real store, its goods the objects he had made. Although visitors to *18 Happenings in 6 Parts* were denied the usual framing signifiers, they knew that some kind of performance was taking place. But as the Happening moved into social space even this was lost, with passers by experiencing the event having no clear idea of what it was.

One result of this invasion of ordinary social space was that the 'audience' became part of the event. With responses unmediated, the boundaries of the symbolic space are dissolved, so that, whereas Cage's *4' 33"* rendered social space symbolic, in *Courtyard* everything was potentially a feature of the performance. This dimension of the Happening was addressed most directly perhaps in Wolf Vostell's *You* (1964). Invited to the country home of a wealthy couple, spectators walked around the swimming pool and tennis courts along pathways littered with bones. Coming upon a variety of bizarre spectacles – a naked woman embracing a vacuum cleaner, a figure lying between inflated cows' lungs – their sheer viscerality and proximity (the path was narrow and there was no special, 'passive' space demarcated for spectators) provoked responses which became part of everyone's experience. Any vestigial determination on the part of guests to remain neutral observers was undermined by loudspeakers, which blared 'You – You – You ' and issued instructions for them to follow. Spectators watched and were watched by other spectators, were integrated into a piece which made all readable.

THE ERUPTION OF THE REAL

As the Happenings of Kaprow, Oldenburg and Vostell transformed spectators into 'collaborators', they also introduced a crucial new element: spontaneity. Refused interpretative frames, audiences were left without given protocols of response, and so could shape what happened in ways that were unpredictable. Such deliberate courting of chance effects and unforeseen occurrences had antecedents in both the European and American avant-garde. The Surrealists produced literary and visual collages of images using a technique which André Breton called 'psychic automatism'. Although Breton and his associates had read little of Freud's work, psychic automatism was similar in principle to the free association of thoughts that his psychoanalytic patients were encouraged to undertake. A kind of verbal or visual doodling, at random and without apparent purpose, it produced works which, according to Surrealists, eluded the usual forms and structures of meaning, tapping into the deeper, unsocialised truth of the unconscious.

By the late 1940s John Cage had begun his own experiments with what he termed 'chance procedures'. 4' 33" was the ultimate realisation of his notion of 'non-intentional music', for its sounds were produced randomly by the audience. This randomness itself refuted one conventional frame, that of the Author. Often we seek to interpret a work as the product of its creator's intentions, assuming that our own role entails decoding them, finding the 'message'. But with its multiple and inadvertent authorship, 4' 33" advertised the absence of any intended meaning at all.

Thus, although Breton and Cage both employed chance, the principles informing their work were different. Surrealists sought to break free of surface meanings to access a hidden and more profound reality. Viewed in their own terms, their work can therefore still be viewed as the unique, albeit unconscious expression of an individual, its elements read as psychic symbols of material ordinarily suppressed. In contrast, with his non-intentional music Cage sought to eschew individual expression entirely. For the audience of 4' 33" there was not one work, one meaningful, repeatable structure, for it was apparent to each listener that he or she heard a 'composition' which was singular and, in a sense, his or her own creation.

This rejection of intention is illustrated most clearly in Cage's collaborations with other artists, which extended beyond musical composition to incorporate diverse kinds of performance. His 'score' for *Untitled Event*, staged at Black Mountain College in 1952, consisted of precisely defined but overlapping time slots, which other artists were invited to fill; each participant was free to choose what he or she would do, but none knew what the others had planned. Responding to such 'purposeful purposelessness', Robert Rauschenberg played old records while David Tudor first performed on piano then poured water from one bucket to another, and others read poetry from the aisles; a dog chased Merce Cunningham through the audience as film clips were projected onto ceilings and walls. In 1964, Cage collaborated with Cunningham, Tudor and others in a piece entitled *Variation V*, in which performers danced on a stage striated with photo-electric cells, their movements randomly activating light and sound effects. Although both works proceeded within a broadly planned framework, the events as a whole were discernibly unpredictable (although not always unrepeatable – Cage recorded *Variation V* for future performance), and viewers could not therefore view them as the site of organised and intentional meaning.

Non-intentionality of this order has been incorporated into performance in various ways, perhaps most interestingly by using 'authors' who lack all potential for intention. German Joseph Beuys's *Coyote: I Like America and America Likes Me* (1974) 'began' when he arrived in New York wrapped in insulating material, to enter the enclosure which he would share with a live coyote for the next week. Consisting of his interaction with the animal, the performance was emphatically unscripted. Similarly, English performance artist Rose English's 'collaborator' in her show *My Mathematics* (1991) was a fully grown horse. The horse's actions could not be predicted absolutely, and, with the piece performed within the limited span of an ordinary theatre stage, its startled movements periodically threatened to thrust its bulk into the auditorium, constantly reminding onlookers of the randomness of what was taking place.

Like *Variation V*, Beuys's and English's performances comprised planned structures but included elements which advertised their own randomness. They thus encouraged spectators to read events (on the assumption that, being organised, they were purposeful, meaningful) while reminding them that parts could not be read. The actions of the horse and coyote were not merely senseless, for, placed in the midst of an act of sense-making, they constituted *absences* of sense; as we try to interpret the performances, discern what is happening in the representation, the animals' actions remind us that 'it happens' outside of representation. With sense juxtaposed against non-sense, the shows thus demonstrated that the modes of sense available had limits, and that reading/representation is therefore 'incommensurate' with the world. If what we take as 'reality' is readable because it is a construct, then the animals constituted an eruption into the performance of a necessarily indefinable 'something' beyond all possible knowing, a genuine, unformulatable real.

This unreadable real has often been suggested in performance by means of bodily exposure. Those bodies have of course most often belonged to women, a part of that subjection of the female form to the male gaze found throughout western culture. Given that history of subjection, it should be borne in mind that the writer is a man, and that the following comments are made from a necessarily male viewpoint.

Women artists have in recent decades consciously manipulated and redrawn images of the exposed female form. In 1963 Carolee Schneemann created *Eye Body*, an 'environment' in which various objects and materials were displayed, including her own naked and painted body. Her aim was to create an image of natural woman, to reclaim for women's bodies their 'sacred' character, and, perhaps as a consequence, this piece, unlike other of Schneemann's works, largely adhered to the traditional artistic decorum for female nudity. But if *Eye Body* for the most part obeyed that decorum, the work of later performers explicitly rejected it. As part of her 1980s show Annie Sprinkle stripped, asking spectators to touch and put their heads between her breasts, and describe the sensation. The section entitled 'Public Cervix Announcement' was even more transgressive, Sprinkle inserting a speculum into her vagina and inviting onlookers to examine her genitals by torchlight. This mode of transgressive exposure took its most potent form in the work of such as Lydia Lunch, Johanna Went and particularly Karen Finlay. Finlay's fragmented monologues were filled with sexual and scatological references, language which prompted some protest, as the performer herself alternated between controlled aggression and trance-like reverie. This was augmented by an emphatic viscerality. Finlay has apparently defecated into a bucket onstage, and in *Yams Up My Granny's Ass* (1986) did indeed appear to insert sliced yams into her rectum. Her work often entailed manipulating viscous foods with her hands – cream, dog food, eggs, raw minced meat – and sometimes smearing them over her body, to create images which deliberately court disgust.

The human body is not usually disruptive, far from it, for most often the body is heavily incultured. Gesture, posture and movement are bound up with behavioural codes, while clothes signify a host of meanings, indicating gender, class, ethnic origin and, more subtly, aesthetic preferences and the finer subdivisions of social grouping associated with them. Nor is the naked body inherently any less readable. Public nudity is sanctioned only in certain situations, whose context itself dictates what meanings it may be ascribed; a strip show prefers meanings derived from constructions of heterosexual male desire, quite different from those favoured by the context of a life-drawing class.

Nevertheless the body, and the naked body especially, does retain some potential to explode given meanings. Clothes, gesture, context – all these involve reading bodies via cultural codes, interpreting them in reference to other bodies, or ideas of other bodies, which are not physically present. We thus read the *particular* body by locating this individual 'signifier' within wider systems of signs. It is this link, between the unique and the systematic, which is vulnerable to assault. Taken out of those contexts which render it 'safe', its meanings contained, the body is first of all shocking, transgressive. Our culture is pervaded by images of naked women, disseminating ideas of a supposed 'norm' or 'ideal', but women's real bodies offer complex patterns, shapes and features. When we publicly encounter an unclothed body outside of those contexts able to contain it, there is often a moment when it sheds cultural codification, refuting those images that ordinarily cluster about it. That is not to say we encounter the 'reality' of a body, but recognise that it in some degree eludes total containment by the usual frames, is not fully quantified by, 'commensurate' with, the mechanisms available.

But crucial to this is the question of who governs representation. In Annie Sprinkle's performance control of exposure lay with her; it was she who determined who should view and touch her body, and *how* it should be viewed and touched. This was augmented by the framing of the event. With a genuine strip show the power to dictate how a body should be viewed, what meanings may be ascribed it, is firmly located with the viewer. The categorisation of the event – effected by advertising, venue, financial transaction and so on, all clear framing signifiers – establishes an interpretative frame which dictates that meaning be generated in a sexualised heterosexual male gaze. But enacted in a theatrical venue, and categorised as art, the situation in Sprinkle's performance was reversed. In such contexts the performer is accorded the power to dictate the meanings generated, while the role conventionally offered the spectator is a passive one. When Sprinkle drew spectators into the performance, into *signification*, the potential for embarrassment was great, for it was she who determined how *they* were to be read. Sprinkle's performance was not without political ambiguity, but throughout she did make clear that the signifying material that was her body was hers to exploit.

Although Finlay claimed a similar control over meaning, she also effected a rupture of bodily codification via transgression itself. Throughout her pieces Finlay's body, clothed or exposed, was constantly associated with matter; with her sexual and scatological language, the foodstuffs she manipulated, the bodily processes she enacted and, most of all, by the transgression of her body's perimeter with foreign objects. The codification of women's bodies renders them both static and non-corporeal; they are 'fixed' within a system of representation, their materiality subjected to the conceptual. Finlay in contrast emphasised her body as a network of biological processes; material not conceptual, shifting and permeable instead of sealed and static; in the midst of transition and so defiant of the kind of stasis conventional codification requires. Like Sprinkle's, Finlay's work is ambiguous in political terms, as any female exposure must be in our culture, but she did assault given norms of women's bodies in a way that made the framing of her own body problematic.

Such disruptions of representation, of corporeality's abstraction and codification, are effected most forcefully when the body is combined with chance to produce genuine physical hazard. The performances of Chris Burden entailed physical discomfort, danger and even damage. In his most extreme work, *Shooting*

Piece (1971), Burden indeed had a collaborator shoot him, for, by enacting real violence, he hoped to change attitudes to the sanitised images of violence perpetuated throughout western culture. In *The Conditioning* (1972) Gina Pane lay on an iron bed frame while being burned by candles positioned beneath, like Burden seeking to overcome the modern individual's alienation to elicit genuine, unmediated responses. Harrowing as they are, such acts are emphatically real, of the here and now. For all practical purposes it is impossible for the spectator to separate them from social space, to abstract them into a symbolic realm as mere representation.

This strategy has been exploited more subtly by German choreographer Pina Bausch. Bausch was instrumental in developing a relatively new mode of performance termed *Tanztheater* or 'dance-theatre', literally dance with a greater narrative component. The subject of her *1980* was culture's shaping of the body. Throughout the piece the audience was presented with short, often funny scenes of childhood, collectively proffering that familiar image of infancy as a time of naturalness and freedom, one unburdened by social pressures. But these were enacted alongside scenes which indicated the opposite. One performer stood in passive sufferance while another repeatedly applied lipstick to her mouth and kissed his face. Initially comic, reminiscent perhaps of the unwanted attentions of fearsome aunts, the act began to take on more sinister overtones as the red lip prints clustered about his face like bruises or lesions. Standing on a chair while a man changed her clothing, a woman explained that this was how her father dressed her as a child; she then went on to describe how he would brush her hair and become frustrated when it refused to straighten. Far from being a period free of social constraints, such scenes suggested infancy to be the time of enculturation, when bodily appearance and movement is coercively shaped by adults to conform to socially derived norms.

This enculturation was traced through to its effects in adulthood. *1980* depicted a host of different situations in which behaviour – and especially movement – was shaped into conventional, overtly artificial forms: parties, dances, leave-takings, a beauty contest and afternoon tea, familiar social roles such as a waiter, salesman, fashion model and so on. A male dancer in an evening suit and one woman's high-heeled shoe limped across the stage, highlighting the way 'natural' gender differences are constructed with conventions of dress; the same performer was stripped, dressed in a single black stocking, had make-up applied to his face, and was finally arranged in a familiar 'seductress' pose. Perhaps most emblematic was the 'Beach Scene' in which the entire company adopted the postures of farcical sunbathers: one dancer swathed himself in towels to reveal only his buttocks, another similarly exposed only her eyes, while a third faced the sun naked but for small pieces of paper stuck to her nose and nipples. By exposing the bathers' bodies in such impractical ways, Bausch's choreography revealed the arbitrariness of such rules of 'decency'.

As a combination of dance and theatrical mimesis, Tanztheater tends to interpretative uncertainty, for it brings into play the distinct reading conventions of both forms. Bausch augmented this by having dancers interact with spectators directly – serving them tea, telling jokes, weaving through the auditorium in a coordinated 'crocodile' of dance – so that the locus's separation from social space was undermined.

But the symbolic space's separation was also subverted in more direct fashion. A dancer entered in the persona of a child to skip round in a circle, waving her handkerchief and chanting 'I'm tired' in an infantile, sing-song tone. The humour waned, however, as the action continued for several minutes, until the performer, now genuinely exhausted, began to stumble, her voice reduced to a breathless croak. A second dancer rushed on to pick her up and carry her through the circle, but he too tired quickly. In a comparable scene a middle-aged man attempted to execute gymnastic exercises on parallel bars. He crumpled painfully onto the apparatus when his strength proved inadequate – only to rise and try again, and again, meeting with the same lack of success.

Scenes such as these provide spectators with an uncomfortable experience. The dancer's circling began as a fiction, occupying a symbolic space of 'art' demarcated from the real social space of the audience. But as her genuine discomfort became apparent, our view necessarily altered. Like the pain experienced by Gina Pane, or the unpredictability of Rose English's horse, the discomfort felt by the performer ruptures the frame of symbolisation; 'it happens' with a potency that goes beyond representation. Just a few scenes of this kind are enough to permeate the show, so

226

that spectators begin to scrutinise every scene to determine whether it too is 'real'. The change is perhaps built upon the spectator's empathy with the suffering performer, but it illustrates the inadequacy of attempts to view the event solely in terms of 'meaning'; real discomfort erupts into the *representation* of reality that is the work.

EXCEEDING THE FRAME

As we have noted, performance art is a form without a fixed form. To stay free of given modes of sense-making, it must acknowledge no generic boundaries, for only by doing so does it elude the frames associated with genres. Paradoxically, this includes those boundaries established by any 'tradition' that may accrue to performance art itself. Some of the performers we have examined operate beyond the limits of 'live art' as usually conceived, in the space of other cultural forms, with Monk employing the conventions of cabaret, Bausch collapsing dance and theatre, and Rose English evoking the codes of circus with an elaborate 'ringmaster' costume and performing horse. Perhaps the most effective of such works was Laurie Anderson's record *O Superman* (1982), a successful invasion of the realm of pop music.

None of these artists or works stayed within the limits of the forms they invaded, of course; 'Turtle Cabaret' was not a cabaret in the accepted sense, any more than *O Superman* obeyed the conventions of the pop song. This is central to their status as postmodern works in the Lyotardian sense. In order to nurture an experience of 'it happens' in the viewer's gaze, it is first necessary to establish a context of sense-making; it is by provoking attempts at symbolic interpretation that the limits of symbolisation are made evident. The gallery space in which *Fountain* was exhibited, surmounted with a title and the artist's name, the planned framework of *Untitled Event*, Gilbert and George's announcements and Vostell's invitations – all these conjure the expectation of a readable text, which the artist then punctures with the unreadable. But while employing the same principle, Bausch, Monk and Anderson used a slightly different strategy, evoking the frames of other given forms precisely so that they might be exceeded, and by this means creating works which elude the sense they seemed to offer.

Most significant for our purposes is that this latter strategy has resulted in works which straddle the spaces of live art and theatre proper. The Wooster Group's *Brace Up!* (1993) was ostensibly a version of Chekhov's *Three Sisters*. But Chekhov's text played little part in the production, for his dialogue was used only occasionally, and whole sections of the plot were not performed, merely summarised by a compère figure. Indeed, towards the end the compère announced that there was no time to complete the play; she then described its resolution to the audience, and *Brace Up!* concluded with a dance. As we noted, the figure of the Author, that notional individual in whose mind the work's meanings are deemed to have cohered, itself constitutes a potent frame, a means of channelling and containing the spectator's interpretative activities. This is particularly so with authors of Chekhov's standing, for, so great is his status, the spectre of his 'intentions' haunts our reading. By choosing a Chekhov play but barely using it, the Wooster Group drew the figure of the Author into the centre of the spectator's interpretative considerations in order then to marginalise him or her.

We may call this device 'exceeding the frame', for it involves evoking, then stepping beyond the limits of recognisable interpretative strategies. *Brace Up!*'s disregard of Chekhov's text was merely the first of a series of decentring devices, perhaps the most extraordinary of which was of the playing space itself. *Three Sisters* is an example of classic naturalism, a form which requires a firmly defined locus, and one of the primary, traditional means of conjuring a locus is by demarcating a separate physical space. *Brace Up!* did use such a space, a raised rectangular platform with open avenues at either side. But having offered these framing signifiers, the production continually disregarded them. Throughout the play production personnel milled about the stage's edge, actors entered and left, and props were handed onto the stage, so that the physical limits of the symbolic otherplace were unclear. This erosion of the limits of symbolic space from without was accompanied by erosion from within. Along the back of the stage ran a long table, about which sat a number of actors/characters. They drank and joked but their words were inaudible, and their actions played no discernible part in the fiction being created in the main stage area. Equally, performances often featured what appeared to be 'real' behaviour; actors relaxed, prepared and discussed their roles, and even arranged props. The overall effect was to break down the distinction between locus and platea, offering the audience no coherent other-place.

It was with video, however, that this breakdown of spatial framing was completed. The character of Natalya did not appear for the first half of *Brace Up!* but waited out of sight offstage, her words and face transmitted live via an onstage television monitor. Similarly, although the actress playing Olga was visible, she sat with her back to the audience, also 'appearing' on video, as did the performers seated at the rear table. The locus, the 'onstage', could be offstage in *Brace Up!*, just as characters about the onstage table only entered the fictional world via the offstage channel of the video link, so that the location of symbolic space was rendered indistinct.

If such devices problematised spatial perimeters, they also exceeded the frame of time. The raising of the curtain and lowering of the lights, the actor's focus within the playing space, ignoring the audience – such signs tell us *when* the demarcated space is to be read as symbolic, as a separate continuum, an other-place. In *Brace Up!*, however, performers ascended the stage singly or in groups over the first fifteen minutes, drifted in and out of character, and spoke to the audience throughout, offering spectators no clear division between fictional and non-fictional time. The compère explained that, being too old to make the journey, the actress playing Anfisa would not appear but would instead present her character on video. But when the tape was played it appeared to show not an actress but a woman speaking to an interviewer; not only did it derive from beyond the time/space of the locus, it was not of fictional time/space at all. Similarly, during much of the show a Japanese samurai film was played on one of the television monitors. Although fictional, it was created by other hands, in another culture; a 'found object"' with no relation to the show's time and space, nor to any intentional meaning.

Perhaps the most continuous assault against the locus, however, figured in the performances themselves. As we have seen, many of the actors appeared not to be acting at all but 'behaving' for much of the time, even interacting with production personnel. Indeed, one actress spent a portion of the show sitting quietly while a second coiffured her hair. The compère's role itself demanded that she be viewed as outside the fiction;

she interviewed actors, tidied the stage and explained proceedings to the audience. At one point she expressed doubt as to the meaning of a scene, asking the opinion of another actor whom she introduced as the Wooster Group's 'literary advisor'. Speaking from the rear table, he described the text's socio-historical context, a perspective not merely upon the play but upon the circumstance of its creation, voiced from within it. At another point the compère asked an actress about her character; she replied, 'I'm not working on character'. Character, the fictional occupant of the symbolic space, was not a part of the exchange; or more accurately, the character that actress proffered, the 'role' she played, was of an actress *not* playing a role.

Space, time, author, character, fictionality itself – all these were problematised in *Brace Up!*. Presenting itself as theatre, the piece evoked within the audience's gaze appropriate frames, none of which could interpretatively encompass its parts: a series of concentric circles for containing sense were proffered, all of which were exceeded. *Brace Up!* finally declined to demarcate a text, a symbolic coherency, with the result that audience's attempts at sense-making continually demonstrated their own inability to confer upon the event a meaning. Perhaps the ultimate experience of the piece was one which, as we have seen, is common to radical performance; an uncertainty as to the nature of the event. All performers clearly were acting, the piece evidencing the kind of polish so characteristic of the Wooster Group; *what* they were acting, what was a fiction and what was not, however, remained elusive.

BIBLIOGRAPHY

Althusser, L. (1971) *Essays on Ideology*, London: Verso.

Artaud, A. (1974) *Antonin Artaud: Collected Works*, vol. 4, trans. Victor Corti, London: Calder & Boyars.

Banu, G. (1987) 'Peter Brook's Six Days: Sharing Theatrical Exploration with the Public', *New Theatre Quarterly* 3, 10: 99–106.

Beckett, S. (1965) *'Proust' and Three Dialogues (with Georges Duthuit)*, London: John Calder.

—— (1985) *Happy Days: Samuel Beckett's Production Notebook*, ed. James Knowlson, London: Faber & Faber.

Belsey, C. (1980) *Critical Practice*, London: Routledge.

Benedetti, J. (1982) *Stanislavski: An Introduction*, London: Methuen.

Berliner Ensemble (1986) 'A Pictorial Retrospective, 1949–84', *New Theatre Quarterly* 2, 6: 99–106.

Bigsby, C. W. E. (1985) *A Critical Introduction to Twentieth-Century American Drama*, vol. 3, Cambridge: Cambridge University Press.

Boleslavsky, R. (1975) *Acting: The First Six Lessons*, New York: Theatre Arts Books.

Bradbury, M. and McFarlane, J. (eds) (1976) *Modernism*, Harmondsworth: Penguin.

Braun, E. (1979) *The Theatre of Meyerhold: The Revolution on the Modern Stage*, London: Eyre Methuen.

—— (1982) *The Director and the Stage*, London: Methuen.

Brecht, B. (1964) *Brecht on Theatre: The Development of an Aesthetic*, ed. and trans. John Willett, London: Methuen.

—— (1965) *The Messingkauf Dialogues*, trans. John Willett, London: Methuen.

Brecht, S. (1978) *The Theatre of Visions: Robert Wilson*, London: Methuen.

Brook, P. (1972) *The Empty Space*, Harmondsworth: Penguin.

—— (1987) *The Shifting Point: Forty Years of Theatrical Exploration*, London: Methuen.

Butler, C. (1994) *Early Modernism*, Oxford: Oxford University Press.

Calandra, D. (1974) 'Karl Valentin and Bertolt Brecht', in *The Drama Review*, 18, 1: 86–98.

Clurman, H. (1983) *The Fervent Years: The Group Theatre and the Thirties*, New York: De Capo Press.

231

Coger, L. I. (1964) 'Stanislavski Changes his Mind', in *Tulane Drama Review*, 9, 1: 48–62.

Cohen, P. (1991) 'Peter Brook and the "Two Worlds" of Theatre', *New Theatre Quarterly* 7, 26: 147–59.

Connor, S. (1989) *Postmodernist Culture: An Introduction to Theories of the Contemporary*, Oxford: Basil Blackwell.

Culler, J. (1982) *On Deconstruction: Criticism after Structuralism*, London: Routledge & Kegan Paul.

Davis, R. J. and Butler, L. S. (eds) (1988) *'Make Sense Who May': Essays on Samuel Beckett's Later Works*, Gerrard's Cross: Colin Smyth.

Deák, F. (1974) 'The Byrd Hoffman School of Byrds: Robert Wilson', *The Drama Review* 18, 2: 67–73.

Debord, G. (1977) *Society of the Spectacle*, Detroit: Red & Black.

Elam, K. (1980) *The Semiotics of Theatre and Drama*, London: Methuen.

Esslin, M. (1968) *The Theatre of the Absurd*, Harmondsworth: Penguin.

Fitzgerald, F. (1987) *Cities on a Hill: A Journey Through Contemporary American Cultures*, London: Pan.

Foster, H. (ed.) (1985) *Postmodern Culture*, London: Pluto Press.

Garfield, D. (1980) *A Player's Place*, New York: Macmillan.

Goldberg, R. (1988) *Performance Art: From Futurism to the Present*, London: Thames & Hudson.

Gontarski, S. E. (ed.) (1986) *On Beckett: Essays and Criticism*, New York: Grove Press.

Grotowski, J. (1969) *Towards a Poor Theatre*, ed. E. Barba, London: Methuen.

Heilpern, J. (1989) *The Conference of the Birds: The Story of Peter Brook in Africa*, London: Methuen.

Hirsch, F. (1984) *A Method to their Madness: A History of the Actors' Studio*, New York: W. W. Norton.

Holland, P. (1984) '*Hamlet* and the Art of Acting', in J. Redmond (ed.), *Drama and the Actor*, Cambridge: Cambridge University Press.

Innes, C. (1972) *Erwin Piscator's Political Theatre: The Development of Modern German Theatre*, Cambridge: Cambridge University Press.

—— (1993) *Avant Garde Theatre*, London: Routledge.

Jefferson, A. and Robey, D. (eds) (1982) *Modern Literary Theory: A Comparative Introduction*, London: Batsford Academic.

Jones, D. R. (1986) *Great Directors at Work: Stanislavski, Brecht, Kazan, Brook*, London: University of California Press.

Kalb, J. (1989) *Beckett in Performance*, Cambridge: Cambridge University Press.

Kumiega, J. (1985) *The Theatre of Grotowski*, London: Methuen.

Lacan, J. (1977) *Ecrits: A Selection*, trans. A. Sheridan, London: Routledge.

Langton, B. (1973) 'Journey to Ka Mountain', *The Drama Review* 17, 2: 48–57.

Lévi-Strauss, C. (1966) *The Savage Mind*, London: Weidenfeld & Nicolson.

Lyotard, J.-F. (1984) *The Postmodern Condition: A Report on Knowledge*, trans. G. Bennington and B. Massumi, Manchester: Manchester University Press.

BIBLIOGRAPHY

—— (1989) *The Lyotard Reader*, ed. A Benjamin, Oxford: Basil Blackwell.
Matejka, L. and Titunik, I. R. (eds) (1976) *Semiotics of Art*, Cambridge, Mass: MIT Press.
Nuttall, J. (1979) *Performance Art: Memoirs*, London: John Calder.
Pavis, P. (1982) *Languages of the Stage: Essays in the Semiology of Theatre*, New York: Performing Arts Journal Publications.
Richardson, T. (1956) 'An Account of the Actors' Studio', in *Sight and Sound* 26, 3: 22–39.
Rogoff, G. (1964) 'Lee Strasberg: Burning Ice', *Tulane Drama Review* 9, 2: 128–45.
Roose-Evans, J. (1989) *Experimental Theatre: From Stanislavski to Peter Brook*, London: Routledge.
Rülicke-Weiler, K. (1991) 'Brecht and Weigel at the Berliner Ensemble', *New Theatre Quarterly* 7, 25: 3–19.
Saussure, F. de (1974) *Course in General Linguistics*, trans. W. Baskin, London: Fontana.
Schall, E. (1986) 'Acting with the Berliner Ensemble: Elements of Brechtian Acting Discussed by an Acknowledged Master', *New Theatre Quarterly* 2, 6: 99–106.
Schechner, R. and Gray, P. (1964) 'Working with Live Material: An Interview with Lee Strasberg', *Tulane Drama Review* 9, 1: 123–35.
Selbourne, D. (1982) *The Making of* A Midsummer Night's Dream, London: Methuen.
Sellin, E. (1968) *The Dramatic Concepts of Antonin Artaud*, Chicago: University of Chicago Press.
Shank, T. (1982) *American Alternative Theatre*, London: Macmillan Press.
Shyer, L. (1989) *Robert Wilson and his Collaborators*, New York: Theatre Communications Group.
Simmer, B. (1976) 'Robert Wilson and Therapy', *The Drama Review* 20, 1: 99–110.
Sinfield, A. (1989) *Literature and Politics in Post War Britain*, Oxford: Basil Blackwell.
Smith, A. C. H. (1972) *Orghast at Persepolis: An Account of the Experiment in Theatre Directed by Peter Brook and Written by Ted Hughes*, London: Methuen.
Stanislavski, C. (1968) *Building a Character*, trans. E. Hapgood Reynolds, London: Methuen (first published 1950).
—— (1980) *An Actor Prepares*, trans. E. Hapgood Reynolds, London: Methuen (first published 1936).
—— (1981) *Creating a Role*, trans. E. Hapgood Reynolds, London: Methuen (first published 1957).
Strasberg, L. (1966) *Strasberg at the Actors' Studio: Tape-Recorded Sessions*, ed. R. Hethmon, London: Jonathan Cape.
—— (1988) *A Dream of Passion: The Development of the Method*, ed. E. Morphos, London: Methuen.
Styan, J. L. (1981) *Modern Drama in Theory and Practice*, 3 vols, Cambridge: Cambridge University Press.
Trilling, O. (1973) 'Robert Wilson's *Ka Mountain* and *Guardenia Terrace*', *The Drama Review* 17, 2: 34–47.

Turner, V. (1987) *The Anthropology of Performance*, New York: Performing Arts Journal Publications.

Weimann, R. (1978) *Shakespeare and the Popular Tradition: Studies in the Social Dimension of Dramatic Form and Function*, trans. R. Schwartz, London: Johns Hopkins University Press.

Willett, J. (1964) *The Theatre of Bertolt Brecht: A Study from Eight Aspects*, London: Methuen.

Williams, D. (1985) '"A Place Marked by Life": Brook at the Bouffes du Nord', *New Theatre Quarterly* 1, 1: 39–74.

—— (ed.) (1991) *Peter Brook and the* Mahabharata, London: Routledge.

Williams, R. (1977) *Marxism and Literature*, Oxford: Oxford University Press.

Wright, E. (1989) *Postmodern Brecht: A Re-Presentation*, London: Routledge.

INDEX

235